Palgrave Studies in Pragmatics, Language and Cognition

Series Editors

Richard Breheny, Psychology and Language Sciences, University College London, London, UK

Nicole Gotzner, Cognitive Science, University of Osnabrück, Osnabrück, Germany

Palgrave Studies in Pragmatics, Language and Cognition is a series of high quality research monographs and edited collections of essays focusing on the human pragmatic capacity and its interaction with natural language semantics and other faculties of mind. A central interest is the interface of pragmatics with the linguistic system(s), with the 'theory of mind' capacity and with other mental reasoning and general problem-solving capacities. Work of a social or cultural anthropological kind is included if firmly embedded in a cognitive framework. Given the interdisciplinarity of the focal issues, relevant research comes from linguistics, philosophy of language, theoretical and experimental pragmatics, psychology and child development. The series aims to reflect all kinds of research in the relevant fields - conceptual, analytical and experimental.

Nicole Gotzner · Jesse A. Harris ·
Richard Breheny · Yael Sharvit
Editors

Alternatives in Grammar and Cognition

palgrave
macmillan

Editors
Nicole Gotzner
Institute of Cognitive Science
Osnabrück University
Osnabrück, Germany

Jesse A. Harris
Department of Linguistics
University of California, Los Angeles
Los Angeles, CA, USA

Richard Breheny
Department of Linguistics
University College London
London, UK

Yael Sharvit
Department of Linguistics
University of California, Los Angeles
Los Angeles, CA, USA

ISSN 2946-2576 ISSN 2946-2584 (electronic)
Palgrave Studies in Pragmatics, Language and Cognition
ISBN 978-3-031-76675-6 ISBN 978-3-031-76676-3 (eBook)
https://doi.org/10.1007/978-3-031-76676-3

This Palgrave Macmillan imprint is published by the registered company Springer Nature Switzerland AG
The registered company address is: Gewerbestrasse 11, 6330 Cham, Switzerland

Acknowledgments

All contributions have been reviewed anonymously by at least one other author in the volume. We thank those authors who volunteered for this task, and also thank further external reviewers, in particular Taka Nakamura. We are grateful to Stella Maria Avila and Berit Reise for editorial support. This work was supported by the German research council DFG (Emmy Noether grant awarded to NG, GO 3378/1-1).

Contents

Editors and Contributors

About the Editors

Nicole Gotzner is a Full Professor at Osnabrück University, Germany, and co-editor of Palgrave Studies in Pragmatics, Language and Cognition. She is an expert in alternative semantics, the mental representation of alternatives and pragmatic inferences. She has published on a wide range of topics relating to alternatives and received the most important early-career award by the DFG (German Research Foundation) for her work in this domain.

Jesse A. Harris is an Associate Professor in the Linguistics Department of University of California, Los Angeles, USA. He has published widely on the processing of focus-sensitive structures and other topics in experimental pragmatics. His research centers on interpretation during online sentence comprehension, with specific interests in focus, prosody, ellipsis and information structure.

Richard Breheny is a Professor of Experimental Linguistics at University College London, UK, and co-editor of Palgrave Studies in Pragmatics,

Language and Cognition. He has established one of the first labs in the area of Experimental Pragmatics and is widely recognized for his work on numerals and pragmatic inferences. He recently led a Leverhulme grant on alternatives.

Yael Sharvit is a Professor in the Linguistics Department of UCLA, USA. Her research focuses on formal semantics and the syntax-semantics interface. She has worked on many topics, including local implicatures, NPIs and tense semantics.

Contributors

Sam Alxatib is an Assistant Professor in the Linguistics Department of the CUNY Graduate Center. He specializes in the formal study of semantics and pragmatics and has worked on degree semantics, the semantics of the particle *only*, focus, and on disjunction and free choice inferences.

Alexander Göbel is a Lecturer at the University of Manchester. His work ranges from investigations into the prosodic realization of focus to its reflexes in interpretation and discourse processing.

Yael Greenberg is an Associate Professor in the Department of English Literature and Linguistics of Bar-Ilan University. She has worked on the semantics-pragmatics interface with various expressions and constructions in English and Hebrew, including focus-sensitive, aspectual and incremental particles, and on using tools from degree semantics in analyzing scalar alternative-sensitive phenomena.

E. Matthew Husband holds a Professorship in the Faculty of Linguistics, Philology and Phonetics at the University of Oxford and a Tutorial Fellowship at St. Hugh's College. He has worked on many issues in the syntax-semantics interface and language processing, including how focus alternatives are generated during online processing.

Radim Lacina is a PhD student in the Emmy Noether Project on Scales in Language Processing and Acquisition (led by Nicole Gotzner) at Osnabrück University. He researches the processing of alternatives in focus and scalar implicatures in his dissertation.

Christian Muxica is currently pursuing a PhD in Linguistics at UCLA and is researching the real-time processing of focus. Prior to his graduate studies, he studied Psycholinguistics at the University of Massachusetts Amherst.

Paul Marty is an Assistant Professor of Linguistics at University of Malta. He has done theoretical and experimental work on fee choice inferences, scalar implicated and alternatives in determiner phrases.

Andreea Nicolae is a Senior Researcher at the Leibniz-Zentrum für Allgemeine Sprachwissenschaft in Berlin. In her research, she has focused on polarity phenomena, the grammatical encoding of implicature calculation as well as on the semantics of questions.

Nikole D. Patson is a Professor of Psychology at the Ohio State University. She specializes in psycholinguistics and her research focuses on language comprehension, particularly how people process and understand sentences in real time.

Jacopo Romoli is Professor of Linguistics at University of Düsseldorf. He has published on both the formal analysis of language and experimental research on language processing and development in the fields of semantics/pragmatics.

Raj Singh is Professor in the Department of Cognitive Science at Carleton University. He works on formal semantics, pragmatics, language processing and language acquisition.

Yasutada Sudo is Professor of Linguistics at University College London. He has conducted theoretical and experimental research on various semantic and pragmatic topics, including presupposition, scalar implicature and other alternative-based phenomena.

List of Figures

List of Tables

Part I

Introduction

1

Introduction

Nicole Gotzner and Jesse A. Harris

1.1 Background

A fundamental principle of pragmatic reasoning is that natural language users come to understand the intent of a message not only by what was said, but what alternative expression was left unsaid (Grice, 1975). Since at least Jackendoff (1972), alternative expressions have come to occupy a central role in the calculation of linguistic meaning and communication. The intuition that alternative forms and utterances enter the computation of linguistic meaning can be formalized in many ways, though perhaps none more influential than the Alternative Semantics framework of Rooth (1985, 1992), in which alternative expressions enter the formal semantic computation of focused content. This account posits that, in

N. Gotzner (✉)
Institute of Cognitive Science, Osnabrück University, Osnabrück, Germany
e-mail: nicole.gotzner@uni-osnabrueck.de

J. A. Harris
Department of Linguistics, University of California, Los Angeles, CA, USA
e-mail: jharris@humnet.ucla.edu

N. Gotzner et al. (eds.), *Alternatives in Grammar and Cognition*, Palgrave Studies in Pragmatics, Language and Cognition, https://doi.org/10.1007/978-3-031-76676-3_1

addition to their ordinary meanings, expressions also denote a set of alternatives to the ordinary semantic value when focused (see also Jackendoff, 1972). The alternative set is ultimately used to generate a set of propositions against which the actual utterance is interpreted. Alternative meanings were further recognized to be necessary to properly account for the truth-conditional effect of focus placement and certain focus-sensitive operators like *only*, *even*, and *also*. Formal alternatives have since come to play a central role in the analysis of various semantic and pragmatic phenomena like focus, free choice, negation, and scalar implicature (Chierchia, 2013; Gajewski & Sharvit, 2012; see Gotzner & Romoli, 2022 for an overview; Katzir, 2007).

In recent years, the investigation of such alternative-based phenomena has been subject to an experimental turn, largely due to two main developments. First, experimental research into scalar implicature spearheaded the creation of a field now known as Experimental Pragmatics (since Chemla & Singh, 2014; Noveck, 2018, 2001 for an overview). Second, linguistic focus has been found to trigger the generation of a set of alternatives in comprehenders, consistent with the framework of Rooth's Alternative Semantics (e.g., Braun & Taglipaietra, 2010; see Gotzner & Spalek, 2019; Gotzner et al., 2016; Husband & Ferreira, 2015 for review). Thanks to the finding that alternative meanings are indeed computed during incremental processing, experimental linguists have begun to apply experimental paradigms to address how alternatives are generated and restricted over time during online comprehension.

Despite the remarkable progress on linguistic focus and scalar implicature made in recent years, foundational issues regarding the mechanisms by which alternatives are computed, both formally and in online language processing, remain open. To name just a few: How are alternatives generated and constrained by the grammar? What determines that one expression should count as an alternative to another? In what ways do grammar and context interact? How are alternatives accessed during real-time processing, and at what point in interpretation does contextual information determine which alternatives are relevant? Are such mechanisms unique to linguistic representations or do they recruit more domain-general mechanisms? To address some of these questions, the present volume "Alternatives in Grammar and Cognition" gathers contributions by leading scholars in semantics, pragmatics, and psycholinguistics who work on the generation and contextual restriction of alternatives. The contributions center around several of the core alternative-based phenomena: prosodic focus, focus-sensitive operators, indefinites, modals, and scalar implicature. This volume brings together a diverse array of scholars investigating the generation and restriction of alternative sets from theoretical and empirical perspectives. The editors compiled contributions from noted scholars in the field to provide theoretical arguments, opinionated perspectives synthesizing existing positions, or empirical evidence from experimentation and fieldwork in support of a theoretical framework. In the remaining sections, we briefly introduce two key threads of the volume: (i) the generation and restriction of alternatives and (ii) operations on salient alternatives.

1.2 Generation and Restriction of Alternatives

The first theme of the volume concerns the formal generation of alternative sets; in particular, whether members of the alternative set (i) constitute a type-theoretic semantic class (as proposed in Rooth, 1985 and adopted in many subsequent accounts), (ii) range over syntactic alternatives, derived by constructing alternative structures (e.g., as proposed in Fox & Katzir, 2011; Katzir, 2007), or (iii) are based on a broader cohort of lexical expressions (as proposed by Gotzner, 2017 and Husband & Ferreira, 2015). The first three chapters of our volume focus on the generation and restriction of alternatives during processing, as inspired by different theoretical accounts. The main theme revolves around the question whether initially a broad set of elements is generated and then contextually restricted or whether only a limited set of relevant expressions plays a role in meaning computation. For example, in the case of scalar implicature, only expressions on the same entailment-based scale (e.g., *some* and *all*) should be considered for inference making.

Gotzner and Lacina provide an overview of different theories about the nature of alternatives involved in scalar implicatures. They argue that the mechanism for activating and selecting alternatives needs to be separated from the inferential mechanism itself. Inspired by work on focus (Gotzner, 2017 and Husband & Ferreira, 2015), Gotzner and Lacina develop a two-stage account for activating scalar alternatives. The chapter also discusses findings that cast doubt on the view that scalar implicatures are computed via the negation of relevant alternatives.

Husband and Patson review the literature on the role of prior mention and the semantic relation of alternatives and the triggering expression. They discuss which cognitive mechanisms could underpin the construction of alternatives in processing ranging from early processing stages to later memory encoding for focus and scalar alternatives. Husband and Patson highlight gaps in our theories of alternative generation, specifically focusing on the relation between how active an alternative is and how it is used in comprehension. They conclude that future research should link activity and use more closely both in theory and within the experimental paradigm.

Muxica and Harris further evaluate a core prediction of a two-stage view, in which the focus processor is initially insensitive to the discourse status of focus alternatives (adopted by Husband & Ferreira, 2015 and Gotzner, 2017). In particular, semantically-related, but contextually-irrelevant, alternatives are said to be available to the focus processor at an initial, context-insensitive stage of semantic priming, and are only later eliminated by contextual constraint. Counter to this prediction, they find evidence from a cross-modal priming study that the availability of alternatives is distinguished by their contextual relevance even in early moments of discourse processing, and advance a *constructive* model of alternative generation, in which contextual information immediately influences the constitution of an alternative set.

1.3 Operations on Salient Alternatives

Although certain alternatives may be generated by the grammar or otherwise salient, they do not necessarily enter into compositional interpretation. Accordingly, scholars have distinguished *formal* alternatives, which are generated by the grammar, from *relevant* alternatives, which feed interpretive operations in context. One area where the distinction is relevant is the so-called *symmetry problem* in scalar implicature, in which, on a neo-Gricean account, stronger alternative utterances are negated—e.g., *some* implicates *not all* by the negation of more informative alternative *all (2-a)*. The problem arises when an alternative sentence A (2-b) for an utterance U (1) is negated in the computation of a scalar implicature in the form $U \wedge \neg A$. The literal meaning of the utterance (1) and the negation of the symmetric alternative (2-b) lead to direct contradiction (*Mary drank some of the coffee and she didn't drink some but not all of the coffee*).

(1) *Utterance:* Mary drank some of the coffee
Implicates: Mary drank some but not all of the coffee

(2) a. *Stronger relevant alternatives:* Mary drank all of the coffee
b. *Symmetric alternative:* Mary drank some but not all of the coffee

To avoid deriving contradictions with symmetric alternatives, it is often assumed that only informationally stronger alternatives like (2-a) are negated via scalar implicature (Breheny et al., 2018; Fox & Katzir, 2011; Horn, 1972). Part II of the volume includes four chapters that address this question looking into how and whether salient alternatives are being operated on.

The chapter by Marty, Romoli, Sudo, and Breheny presents experimental evidence using an inference task that the mere salience of alternatives is not a factor in the computation of scalar implicatures. Their main conclusion is that the salience of an alternative does not increase the derivation of scalar implicatures if that alternative is already relevant.

It is often assumed that intonational tunes are associated with a distinct meaning or set of meanings (Pierrehumbert & Hirschberg, 1990). It is an empirical question whether a particular tune contributes a meaning distinct from items in the lexicon. Gobel investigates the meanings associated with a late rise (L* + H) pitch accent in English, finding experimental support that it imposes an evaluative ranking of alternatives in a way similar to, but nonetheless distinct from, the evaluative interpretation associated with *at least*. The paper raises important questions about how intonation guides the interpretation of alternatives.

The chapter by Greenberg discusses the division of labor between formal and contextual restriction and whether all salient alternatives in the preceding discourse affect the construction of alternative sets. She presents a range of empirical data indicating that salient sentences can only introduce alternatives into the set if they answer the same question, arguing for an answerability-constraint on salient alternatives.

Alxatib and Nicholae focus on whether indefinites and modals behave differently with respect to local implicatures. They present a dynamized account of exhaustification where alternatives for indefinites need to be anaphoric to it.

1.4 Conclusion

A final commentary chapter in our volume by Singh synthesizes the claims and outstanding questions regarding the interaction between grammar and context. Our collection of papers brings together current theoretical and empirical approaches to alternative-based phenomena, showing a common set of interwoven themes and issues. Theoretical accounts have inspired numerous experimental investigations into the generation and constraint of alternatives during online processing. At the same time, experimental findings are ever-more incorporated into theoretical approaches, informing new incremental accounts of alternatives. We believe that the collection of essays here attests to the importance and fruitfulness of an ongoing dialogue between approaches using various methodological tools to determine the construction of alternatives in grammar and cognition.

References

Braun, B., & Tagliapietra, L. (2010). The role of contrastive intonation contours in the retrieval of contextual alternatives. *Language and Cognitive Processes, 25*(7–9), 1024–1043.

Breheny, R., Klinedinst, N., Romoli, J., & Sudo, Y. (2018). The symmetry problem: Current theories and prospects. *Natural Language Semantics, 26*, 85–110.

Chemla, E., & Singh, R. (2014). Remarks on the experimental turn in the study of scalar implicature, Part I. *Language and Linguistics Compass, 8*(9), 373–386.

Chierchia, G. (2013). *Logic in grammar: Polarity, free choice, and intervention.* OUP Oxford.

Fox, D., & Katzir, R. (2011). On the characterization of alternatives. *Natural Language Semantics, 19*(1), 87–107.

Gajewski, J., & Sharvit, Y. (2012). In defense of the grammatical approach to local implicatures. *Natural Language Semantics, 20*, 31–57.

Gotzner, N. (2017). *Alternative sets in language processing: How alternatives are represented in the mind*. Palgrave studies in Pragmatics, Language and Cognition, Palgrave Macmillan.

Gotzner, N., & Romoli, J. (2022). Meaning and alternatives. *Annual Review of Linguistics, 8*, 213–234.

Gotzner, N., & Spalek, K. (2019). The life and times of focus alternatives: Tracing the activation of alternatives to a focused constituent in language comprehension. *Language and Linguistics Compass, 13*(2), e12310.

Gotzner, N., Wartenburger, I., & Spalek, K. (2016). The impact of focus particles on the recognition and rejection of contrastive alternatives. *Language and Cognition, 8*(1), 59–95.

Grice, H. P. (1975). Logic and conversation. In P. Cole & J. Morgan (Eds.), *Syntax & Semantics* Speech Acts (Vol. 3, pp. 41–58). New York: Academic Press.

Horn, L. (1972). *On the semantic properties of logical operators in English.* University of California.

Husband, E. M., & Ferreira, F. (2015). The role of selection in the comprehension of focus alternatives. *Language, Cognition and Neuroscience, 31*(2), 217–235.

Jackendoff,. (1972). *Semantic interpretation in generative grammar*. MIT Press.

Katzir, R. (2007). Structurally-Defined Alternatives. *Linguistics and Philosophy, 30*, 669–690.

Noveck, I. (2018). *Experimental pragmatics: The making of a cognitive science.* Cambridge University Press.

Noveck, I. A. (2001). When children are more logical than adults: Experimental investigations of scalar implicature. *Cognition, 78*(2), 165–188.

Pierrehumbert, J. B., & Hirschberg, J. (1990). The meaning of intonational contours in the interpretation of discourse. In P. R. Cohen, J. Morgan, & M. E. Pollack (Eds.), *Intensions in communication* (pp. 271–311). MIT Press.
Rooth, M. E. (1985). *Association with focus (montague grammar, semantics, only, even)*. University of Massachusetts Amherst.
Rooth, M. (1992). A theory of focus interpretation. *Natural Language Semantics, 1*(1), 75–116.

Part II

The Online Generation and Selection of Alternatives in Context

2

Generating and Selecting Alternatives for Scalar Implicature Computation: The Alternative Activation Account and Other Theories

Nicole Gotzner and Radim Lacina

2.1 Introduction

Scalar implicature is one of the key phenomena involving reasoning about alternatives. Fifty years of research has looked at the mechanisms underlying scalar implicature computation focusing on whether those are pragmatic or semantic in nature (see Sauerland, 2012; Chemla & Singh, 2024a and 2024b; and Gotzner & Romoli, 2022, for an overview). Closely intertwined with this is the key question of the current paper about the nature of alternatives that serve as the basis for scalar implicature computation.

N. Gotzner (✉) · R. Lacina
Institute of Cognitive Science, Osnabrück University, Osnabrück, Germany
e-mail: nicole.gotzner@uni-osnabrueck.de

R. Lacina
e-mail: radim.lacina@uni-osnabrueck.de

R. Lacina
Department of Czech Language, Faculty of Arts, Masaryk University, Brno, Czech Republic, Czechia

N. Gotzner et al. (eds.), *Alternatives in Grammar and Cognition*, Palgrave Studies in Pragmatics, Language and Cognition, https://doi.org/10.1007/978-3-031-76676-3_2

While different in their architecture, most formal theories assume that scalar implicatures involve three computational steps: (1) the computation of the literal meaning of an utterance, (2) the activation of alternatives and (3) the negation of relevant alternatives.

The key controversy in the literature has surrounded step (3) and the question of how relevant alternatives are being negated: Either via a Gricean mechanism in which the listeners reason about alternative utterances the speaker could have said (Grice, 1975; Horn, 1972; Sauerland, 2004) or a grammatical exhaustification mechanism (e.g., Chierchia et al., 2012; Fox & Katzir, 2011). According to Horn's view, scalar implicatures involve dedicated scales of weak and strong expressions that are stored in the lexicon. In the grammatical framework, different constraints on alternatives have been proposed, also allowing for logically independent alternatives (e.g., in the case of embedded implicatures, Chemla & Spector, 2011). Chierchia (2013) and others explicitly incorporate a notion of activated alternatives in their mechanism for scalar implicature but do not spell out the mechanism underlying activated alternatives. Typically, the set of alternatives is assumed to be given or inferable based on the attested scalar implicatures (Gotzner & Romoli, 2022; Trinh, 2019). Thus, little is known about which alternatives are activated and when during the comprehension process.

Inferring relevant or activated alternatives from attested inferences creates a problem of circularity. In this paper, we argue that we need to separate the mechanisms by which alternatives are being selected from the inferential mechanism itself (see also Gotzner, 2017, 2019). To do so, we draw on work from psycholinguistics on the mechanisms of generating and restricting alternative sets. Work on focus processing has integrated theoretical assumptions about alternatives with insights about semantic activation spreading (Gotzner, 2017; Husband & Ferreira, 2015). On this view, generating alternatives also involves domain-general mechanisms that determine which alternatives are activated and become salient. We adapt this so-called Alternative Activation Account for scalar implicature with the following subsequential steps: (1) domain-general mechanisms determine the salience and lemma-level activation of a broad cohort of expressions. (2) Dedicated grammatical and pragmatic mechanisms constrain which alternatives are used during scalar implicature computation.

Our main argument is that a cohort of alternatives is being activated as a byproduct of how the brain organizes concepts in semantic networks (e.g., Swinney et al., 1979). Only a subset of these elements are spelled out (receive phonological activation) during implicature computation, i.e., are relevant alternatives. We review the experimental literature in line with this view. We specifically focus on different priming studies that tested the activation of scalar and non-entailed alternatives during scalar implicature computation.

Our paper is structured as follows. First, we present the Alternative Activation for focus alternatives. Then, we develop a corresponding account for scalar implicature while discussing the nature of alternatives assumed in mainstream theories. We review psycholinguistic studies on how listeners generate alternatives during language comprehension. Then, we present evidence for scalar diversity in scalar implicature computation. We discuss theoretical proposals which accommodate this variability by assuming that some scales do not activate alternatives but instead involve a different implicature mechanism. Our concluding remarks provide directions for future research, including novel methods and test cases to answer core questions about the nature of alternatives.

2.2 Theoretical Proposals

2.2.1 Alternative Activation Account for Focus

Grammatical accounts of scalar implicature have been built on the basis of Rooth's alternative semantics (Rooth, 1992) and several accounts assume the alternatives for focus and scalar implicature to be the same (see especially Fox & Katzir, 2011). In the area of focus, concrete proposals have been made for how alternatives are generated and restricted during real-time processing.

One key finding from psycholinguistic studies is that focus activates alternatives that are of the same semantic type as the focused element (see Gotzner & Spalek, 2019 for an overview). The evidence for this comes from lexical priming where the reaction times for deciding whether a target is a word in a given language is faster when this word is related to a preceding word with focal stress (e.g., Braun & Tagliapietra, 2010; Husband & Ferreira, 2015). For example, when participants are presented with a sentence like *Mary ate bananas,* they are faster to react to the target CHERRIES compared to SOCKS. The extent of this priming effect is modulated by focal stress, preceding focus particles like *only,* the discourse context and verb selectional restrictions and the time that elapses between stimulus presentation. For example, there is evidence that the unrelated word SOCKS does receive some level of activation in a sentence frame that forms an ad hoc category for buyable things, that is *Mary bought bananas* (Gotzner, 2015; Jördens et al., 2020).

Husband and Ferreira (2015) spell out psychological mechanisms of activation and selection of relevant alternatives and show that they kick in sequentially during processing. In particular, they found that at the offset of a focused word both semantic associates of BANANA, CHERRIES and YELLOW, become activated while at a later point (750 ms offset) only relevant alternatives remain activated. Concurrently with this literature, Gotzner (2015, 2017) made a proposal in which both domain-general mechanisms and grammatical and pragmatic mechanisms serve the generation and restriction of alternative sets. While Husband and Fereira propose psychological mechanisms such as spreading activation and inhibition in a semantic network, Gotzner integrated such mechanisms with grammatical and pragmatic mechanisms assumed in semantics and pragmatics. We call this view the *Alternative Activation Account*. This account separates a step of initial broad activation spreading from a second step in which only relevant alternatives that are being negated during the inferential process remain:

1. Domain-general mechanisms generate a broad set of alternatives including all semantic associates (words/concepts)

(1) Mary ate [bananas]^{F}-> CHERRIES, SOCKS, YELLOW

2. Grammatical and pragmatic mechanisms single out relevant alternatives (negated alternatives)

(2) Mary ate [bananas]^{F} - > CHERRIES

The Alternative Activation Account is supported by a neuroimaging study by Spalek and Oganian (2019) showing that semantic associates activate different brain areas from proper focus alternatives. Specifically, only relevant alternatives activate areas that have been invoked in discourse processing. Since all the aforementioned studies on focus alternatives tested noun alternatives are single words, it is not clear what level of representation alternatives have.[1] Alternatives could be concepts, lemmas, sub-constituents, phrases or entire utterances. In the following, we will revisit the theoretical literature to make different suggestions about this question for the case of scalar implicature.

2.2.2 Extending the Alternative Activation Account to Horn scales

Similar to focus, theoretical accounts of scalar implicature assume that more alternatives are initially generated and then restricted. Several theoretical accounts in the grammatical tradition following Fox and Katzir (2011) even assume the alternatives for focus and for scalar implicature to be the same. Thus, we propose to extend the Alternative Activation Account to cases of scalar implicature.

---

[1] A study by Lacina, Sturt and Gotzner (2024a, 2024b) has extended the so-called probe recognition paradigm to verbal alternatives. This study provides evidence that larger constituents become activated in focus processing; however, the study did not find a critical interaction with focus particles. So, it remains unclear whether listeners entertain verbal phrases as part of generating alternatives or as a general by-product of memory retrieval.

Starting off from the same assumption about online semantic and pragmatic processing, we can straightforwardly extend the Alternative Activation Account to scalars as follows. In the first step, a broad cohort of alternatives is activated including all associates of a scalar expression. Thus, an expression like *beautiful* should also activate its antonym *ugly*. Due to the entailment condition (e.g., Horn, 1972), antonyms should be deactivated in step 2 so that only the stronger scale-mates remain as part of the proper set of alternatives to *beautiful*. That is, only *gorgeous* should be negated during the inferential process. Thus, the main prediction arising from the Alternative Activation Account is that alternatives beyond scale-mates (of one polarity) should initially be activated as a result of how the brain organizes words in a semantic network.

1. Initial activation of all associates

(3) Mary is beautiful - > UGLY, GORGEOUS

2. Restriction to stronger scale-mates (relevant alternatives)

(4) Mary is beautiful - > GORGEOUS

Let us briefly discuss the nature of relevant alternatives from the view of the theoretical scalar implicature literature. The majority of the literature has assumed that scalar implicatures arise via specialized Horn scales that are ordered with respect to asymmetric entailment (Horn, 1972). These asymmetric entailment relations can be shown with linguistic tests using the scalar particle *even*:

(5) He ate some, he even ate all of the cookies
(6) #He ate all, he even ate some of the cookies
(7) #He ate all, he even ate none of the cookies

The tests show that the statement with *all* entails the one with *some but* not vice versa. *All* also does not entail its antonym *none* and the opposite is not true either. To save the asymmetric entailment condition, negative terms are assumed to be represented on a separate Horn scale (see Hirschberg, 1985). Note also that the ordering relation is reversed for negative scales, for example *none* is stronger than *few*. One of the main reasons to postulate entailment scales was the symmetry problem (Kroch 1972; see Breheny et al., 2017 for a recent overview). Symmetry is said to arise when there is a particular expression that has two alternatives whose disjunction it is equivalent to and these alternatives are in contradiction (Fox & Katzir, 2011). Let us exemplify the problem with the *some-all* scale and its corresponding implicature:

(8) John ate some of the cookies

Sentence (8) has the implicature that John ate some but not all of the cookies due to the negation of the statement with the alternative *all*. However, the expression *some but not all* is in principle a symmetric alternative to *some*. The problem is that if *some but not all* is part of the alternative set, a contradiction would follow. The symmetry problem is how to include *all* as an alternative while excluding the symmetric alternative *some but not all.* In Horn's view, symmetry is broken by stipulating that alternatives are lexical scales ordered by asymmetric entailment. This means that *some but not all* is excluded from the set of relevant alternatives.

Neo-Gricean globalist accounts such as the one by Horn (1972) are globalist in the sense that entire utterances are being negated. For example, to derive a scalar implicature for sentence (8) one would need to negate the sentence *John ate all of the cookies*. This assumption was challenged by cases of embedded implicatures where a triggering expression embedded under another scalar generates a strengthened reading (Chierchia, 2006). To take an example, a sentence like *All girls found some of their marbles* has a reading in which all girls found some but not all of their marbles (e.g., Chemla & Spector, 2011; Potts et al., 2016; Gotzner & Benz, 2018). This reading cannot be derived by globally negating the alternative *All girls found all of their marbles* in a standard way (but see Chemla & Spector, 2011). As a reaction, Chierchia (2006) and others developed the grammatical view of implicatures, which incorporates implicatures locally at the triggering site. This account uses sub-constituents as alternatives, for example when encountering *some* the lexical expression *all* is triggered and negated by a silent operator (see Potts et al., 2016 and Benz & Gotzner, 2021 for non-grammatical accounts to derive embedded implicatures).

While some versions of the grammatical account still use specialized scales (e.g., Chierchia, 2013), other accounts use alternatives that are constrained by complexity considerations (e.g., Trinh & Haida, 2015; Fox & Katzir, 2011). What is common to grammatical accounts is that they use phrases or sub-constituents as the basis of the inferential process. This view prima facie seems to be more compatible with the incremental nature of language processing. But on a Neo-Gricean globalist account, it is also plausible that listeners initially entertain a broader set of alternatives beyond proper scale-mates during real-time processing. On this view, a later pragmatic process would involve the reasoning about entire alternative utterances the speaker could have used (see for example, Chemla & Singh, 2024a and 2024b for an overview of this debate). Importantly, all of the existing accounts would exclude antonyms or more complex alternatives from the relevant set of alternatives to avoid the symmetry problem.

To summarize, the main novel prediction arising from the Alternative Activation Account is that alternatives beyond scale-mates (of one polarity) should be activated during the inferential process. This would be compatible with several accounts of scalar implicature, that is accounts of how alternatives are being negated. Hence, experimental work needs to find a way to distinguish activated and relevant alternatives that are negated during pragmatic processing. We will discuss some suggestions for doing so after reviewing the existing body of experimental research on which alternatives become activated during processing.

2.3 Psycholinguistic Evidence for the Activation of Alternatives for Scalar Implicature

A recent body of research has investigated the nature of alternatives and their underlying mental representation during sentence comprehension. Firstly, we review the evidence on the activation of informationally stronger alternatives that are predicted to be a necessary component of pragmatic inference processes (e.g., Horn, 1972). Next, we turn our attention to the emerging body of literature that aims to test the prediction of the Alternative Activation Account (Gotzner, 2017) that it is not only the stronger, but also the other, weaker alternatives that are active in the process. Additionally, we discuss related research using structural priming and show how it can be related to the questions surrounding the activation of alternatives as well.

2.3.1 Evidence for the Activation of Strong Terms

De Carvalho et al. (2016) were the first to investigate whether informationally stronger terms are in fact activated during comprehension. Using a masked priming paradigm and a lexical decision task, they presented their participants either weak scalar terms (*some*) or strong ones (*all*) as subliminal primes. The targets were either identical (i.e., *some—some*, *all—all*) or the other scale-mate (i.e., *some—all*, *all—some*). There was also a control condition where a sequence of consonants not comprising an existing word was presented. When their French participants performed the task, they were found to be the quickest in the identical condition and the slowest when the prime was a non-word sequence. This suggested that the experimental subliminal priming set up of de Carvalho and colleagues (2016) in fact impacted people's lexical decision times. Crucially, they found a difference between the two scalar word prime conditions. It turned out that weak scalar word primes activated their stronger scale-mate targets more than the latter used as primes did for the weak. In other words, de Carvalho et al. (2016) found a priming asymmetry. This, they argued, was evidence in favor of the psychological reality of lexical scales, as predicted by accounts such as that proposed by Horn (1972). However, what this research did not address was whether this activation is indicative of anything beyond lexical relations between scale-mates, as their participants were presumably engaged in lexical processing only and were not deriving any scalar implicatures.

Let us now turn to discussing the recent study by Ronai and Xiang (2023), which attempted to fill this gap. These researchers were interested in the "psycholinguistic reflexes" of pragmatic inferential processes. More concretely, they set out to test whether in the context of SI-triggering sentences, the stronger alternatives are retrieved from memory and activated. They did this for a variety of scales, which they took from their research on the inference rates of these different scales (Ronai & Xiang, 2024). These included scalar words of many different categories, among which were quantifiers such as the pair *some* and *all*, the conjunctions *or* and *and*, adverbs such as *partially* and *completely*, verbs (for example, *slowed* and *stopped*), and adjectives (for example, *warm* and *hot*), which made up more than half of all items used. They included 60 scalar pairs altogether.

They conducted several web-based experiments in which their participants had the task of performing lexical decision on the strong term of each item pair. The prime words were either the weak scale-mate of the given scale (e.g., *warm* with *hot* as the target) or an unrelated word (e.g., *mercurial*). Their Experiment 3 was the crucial one for testing whether the stronger scalar terms are activated in real-time comprehension. Ronai and Xiang (2023) embedded their weak scalars and unrelated words within sentential contexts that could give rise to a scalar implicature (*The weather is warm/mercurial*). The sentence was presented in the rapid-serial visual presentation mode and was followed by 650 ms of a blank screen, at which point the target word appeared.

What the results of this experiment showed was that strong terms (*hot*) were indeed activated by the presence of their weaker scale-mates (*warm*), evidenced by the fact that comprehenders reacted to the strong scalar target quicker when the weak scalar was the prime compared to when it was the unrelated word. In order to ascertain that this was in fact the work of pragmatic inferential processes and not just a result of lexical-based priming, they conducted their Experiment 2, in which the prime words were presented in isolation without any sentential context. Here, no priming was observed. What Ronai and Xiang (2023) take these results to mean is that weak scalar terms activate their stronger scale-mates only in SI-triggering contexts, while this activation cannot be assigned to simple lexical factors unrelated to pragmatics, and thus, that comprehenders in fact entertain the stronger terms during online scalar implicature derivation processes.[2]

What these two studies taken together show is that strong scalar terms are activated in the minds of comprehenders and that this effect is specific to sentential contexts, which could in principle give rise to scalar implicatures, and that they are primed asymmetrically when compared to their weaker counterparts, or in other words that priming seems to be stronger when going up the scale in terms of informational strength as opposed to downward. This evidence points toward the psychological reality of scalar alternatives and to them being employed in a similar way to focus ones.

There is another strand of research that operates with the activation of alternatives within their both experimental and explanatory frameworks. This is the examination of scalar implicature derivation by means of *structural priming* methods, ultimately derived from language production studies (Branigan & Pickering, 2017). Here, visual stimuli or linguistic material (often both) are presented as primes with the target being a sentence (often accompanied by a visual scene), which could give rise to a scalar implicature (e.g., Bott & Chemla, 2016). Different tasks and measures such as the truth-value task or the covered box paradigm are used to assess whether the participant in question derived a scalar implicature in a given trial. In the study of Rees and Bott (2018), participants were found to be more likely to derive an implicature (e.g., *some of the shapes are circles*) when the prime sentence preceding this trial contained the stronger alternative (e.g., *all of the shapes are squares*). Rees and Bott (2018) interpreted these results as supporting a particular model of implicature derivation, in which the activation of the stronger

---

[2] Ronai and Xiang (2023) also tested whether the inclusion of the particle *only* had an effect on the activation of strong scalars, since the particle had been found to create additional interference in the case of focus (e.g., Gotzner et al., 2016). However, no such effect was found.

alternative is key. They proposed a theory in which scalar implicature derivation is initiated only when the alternative is made sufficiently salient, i.e., activated. These data and theoretical suggestions were further corroborated by Bott and Frisson (2022), who showed that when their participants were shown the alternative in the same paradigm, the time it took them to derive the implicature in the subsequent trial decreased.

All in all, studies using both types of priming seem to coalesce around the idea that the activation of the stronger alternative within the minds of comprehenders is key to deriving scalar implicatures.

2.3.2 Evidence for the Role of Non-Entailed Alternatives

While the research reviewed above focused on the question whether informationally stronger terms are active during online scalar implicature derivation, an element that most of the theoretical accounts consider to be necessary, there has also been recent research asking whether other, informationally weaker alternatives also appear within the process or even participate in it.

Working within the Rational Speech Act framework, Peloquin and Frank (2016) attempted to model participants' judgments regarding scalar implicatures on different scales. They tested several models that included either only the stronger alternatives, as predicted by the classical treatments discussed above (e.g., Horn, 1972), or other alternatives, such as antonyms and middling terms (e.g., *okay* for the scale < *good, excellent* >). They found that contrary to the predictions, the models that included these other alternatives provided a better fit for participants' judgments. Peloquin and Frank (2016) took this as evidence that other informationally not stronger alternatives might also play a role in people's reasoning about pragmatic meanings and deriving scalar implicatures.

Additionally, Degen and Tanenhaus (2016) showed that in scalar implicature processing with quantifiers (i.e., *some*), including exact numbers (*one, two*) as alternatives that could be entertained by the comprehender, people judged the quantifier *some* as less appropriate within the given discourse, thus giving these researchers evidence that alternatives that are not stronger and are even from a different category could be playing a role in the process.

Another empirical suggestion for the relevance of non-entailed alternatives comes from the domain of the acquisition of pragmatics. In the research of Skordos and Papafragou (2016), which examined the derivation of scalar implicatures by preschool children and the role of alternatives therein, it was found that when their children participants were explicitly provided the non-entailed alternative *none*, they were more likely to interpret the quantifier *some* in a pragmatic way. In fact, the strength of this priming was similar to when the strong term *all* was cued. Such findings are surprising given standard accounts which assume that negative and positive quantifiers are represented on separate Horn scales.

To directly test whether non-entailed alternatives could play a role in scalar implicature derivation, a recent study by Lacina et al. (2024a) probed the activation of antonyms and of scale-mates under negation. They took the method and stimuli from the above-discussed research by Ronai and Xiang (2023) as their starting point. The main question being answered in their research was whether the priming observed by Ronai and Xiang (2023) was indeed indicative of scalar implicature derivation and whether even in situations where the target word, i.e., the strong scalar term *hot* in the previous study, would also be activated when it ceased to be informationally stronger due to manipulations to the sentence context and the prime word.

Negation is a downward entailing operator. When a sentence includes constituent negation of, say, a predicative adjective, i.e., *not warm*, no scalar implicature to the effect of *warm but not hot* is expected to arise (e.g., Horn, 1972). This is due to the fact that *hot* is no longer informationally stronger within the negated context. The meaning *not hot* is not implicated here, but entailed. In their first experiment, Lacina, Ronai, Alexandropoulou and Gotzner (2024a) used this to test for the activation of strong scalar target words (*hot*). What they found was that negating the weak scalar term canceled the priming effect for the scale-mate. In other words, when negated, *warm* no longer activated *hot*.

Next, they conducted two experiments where the weak scale-mate prime (*warm*) of Ronai and Xiang (2023) was replaced with its antonym (*cool*), while the target word was the same (*hot*). In one experiment, they embedded these antonyms into the same sentential frames that were used in the study of Ronai and Xiang (2023) in their Experiment 3. In the other experiment, they presented the same antonymic primes as isolated lexical items, mirroring the lexical Experiment 2 from Ronai and Xiang (2023). What they found out was that the antonyms (*cool*) activated the strong terms of opposite polarity (*hot*) both when inside a sentential context and when presented as isolated words.

Finally, the researchers also conducted an experiment where antonymic primes were used but constituent negation was also added. Their participants were therefore exposed to sentences containing *not cool* and were to react to the target *hot*. Here, no priming was observed, similar to the negated weak scale-mate experiment. In order to test whether the lack of activation observed in the two negated experiments was only due to the presence of negation rather than due to any implicature or informational strength factors, Lacina et al. (2024a) conducted a joint analysis of their experiments with sentential context and of Experiment 3 from Ronai and Xiang (2023). They found that negation had a different impact on the lexical decision times to the targets depending on whether the prime was a weak scale-mate or its antonym. Negation interacted with the weak scalar primes, but not with the antonymic ones. This in turn suggested that while antonyms might activate the strong scalar targets, negation does not seem to be effecting this activation in the same way that it does when the target is informationally stronger and is the locus of a possible scalar implicature. Consequently, we interpret these results to be in line with the Alternative Activation Account discussed above, since these data suggest that associative links do activate a slew of alternatives, some informationally stronger, some weaker, yet that a selection process follows that, depending on the context and grammatical restrictions, proceeds to pick out only those alternatives that are directly relevant to implicature derivation.

What we have attempted to show and highlight in this section is that alternatives beyond the stronger, entailed scale-mates play a role in the process of scalar implicature derivation, which goes against the predictions of most standard accounts of scalar implicature. On the contrary, it appears that modeling data suggest that including non-entailed alternatives improves accuracy with regard to matching human data and that experimental studies show that non-entailed alternatives such as antonyms are active in the process of real-time scalar implicature derivation. The Alternative Activation Account presents us with an explanation—it might be that non-entailed alternatives are activated during the process via the semantic network. Those should be discarded later in order for the relevant alternatives to be worked upon in further stages to achieve the final pragmatic meaning.

Relating these findings back to the theories of scalar implicature outlined in Sect. 2.2, one should note that all accounts would exclude antonyms from the set of relevant alternatives. At this point, we cannot distinguish whether antonyms are activated as part of the broader activation spreading mechanism (step 1 in the Alternative Activation Account) or whether they are part of the relevant set of alternatives. This would mean that antonyms are being explicitly negated during the inferential process or that there is another scalar implicature mechanism that is not sensitive to lexical Horn scales. In the following, we review evidence that casts doubt on the role of lexical alternatives in scalar implicature and we briefly sketch some novel scalar implicature mechanisms.

2.4 Different Alternatives or Different Implicature Mechanisms?

While the theoretical and experimental literature reviewed so far indicated that alternatives play a crucial role in pragmatic reasoning, there are also studies that cast doubt on this assumption. Especially when considering scales beyond the quantificational ones involving *some* and *all*, alternatives may be invoked differently or not at all. In the following section, we first review evidence suggesting that alternatives are invoked differently across triggering expressions and then we sketch recent proposals that could explain these results via a scalar implicature mechanism that does not involve lexical alternatives.

2.4.1 Scalar Diversity and the Role of Semantics in Scalar Implicature Computation

The first study showing variation across triggering expressions was carried out by Doran et al. (2009). They manipulated whether a contextual question evoked alternatives on a scale and how many scale-mates were mentioned. This manipulation was only effective for adjectival scales. For example, when the stronger scale-mate *gorgeous* was mentioned in the contextual question, participants were most likely to endorse the scalar implicature *Kate is pretty but not gorgeous*. In fact, the highest rates were observed in the condition where both the stronger scale-mate *gorgeous* and a non-entailed alternatives *average-looking* were mentioned. For quantifiers like *some* the endorsement of the scalar implicature was equally high in all contextual conditions. This could mean that quantifiers like *some* more automatically activate their stronger scale-mate than adjectives. The adjective results, in turn, might suggest that non-entailed alternatives play a role in the inferential process, as argued in Sect. 3.2.

Building on Doran et al.'s study, van Tiel et al. (2016) constructed a set of Horn scales involving different grammatical classes and demonstrated large variability in scalar implicature endorsement rate across triggering expressions—an effect that became known as *scalar diversity*. To measure the extent to which activated alternatives predict inference rates, van Tiel et al. used several predictors such as the likelihood of mentioning the strong term in a cloze task and relative frequencies in the COCA corpus. Under the hypothesis that inference rates vary as a function of whether alternatives are available to the listener, one would expect that cloze probabilities predict inference rates. However, no such effect was not observed. What did predict inference rates was the boundedness of the strong term and the distance between scalar expressions. That is, when the strong term denoted an endpoint (e.g., *certain* representing 100% percent on a degree scale), inference rates were relatively higher. Semantic distance was measured via a rating of the relative strength of corresponding expressions and the stronger a scale-mate was judged, the more likely participants were to endorse a scalar implicature. While these factors did explain some of the variability, a large amount still remained unexplained.

In a study using the same items, Ronai and Xiang (2024) tested whether the variability in scalar implicature disappears entirely when *only* is used. Since *only* requires alternatives due to its semantics, one would expect that with any scalar trigger, participants endorse the negation of its stronger alternative. For example, *only some* should mean *not all* on its semantic meaning. Contrary to expectation, *only* did not fully eliminate the scalar diversity effect. Providing a contextual question with the strong scale-mate also left some of the variability unexplained. Interestingly, a combination of both manipulations led to almost 100% endorsement rates across all scalar triggers. This indicates that for certain scalars, listeners do not automatically generate the strong alternative and that simply providing it in the context does not necessarily lead listeners to negate the strong alternatives. In line with this, modeling work by Hu et al. (2022) finds that a corpus measure quantifying the uncertainty over evoked alternatives predicts the scalar diversity effect. That is, the more listeners are uncertain about which alternatives are crucial, the less they endorse a pragmatic inference.

In all of the aforementioned studies, the scalar implicature endorsement rates were relatively low for adjectival scales. However, it is implausible that this is due to the nature of this grammatical category, as a study by Gotzner et al. (2018a) indicates. The authors constructed a set of 70 adjective scales that were balanced with respect to the scale structure underlying the semantics of adjectives (Kennedy & McNally, 2005). The authors reasoned that quantifiers may not differ from adjectives per se as a grammatical class but instead that certain adjectives have a similar semantics as the quantificational scales (e.g., < *possible, certain* >) and others involve a completely different semantics. Gotzner et al. hypothesized that these semantic factors should play a key role in scalar implicatures and classified their test set according to the types of standards their scale structure invokes, their polarity and extremeness. The factors relating to the semantics of adjectives explained around 67% of the variability in the endorsement of scalar implicature. While van Tiel et al. (2016) only looked at the boundedness of the stronger scale-mate, the study by Gotzner et al. (2018a) took into account additional semantic factors concerning both scale-mates (weak and strong) and used linguistic tests from the formal literature on adjective semantics to classify expressions. The study by Ronai and Xiang (2024) showed that not all expressions automatically activate their stronger scale-mates. It remains to be determined whether this is a factor that operates independently of the role of adjective semantics.

A study by Alexandropoulou, Herb, Discher and Gotzner (2022) investigated the role of adjective semantics to the incremental processing of scalar implicature. The study compared relative adjectives (e.g., *warm*) that involve context-dependent standards to minimum standard adjectives that impose a lower bound by their semantics (e.g., *breezy*) in a visual world setup (building on Sedivy et al., 1999). Participants clicked on a target picture over a competitor representing the stronger scale-mate were taken to indicate a scalar implicature. As hypothesized, the authors found an interaction of the adjective semantics with the context-dependence of the scalar implicature. Specifically, the presence of a contextual contrast (e.g., a picture of cold water) facilitated the derivation of scalar implicature involving relative adjectives, presumably by setting the threshold of the adjective meaning. In contrast, the scalar implicature was computed independently of the contextual contrast manipulation for minimum standard adjectives. Overall, the study indicated that semantic thresholds and pragmatic upper bounds are computed in parallel.

To summarize, there is evidence that alternatives are evoked to a different extent in the minds of listeners when considering different scalar expressions. What is more, the semantics especially of adjectival scales systematically affects the computation of scalar implicature. What we can conclude at this point is that the traditional mechanisms for scalar implicature are either incomplete to account for the processing findings or they only apply to a subset of scalar expressions such as quantifiers.

2.4.2 Semantic and Conceptual Representations

Most work reviewed so far tries to rescue the assumption that alternatives are evoked in scalar reasoning to some extent, for example by postulating that alternatives are activated to a different extent across triggering expressions. But there is also a way to make sense of the above-mentioned results without appealing to alternatives.

Given the findings that measurement scales play a role in pragmatic reasoning, Gotzner (2022) proposes a different mechanism for scalar implicatures involving adjectival scales without reference to alternatives. Instead the so-called *measurement mechanism* postulates that listeners reason about positions on an underlying measurement scale. A term like *warm* would exclude degrees that are above the degree interval denoted by *warm*. Thus, listeners may not be reasoning about stronger expressions that could have been used but rather about where to order a given expression on a degree scale. Since the meaning of certain adjectives involves relative context-dependent thresholds, the upper bounded meaning (corresponding to a scalar implicature) will also vary as a function of context. This would account for the boundedness and scalar distance findings (Gotzner et al., 2018a; van Tiel et al., 2016) and the role of contextual contrast in incremental processing (Alexandropoulou et al., 2022) without appealing to activated alternatives. For example, the effect of a contextual contrast could be akin to the role of comparison classes in determining the threshold of a relative adjective. If a contrast is contextually salient, the bounds are placed lower such that the ranges denoted by different expressions are more distinguishable. Considering the findings mentioned in Sect. 3.2., which indicated a role of non-entailed alternatives, the measurement mechanism would state that antonyms play a role in the inferential process but not their lexical representation per se. Instead it is the degree scale onto which different expressions may be mapped.

There are several other proposals in the literature which have a resemblance with the measurement mechanism. For example, Magri (2017) proposed to model Hirschberg scales (e.g., Bachelor's degree, Master's degree) via the negation of elements that are ranked higher on a partial order. Based on modeling results, Hu et al. (2023) conjecture that listeners may not have the strong scale-mate in mind but rather a concept of a more extreme case. To summarize, different proposals have been made that do not involve lexical alternatives but some other semantic or conceptual basis for scalar implicature reasoning (see also Buccola et al.,

2022 for a view involving conceptual alternatives for quantificational scales).

At this point, none of the existing work can pinpoint exactly the nature of the representation of alternatives. While different inference computation mechanisms may be involved for different scalars, another possibility is that there is only one mechanism but different kinds of alternatives. To make progress on these debates, we outline the key outstanding questions and how they can be addressed experimentally in the next section.

2.5 Future Research on Key Test Cases

We began this paper by showing that alternatives are represented in the mind of listeners in real-time processing and that initially expressions beyond scale-mates are invoked. We accounted for these findings via the Alternative Activation Account, which assumes two steps for generating and selecting alternatives (Gotzner, 2017). On this view, a broad cohort of semantically-related expressions is activated and subsequently pragmatic and grammatical mechanisms narrow down this broad set to the relevant alternatives. Several existing studies have shown that non-entailed alternatives become activated during processing but it is unclear which precise role they play during the inferential process.

According to the Alternative Activation Account, only relevant alternatives should be detected at later processing stages. Thus, it is crucial to test the evolving set of alternatives over the course of real-time processing. For this purpose, the paradigms of focus can be borrowed employing stimulus onset asynchrony (Husband & Ferreira, 2015) and memory (Gotzner, 2019) manipulations for activated alternatives and corresponding inference computation.

The second main point of this article was that theoretical accounts make different assumptions about the nature of alternatives: they could be entire sentences, phrases, lemmas or concepts. While the assumption that listeners reason about entire alternative utterances is implausible given current findings, none of the existing work can tease apart the other existing proposals since only nouns were tested in lexical tasks. In case alternatives are phrases, how can they be constructed online? Future processing studies need to test whether listeners activate alternatives beyond lexical expressions and to what extent grammatical restrictions guide the selection of alternatives. A recent study, Lacina, Sturt and Gotzner (2024b), showed that probe recognition can be used for phrasal alternatives in the case of broad focus. Such paradigms can be used to tackle grammatical constraints and phrases of different levels of complexity, for example to tackle the symmetry problem (see Breheny et al., 2017 for a recent overview).

To test new accounts that assume lemma-level or conceptual alternatives, visual paradigms can be used. The existing studies in this domain (e.g., Tieu et al., 2019; Chung et al., 2022) do seem to indicate that scalar implicature reasoning can be done without linguistic stimuli and the involvement of language. However, it cannot be excluded that participants also activate some lexical representations. Hence, distinguishing conceptual from lemma-level or some other form of lexical representation will require researchers to design new paradigms that do for example inhibit aspects of the representation.

Furthermore, two recent proposals make reference to measurement scales (Gotzner, 2022) and ranked orders (Magri, 2017) and discard the role of alternatives for certain scales. To test these accounts, cross-linguistic studies on languages that do not involve degrees or that involve different alternative sets (e.g., Dionne & Coppock, 2022; Stateva et al., 2019) could shed light. The other main prediction of the measurement mechanism is that scalar implicature should be possible when even access to lexical alternatives is interrupted. For example, production interference paradigms or transcranial magnetic stimulation (TMS) used to inhibit areas of the brain responsible for lexical access could be used to test this assumption. Finally, testing scalar implicature for novel expressions in an artificial learning paradigm (e.g., Buccola et al., 2022) or in developing children is promising avenue to tease apart lexical alternatives from other degree-based representations.

The key piece missing in all existing work is evidence that alternatives play a causal role in reasoning. The structural priming paradigms (Bott & Frisson, 2022) are currently the closest to providing an answer to this question. However, a more direct online measure is needed to study the evolving set of alternatives and the inference making process in tandem.

2.6 Concluding Remarks

In this paper, we have reviewed recent work on the nature of alternatives underlying scalar implicature computation. Contrary to existing theoretical proposals, studies have shown that listeners entertain alternatives beyond scale-mates during processing. These findings are expected based on domain-general mechanisms that subserve semantic networks in the brain. The literature indicates that sentence processing is incremental and so is the generation of alternatives. For this reason, the key questions about the nature of alternatives and the mechanisms underlying scalar implicature computation need to be addressed in real-time processing and probed at different time points.

We have highlighted that different scalar expressions may invoke alternatives to a different extent. It is an open question whether this means that different mechanisms underlie the computation of scalar implicature for different scalar triggers. Therefore, future work needs to use paradigms that distinguish activated alternatives from those alternatives that an inference is made on.

References

Alexandropoulou, S., Discher, H., Herb, M., & Gotzner, N. (2022). Incremental pragmatic interpretation of gradable adjectives: The role of standards of comparison. *Semantics and Linguistic Theory, 1*, 481–497.

Benz, A., & Gotzner, N. (2021). Embedded implicature: what can be left unsaid?. *Linguistics and Philosophy, 44*(5), 1099–1130.

Bott, L., & Chemla, E. (2016). Shared and distinct mechanisms in deriving linguistic enrichment. *Journal of Memory and Language, 91*, 117–140.

Bott, L., & Frisson, S. (2022). Salient Alternatives Facilitate Implicatures. *PLoS ONE, 17*(3), e0265781.

Branigan, H. P., & Pickering, M. J. (2017). Structural priming and the representation of language. *Behavioral and Brain Sciences, 40.*

Braun, B., & Tagliapietra, L. (2010). The role of contrastive intonation contours in the retrieval of contextual alternatives. *Language and Cognitive Processes, 25*(7–9), 1024–1043.

Breheny, R., Klinedinst, N., Romoli, J., & Sudo, Y. (2017). The symmetry problem: Current theories and prospects. *Nat Lang Semantics, 26*, 85–110.

Buccola, B., Križ, M., & Chemla, E. (2022). Conceptual alternatives: Competition in language and beyond. *Linguistics and Philosophy, 45*(2), 265–291.

Chemla, E., & Singh, R. (2024a). Remarks on the experimental turn in the study of scalar implicature. *Part I. Language and Linguistics Compass, 8*(9), 373–386.

Chemla, E., & Singh, R. (2024b). Remarks on the experimental turn in the study of scalar implicature. *Part II. Language and Linguistics Compass, 8*(9), 387–399.

Chemla, E., & Spector, B. (2011). Experimental evidence for embedded scalar implicatures. *Journal of Semantics, 28*(3), 359–400.

Chierchia, G. (2006). Broaden your views: Implicatures of domain widening and the "logicality" of language. *Linguistic inquiry, 37*(4), 535–590.

Chierchia, G. (2013). *Logic in grammar: Polarity, free choice, and intervention.* OUP Oxford.

Chierchia, G., Fox, D., & Spector, B. (2012). Scalar implicature as a grammatical phenomenon. In *Handbücher zur Sprach-und Kommunikationswissenschaft/Handbooks of Linguistics and Communication Science Semantics* (Vol. 3). de Gruyter.

Chung, W., Bade, N., Blanc-Cuenca, S., & Mascarenhas, S. (2022). Question-answer dynamics in deductive fallacies without language. In *Proceedings of the Annual Meeting of the Cognitive Science Society* (Vol. 44, No. 44).

De Carvalho, A., Reboul, A. C., der Henst, V., Cheylus, A., & Nazir, T. (2016). Scalar implicatures: The psychological reality of scales. *Frontiers in Psychology, 7*, 1500.

Degen, J., & Tanenhaus, M. K. (2016). Availability of alternatives and the processing of scalar implicatures: A visual world eye-tracking study. *Cognitive Science, 40*(1), 172–201.

Dionne, D., & Coppock, E. (2022). Complexity vs. salience of alternatives in implicature: A cross-linguistic investigation. *Glossa Psycholinguistics, 1*(1).

Doran, R., Baker, R. E., McNabb, Y., Larson, M., & Ward, G. (2009). On the non-unified nature of scalar implicature: An empirical investigation. *International Review of Pragmatics, 1*, 211–248.

Fox, D., & Katzir, R. (2011). On the characterization of alternatives. *Natural Language Semantics, 19*(1), 87–107.

Gotzner, N., & Romoli, J. (2022). Meaning and alternatives. *Annual Review of Linguistics, 8*, 213–234.

Gotzner, N., & Spalek, K. (2019). The life and times of focus alternatives: Tracing the activation of alternatives to a focused constituent in language comprehension. *Language and Linguistics Compass, 13*(2), e12310.

Gotzner, N. (2022). All you ever wanted to know about scales but were afraid to ask. Invited talk, September 22, 2022–September 23, 2022. Biennial XPRAG, Pavia.

Gotzner, N., Wartenburger, I., & Spalek, K. (2016). The impact of focus particles on the recognition and rejection of contrastive alternatives. *Language and Cognition, 8*, 59–95.

Gotzner, N. (2015). What's included in the set of alternatives? Psycholinguistic evidence for a permissive view. In *Proceedings of Sinn und Bedeutung* (Vol. 19, pp. 252–267).

Gotzner, N. (2017). *Alternative sets in language processing: How alternatives are represented in the mind*. Palgrave studies in Pragmatics, Language and Cognition, Palgrave Macmillan.

Gotzner, N., & Benz, A. (2018). The best response paradigm: A new approach to test implicatures of complex sentences. *Frontiers in Communication*, 2, 21.

Gotzner, N. (2019). The role of focus intonation in implicature computation: A comparison with only and also. *Natural Language Semantics, 27*(3), 189–226.

Gotzner, N., Solt, S., & Benz, A. (2018a). Scalar diversity, negative strengthening and adjectival semantics. *Frontiers in Psychology, 9*, 1659.

Gotzner, N., Solt, S. & Benz, A. (2018b). Adjectival scales and three types of implicature. *Proceedings of SALT 28*, 409–423. MIT.

Grice, H. P. (1975). Logic and conversation. In Cole, P., & Morgan, J. (Eds.), *Syntax & Semantics* (3).

Hirschberg, J. L. B. (1985). *A theory of scalar implicature.* PhD Dissertation, University of Pennsylvania.

Horn, L. (1972). *On the semantic properties of logical operators in English.* University of California.

Hu, J., Levy, R., & Schuster, S. (2022). Predicting scalar diversity with context-driven uncertainty over alternatives. Association for Computational Linguistics (ACL).

Hu, J., Levy, R., Degen, J., & Schuster, S. (2023). Expectations over unspoken alternatives predict pragmatic inferences. *arXiv preprint* arXiv:2304.04758.

Husband, E. M., & Ferreira, F. (2015). The role of selection in the comprehension of focus alternatives. *Language, Cognition and Neuroscience, 31*(2), 217–235.

Jördens, K. A., Gotzner, N., & Spalek, K. (2020). The role of non-categorical relations in establishing focus alternative sets. *Language and Cognition, 12*(4), 729–754.

Kennedy, C., & McNally, L. (2005). Scale structure, degree modification, and the semantics of gradable predicates. *Language, 81*, 345–381.

Kroch, A. (1972). Lexical and inferred meanings for some time adverbs, *Quarterly Progress Report of the Research Laboratory of Electronics, 104*. Cambridge, MA: MIT.

Lacina, R., Alexandropoulou, S., Ronai, E., & Gotzner, N. (2024a). Scalar alternative activation in implicature processing: A lexical decision study with antonyms and negation. Preprint available at https://osf.io/preprints/psyarxiv/r3q79.

Lacina, R., Sturt, P., & Gotzner, N. (2024b). The comprehension of broad focus: Probing alternatives to verb phrases. In Lemke, Robin, Schäfer, Lisa & Reich, Ingo (eds.) *Information structure and information theory*. (Topics at the Grammar-Discourse Interface 10). Berlin: Language Science Press. https://doi.org/10.5281/zenodo.12784266

Magri, G. (2017). Blindness, short-sightedness, and Hirschberg's contextually ordered alternatives: A reply to Schlenker (2012). *Linguistic and psycholinguistic approaches on implicatures and presuppositions*, 9–54.

Peloquin, B. N., & Frank, M. (2016). Determining the alternatives for scalar implicature. *CogSci*.

Potts, C., Lassiter, D., Levy, R., & Frank, M. C. (2016). Embedded implicatures as pragmatic inferences under compositional lexical uncertainty. *Journal of Semantics, 33*, 755–802.

Rees, A., & Bott, L. (2018). The role of alternative salience in the derivation of scalar implicatures. *Cognition, 176*, 1–14.

Ronai, E., & Xiang, M. (2023). Tracking the activation of scalar alternatives with semantic priming. *Experiments in Linguistic Meaning, 2*, 229–240.

Ronai, E., & Xiang, M. (2024). What could have been said? Alternatives and variability in pragmatic inferences. *Journal of Memory and Language, 136*, 104507.

Rooth, M. E. (1985). *Association with focus (montague grammar, semantics, only, even)*. University of Massachusetts Amherst.

Rooth, M. (1992). A theory of focus interpretation. *Natural Language Semantics, 1*(1), 75–116.

Sauerland, U. (2004). Scalar implicatures in complex sentences. *Linguistics and Philosophy, 27*(3), 367–391.

Sauerland, U. (2012). The computation of scalar implicatures: Pragmatic, lexical or grammatical? *Language and Linguistics Compass, 6*(1), 36–49.

Sedivy, J. C., Tanenhaus, M. K., Chambers, C. G., & Carlson, G. N. (1999). Achieving incremental semantic interpretation through contextual representation. *Cognition, 71*(2), 109–147.

Skordos, D., & Papafragou, A. (2016). Children's derivation of scalar implicatures: Alternatives and relevance. *Cognition, 153*, 6–18.

Spalek, K., & Oganian, Y. (2019). The neurocognitive signature of focus alternatives. *Brain and Language, 194*, 98–108.

Stateva, P., Stepanov, A., Déprez, V., Dupuy, L. E., & Reboul, A. C. (2019). Cross-linguistic variation in the meaning of quantifiers: Implications for pragmatic enrichment. *Frontiers in Psychology, 10*, 957.

Swinney, D. A., Onifer, W., Prather, P., & Hirshkowitz, M. (1979). Semantic facilitation across sensory modalities in the processing of individual words and sentences. *Memory & Cognition, 7*(3), 159–165.

Tieu, L., Schlenker, P., & Chemla, E. (2019). Linguistic inferences without words. In Proceedings *of the National Academy of Sciences, 116*(20), 9796–9801.

Trinh, T., & Haida, A. (2015). Constraining the derivation of alternatives. *Natural Language Semantics, 23*, 249–270.

Trinh, T. (2019). Exhaustification and contextual restriction. *Frontiers in Communication*. https://doi.org/10.3389/fcomm.2019.00047

van Tiel, B., Van Miltenburg, E., Zevakhina, N., & Geurts, B. (2016). Scalar diversity. *Journal of Semantics, 33*(1), 137–175.

3

Informational Sources and Discourse in the Generation and Maintenance of Alternatives

E. Matthew Husband and Nikole D. Patson

3.1 Introduction

Expressing the complete meaning that is intended by any particular sentence is difficult if not impossible for speakers. Speakers often must leave implicit much of the meaning they intend to express with any specific utterance. Luckily, comprehenders can often recover a speaker's implicit meanings by considering what the speaker could have said but did not. These *alternatives* to what was said are frequently used to enrich a sentence's meaning, and language provides speakers with a variety of devices to mark when such enrichment should take place within a sentence. These include changes in prosody, the use of focus particles or clefts, changes in word order, and the presence of scalar items, among

E. M. Husband (✉)
University of Oxford, Oxford, UK
e-mail: matthew.husband@ling-phil.ox.ac.uk

St. Hugh's College, Oxford, UK

N. D. Patson
The Ohio State University, Columbus, OH, USA

N. Gotzner et al. (eds.), *Alternatives in Grammar and Cognition*, Palgrave Studies in Pragmatics, Language and Cognition, https://doi.org/10.1007/978-3-031-76676-3_3

others. But recognizing that alternatives are relevant is just the beginning for comprehenders. They must use these cues to recover the correct alternatives and use them to infer what the speaker intended them to infer. How is it that comprehenders recover the relevant set of alternatives? In this chapter, we consider how comprehenders use different sources of information to recover different kinds of alternatives. For example, alternatives that are unmentioned may need to be recovered implicitly via semantic associations, scalar relations, or situational familiarity to the utterance, while explicit mention in discourse context can set up alternatives which are anaphorically related to the current sentence's content.

Psycholinguistic research has examined the time course in which comprehenders recover and use alternatives, revealing the cognitive mechanisms at play that generate and shape the set of alternatives that ultimately form a durable part of a sentence's meaning. In this chapter, we frame this literature around whether an alternative is explicitly mentioned or left unmentioned in discourse and propose that this distinction draws upon different cognitive processes. Within this distinction, we also examine the relationship an alternative has to a marked constituent. In doing so, we identify some gaps in what is currently known about alternatives from the psycholinguistic perspective. There are still many open questions for future research to investigate.

The chapter proceeds as follows: Sect. 3.2 explores the landscape of alternatives with an eye to their lexical and discourse sources. Section 3.3 then takes up this framing over the time course of processing, starting with the early processes that play out for unmentioned and mentioned alternatives before turning to their longer-term encoding and maintenance. Two pilot studies will be reported: one on memory retrieval of mentioned alternatives and the other on longer-term maintenance of unmentioned scalar alternatives. Section 3.3 concludes with a call for further theorizing around linking hypotheses tying measures of processing to the products of comprehension.

3.2 The (Processing) Landscape of Alternatives

Speakers must make choices about what to say and how to say it. Some of these choices reflect *alternatives*; when there are options available to speakers, the choice of one option can be used as a signal to communicate about the others. When speakers intend for comprehenders to draw these inferences, they can mark their choices through a variety of linguistic markings, including pitch accents, focus particles, word order, clefts, and scalar items that trigger implicatures. Alternatives are also argued to be involved more widely in the interpretation of negation, questions, and (counterfactual) conditionals, although these constructions are outside the scope of this chapter.

Focus constructions have long been considered primary markers for alternatives. For example, in response to the question, *Did John eat cake?*, a speaker might say, *John ate* PIE. The pitch accent on *pie* suggests that there were multiple dessert options, cake, pie, and perhaps even ice cream, and John chose to eat pie and not the other selections. As this example indicates, pitch accented constituents alone can evoke the relevance of a contrast. However, speakers can also choose to use a focus particle which further identifies a relevant semantic relation, e.g., whether alternatives should be excluded (*only*) or included (*even/also*) as part of the sentence's interpretation.

When speakers use linguistic markers like focus to indicate the relevance of alternatives, comprehenders need to infer what alternatives a speaker had in mind. There are two main sources of alternatives. One source is discourse context in which alternatives that are overtly mentioned can be anaphorically related to the meaning of the current sentence. These alternatives need not be related to the alternative-marked constituent in any particular way apart from their relationship in discourse, and therefore comprehenders must keep the contextual relationships established between discourse entities in mind. Another source for alternatives is implicit recovery of unmentioned alternatives from an alternative-marked constituent which signals some kind of relation (e.g., lexical, semantic, conceptual, or situational) with that constituent's meaning.[1]

Because alternatives can be purely contextual, only requiring that they be mentioned in the discourse, the semantic value of alternative marking such as focus must permit a very wide range of possible alternatives. Rooth (1992) suggests that these need only have the same semantic type of the focused constituent, while Katzir (2007) and Fox and Katzir (2011) propose a somewhat more constrained set of elements, any of which is at most as structurally complex as the focused constituent—still a very unconstrained set of possibilities.

This wide set of possibilities for alternatives may be likely when the source of alternatives is the discourse where there need not be any prior relation established between alternatives and marked constituents. Unmentioned alternatives, however, likely involve more constraint, relying on conceptual/semantic categories, situational knowledge, or scale structure to constrain what would otherwise be too wide a potential set of elements. Scalemates provide one constrained source of alternatives, where the alternative is related to the overt constituent via asymmetric entailment (Horn, 1972), or some ordering by rank, space, or time or underlying scale of quantity or other metric, like size, temperature, luminance, among others (Hirschberg, 1985; Solt, 2015). Other alternatives are related to the way a language carves up different semantic fields such as color, animals, and types of accommodation. Event and situational knowledge built up over a lifetime of experience may also play an important role in accessing alternatives that are not semantically or conceptually associated.

This suggests that the alternative set may be a bit of a mixed bag. Alternatives may enter the set because they are lexically/semantically related to the marked constituent in various ways but may also enter by dint of their discourse relation with the alternative-marked constituent. Often, both lexical/semantic and discourse relations may support certain alternatives, especially in natural everyday speech. Examining these factors

[1] Unmentioned alternatives may also arise from the shared environment, e.g., as visual referents. These require the speaker and comprehender to reason about what is in the common ground more broadly, an issue we will set aside here.

independently, therefore, is important and will play a key role in our theorizing.

While much of the literature on alternative semantics assumes a very wide range of alternatives that arise from the discourse or same semantic type of the focused constituent, most psycholinguistic studies have examined a narrower range of alternative relations (though see Gotzner, 2017; c.f., Gotzner & Romoli, 2022, and Repp & Spalek, 2021, for review).[2] Table 3.1 provides a non-exhaustive survey of the landscape from the viewpoint of discourse status and relational source. As can be seen, the vast majority of studies have investigated alternatives that are lexically related to an alternative-marked word, either because they are semantically associated or related to one another on a scalar dimension. Much less is known about alternatives that are only situationally related to the utterance. While such a narrowing of potential relations may be unsurprising when it comes to unmentioned alternatives, this has also been the case for alternatives mentioned in prior discourse where very few studies have teased these sources apart.

While there are clear gaps in the empirical landscape, the research that has been reported already shows that these different sources of alternatives lead to different processing profiles and long-term meaning representations. We take this up in the next section.

3.3 Alternatives in Time

3.3.1 Recovery of Alternatives in Early Processing

Accessing the relevant alternatives to any utterance and using them to enrich sentence meanings may seem like a demanding time-intensive process, but much psycholinguistic research has found that comprehenders are able to rapidly access and use alternatives very early in the

[2] Current psycholinguistic research has also been primarily limited to nouns and adjectives, though see Gotzner, Sturt, and Lacina (in press) for recent work on verbs and verb phrases.

Table 3.1 Overview of psycholinguistic studies on alternatives investigating mention and relation

		Mentioned	Unmentioned
Lexical relation	Semantic	Byram-Washburn et al. (2011), Calhoun et al. (2023), Fraundorf et al. (2010, 2013), Gotzner (2019), Gotzner and Spalek (2017), Gotzner and Spalek (2019), Gotzner et al. (2013, 2016), Kim et al. (2015), Norberg and Fraundorf (2021), Spalek et al. (2014)	Braun and Tagliapietra (2010), Calhoun et al. (2023), Fraundorf et al. (2010), Fraundorf et al. (2013), Gotzner and Spalek (2016), Gotzner and Spalek (2019), Gotzner et al. (2016), Husband and Ferreira (2016), Káldi et al. (2021), Kim et al. (2015), Koch and Spalek (2021), Norberg and Fraundorf (2021), Spalek and Oganian (2019), Tjuka et al. (2020), Yan et al. (2019, 2023)
	Scalemate		Benz et al. (2018), Bott and Frisson (2022), Chevallier et al. (2008), de Carvalho and et al. (2016), Doran et al. (2009), Lacina et al. (2023), Gotzner et al. (2018), Rees and Bott (2018), Ronai and Xiang (2023), Schwarz et al. (2007), Waldon and Degen (2020), van Tiel et al. (2016)
Contextual Relation	Situational	Byram-Washburn et al. (2011), Jördens et al. (2020)	Kim et al. (2015)
	Ad hoc scale		Rees and Bott (2018), Tomlinson et al. (2017), Waldon and Degen (2020)

time course of language processing (Gotzner & Spalek, 2019). There now exists a body of evidence concerning the cognitive mechanisms that make this possible—which mechanisms, however, depend on the source of alternatives. Fairly clear are unmentioned alternatives, which rely on an activation/selection mechanism that uses some relationship to the marked constituent to access these alternatives. Less well understood are mentioned alternatives, which we will propose rely on retrieval mechanisms that can navigate discourse structure. We will first examine the activation/selection of unmentioned alternatives before turning our attention to the retrieval of mentioned alternatives.

3.3.1.1 Activation/Selection of Unmentioned Alternatives

Activation/selection mechanisms are often proposed as part of the cognitive architecture of language processing. Several lines of research have found that the set of relevant alternatives that comprehenders use is generated and rapidly refined over time in early processing. Evidence has accumulated that at first a very broad set of candidates for the alternative set is initially activated through their relationship to the marked constituent and its context. This initial set of candidates includes both true alternatives and elements that are merely associated. Selection mechanisms have been proposed to weed out mere associates, leaving the comprehender with just those true alternatives that are relevant for comprehension.

Unmentioned Focus Alternatives

Much of the evidence for this rapid activation and selection process comes from lexical decision studies which ask participants to respond whether a letter string forms a word of their language. Response times in lexical decision tasks are known to be quicker when the letter string is a word that is semantically primed by prior stimuli, indicating that the concept related to the word's meaning is already active, or primed, in participant's minds. Braun and Tagliapietra (2010) used a lexical decision task with target strings appearing immediately after the offset of the critical word (SOA[3]: 0 ms) in Dutch sentences like *In Florida fotografeerde hij een FLAMINGO* 'In Florida he photographed a FLAMINGO.' They found that both true alternatives, like *pelikaan* 'pelican,' and mere semantic associates, like *roze* 'pink,' to a contrastively accented word were primed relative to an unrelated word (*beroemdheid* 'celebrity'). This suggests that participants initially activate a wide pool of possible candidates for the alternative set, including those that are appropriate alternative meanings for the focused word, as well as those that are merely present via their semantic association with the focused word. While this could suggest that comprehenders are unclear about which candidate items should be alternatives, it seems that comprehenders ultimately use their representation of a sentence's focus value to select from the set of candidates just those that are true alternatives. Using a similar design in English, Husband and Ferreira (2016) found that priming was maintained only for true alternatives 750 ms after the offset of the contrastively accented word. That is, mere semantic associates were no longer primed. This continued priming of true alternatives was also reported at a later SOA of 1,500 ms in Mandarin Chinese by Yan et al. (2023) who also found that mere semantic associates remain unfacilitated with longer SOAs.

Related results with longer SOAs have also been reported using probe recognition studies where participants were asked if a word appeared in the previous sentence/discourse. Because unmentioned alternatives are, by hypothesis, active in a comprehender's mind but unmentioned in the discourse, response times to probe words related to unmentioned alternatives in probe recognition tasks are inhibited, the slower response times indicating that participants find it more difficult to reject the probe word because it forms part of the sentence/discourse representation. Gotzner and Spalek (2017) manipulated the presence/absence of German focus particles *nur* 'only' /*auch* 'also' in critical sentences, shown in (1), to mark a constituent where alternatives are relevant. Probe words were presented 2,050 ms after the critical sentence. They found that alternative probe words were rejected more slowly when a focus particle was

[3] Stimulus Onset Asymmetry: The amount of time between the start of one stimulus and the start of another.

present compared to when it was absent, while mere semantic associates were rejected at the same rate regardless of a focus particle's presence/absence.

(1) Carsten wollte gern Obst essen und griff in einen Korb.
'Carsten wanted to eat some fruit and reached into a basket.'
Er nahm sich (nur) Äpfel heraus.
'He (only) took out apples out of it.'
Er ernährte sich stets ausgewogen.
'He always lived on a balanced diet.'
Probe: Beeren 'berries' (Contrastive Alternative)/Maden 'maggots' (Non-contrastive Associate)

Spalek and Oganian (2019) investigated even later stages of early processing, with probe words appearing 6,000 ms and 10,000 ms after critical sentences.[4] They used a distinct prosodic pattern, manipulating the presence of a pitch accent falling on the relevant constituent (*Kirschen* 'cherries') or earlier in the sentence (on *Carsten*), shown in (2). They found that the speed with which probe words that are semantically associated with a sentence constituent are rejected depended on the placement of a contrastive accent. When the contrastive accent was on the associated constituent, probe words were rejected at the same speed as unrelated probe words, but when the contrastive accent was elsewhere in the sentence, the same probe words were rejected significantly more slowly. They propose that the inhibition is only found for probes that are generally related to the event but are not good alternatives for the focused constituent.

(2) a. Carsten hat Kirschen vom Baum gepflückt. (Alternative Related)
Carsten has picked cherries from the tree.
b. Carsten hat Kirschen vom Baum gepflückt. (Nonalternative Related)
Carsten has picked cherries from the tree.
c. Thorsten hat die Ziegen auf dem Bauernhof gefüttert. (Unrelated)

[4] The late SOAs were conducive to Spalek and Oganian's (2019) fMRI study where the sluggish hemodynamic response is better detected at jittered longer lags.

Thorsten has fed the goats on the farm.
Probe: Pfirsiche 'peaches'

While the studies reviewed thus far have relied on a semantic relation between a marked constituent and the probed alternative, semantic relations are not the only possible relationships an unmentioned alternative can have. Unmentioned alternatives may also be accessed when they are related situationally to the sentence context of the marked constituent. Kim et al. (2015) investigated whether comprehenders can rapidly access situation-related alternatives by introducing scenarios that are relatively constrained in terms of alternatives given general world knowledge. They used a visual world paradigm where participants view visual displays of objects and listen to spoken language while their eye movements are tracked. Eye movements can rapidly converge on target object images when they become active in the mind during comprehension, sometimes leading to fixations that anticipate spoken language input. Kim et al. reasoned that comprehenders could use the presence of a focus particle in conjunction with a constraining context to rapidly fixate the target object image of a situationally related alternative before receiving auditory input that names that object. They manipulated the context prior to a target sentence to be constraining or neutral, shown in (3). The visual displays were also manipulated to include either four compatible referents in the neutral condition or one compatible referent (target picture: hot dogs) in constraining contexts. The proportion of fixations to the target picture were higher in bias contexts with *only* prior to the onset of the target word, suggesting that comprehenders can rapidly use the presence of a focus particle to activate a relevant situational alternative prior to its overt mention.

(3) a. Constraining Context: Niel and Alex went to a baseball game. Alex wants to buy some Coke and some nachos.
b. Neutral Context: Niel and Alex are at the supermarket. Alex wants to buy some bell peppers and some cherries.

Target Sentence: Neil (only) wants to buy some hot dogs.

Jördens et al. (2020) also investigated situationally related alternatives using contrastive accent manipulation similar to Spalek and Oganian (2019). In their probe recognition study (SOA: 4,000 ms), they found that a probe word like *cows* was rejected at a slower rate when it was situationally related and an alternative to a contrastively accented word but not when it was situationally related but a nonalternative. Response times to situationally related probe words (*Kühe* 'cows') in the nonalternative condition were not significantly different from unrelated probe words (*Aufzüge* 'lifts').

(4) a. Der Bauer hat STROH in den Stall gebracht. (Situationally Related Alternative)
'The farmer has straw into the barn brought.'
b. Der BAUER hat Stroh in den Stall gebracht. (Situationally Related Nonalternative)
'The farmer has straw into the barn brought.'
Probe: Kühe 'cows' (Situationally Related) / Aufzüge 'lifts' (Unrelated)

Unmentioned Scalar Alternatives

A second prominent source for unmentioned alternatives arises from the scalar relations introduced by scalar items. There is now a large psycholinguistics literature investigating scalar implicature, with much of it focused on whether and when comprehenders calculate a scalar implicature (see Chemla & Singh, 2014, for an empirical review). While these studies can be seen as addressing whether and when stronger scalar alternatives are active during comprehension, we focus here on those studies that directly concerned scalar alternatives.

Several studies directed at this source of alternatives have investigated how untimed responses to comprehension questions change when those questions probe an alternative, following important work on scalar implicature variability reported in Doran et al. (2009, 2012). van Tiel et al. (2016) presented participants with a sentence that included a scalar item (*intelligent*) and asked whether they inferred the negation of a stronger scalemate (*not brilliant*), shown in (5). Affirmative responses indicated that participants had adopted a sentence meaning enriched by the scalar implicature. As in Doran et al., they found high variability in the inference rates for different scalar items, but also observed higher implicature rates when the stronger alternative was more semantically distant from its scalemate. This was especially true when the stronger alternative denoted the upper bound of the scale (e.g., *free* as an upper-bounded stronger alternative to *cheap*). Surprisingly, higher word frequency, association strength, and semantic relatedness were not significant factors affecting rates of scalar implicature. This suggests that it is selection, not activation, that is more tightly tied to alternative processing, as these factors that should make the stronger alternative more available to comprehension because they are independently known to facilitate activation during lexical access.

(5) John says: She is intelligent.
Question: Would you conclude from this that, according to John, she is not brilliant?

Following this work, Gotzner et al. (2018) provided further evidence that the variation in scalar implicature rates is more systematic. They investigated how the scale structure of scalemates factors into rates of scalar implicature by adding measures of extremeness (Morzycki, 2012), standard type (Kennedy & McNally, 2005), and polarity to van Tiel et al.'s task. They also investigated rates of negative strengthening, where negation of a stronger scalemate implies a scalar value below that of the weaker scalemate (Horn, 1989), e.g., where *John is not brilliant* is taken to mean that John is 'less than intelligent' or 'rather stupid.' They used van Tiel et al.'s task to measure rates of scalar implicature for scalar pairs and added a second set of stimuli to measure their rate of negative strengthening, shown in (6). They found that scale structure factors influenced implicature rates, suggesting that additional factors related to the distinctness of alternatives matter. They also reported a strong anti-correlation between rates of scalar implicature and negative strengthening, suggesting that comprehenders sometimes do not calculate an implicature because they applied negative strengthening to the stronger scalemate.

(6) Mary says: He is not brilliant.
Question: Would you conclude from this that, according to Mary, he is not intelligent?

How all these factors contribute to comprehension in real time is at present not well understood, though experimental work is beginning to shed light on this issue. de Carvalho et al. (2016) provided some initial evidence for a priming asymmetry between weaker and stronger scalar alternatives using lexical decision with masked priming (34 ms prime + 34 ms pre- and post-prime masks; SOA: 34 ms). They presented participants with 43 scalar items drawn from 18 different scales, with primes being either weaker than the target (prime: *pouvoir* 'can,' target: *devoir* 'must') or stronger than the target (prime: *jamais* 'none,' target: *peu* 'few'). Both prime-target orders showed priming relative to a consonant string control, with the weak-strong order showing greater facilitation over the strong–weak order.

In contrast, Ronai and Xiang (2023) used a lexical decision task with a 650 ms SOA and found that stronger scaler alternatives were not primed in isolation without sentence contexts (just *good/foreign* preceding the target *excellent*), but showed robust priming with sentence contexts (*The movie is good*) and in sentence contexts with focus particles (*The movie is only good*). Lacina et al. (2023) also used a lexical decision task to examine the priming of stronger alternatives, using a subset of the items in Ronai and Xiang (2023). They found that negated weaker scalemates in sentence contexts (*The coffee is not warm*) did not prime their stronger alternative (*hot*), while straightforward antonyms in sentence context (*The coffee is cold*) do.

These studies suggest that unmentioned alternatives related to scalar relations may also rely on the same activation/selection mechanisms investigated more broadly in the domain of focus. Scalemates that are relevant to scalar implicature appear to be active post-selection, while those that are not appear to be deactivated post-selection. Questions remain as to when such alternatives are initially activated and whether their continued priming post-selection truly reflects their use by comprehenders. Studying this will require manipulations that control scalar implicature. For example, in an unpublished lexical decision study with a 0 ms SOA, Husband (2015) found that upward-entailing contexts which encourage scalar implicature (e.g., *The soup was hot…*) actually slowed response times to stronger alternative targets (e.g., *scalding*) relative to downward entailing contexts where such implicature is blocked (*The soup was not hot…*). Weaker alternatives (e.g., *warm*) were unaffected by entailment direction. While this asymmetric processing profile may reflect effects of scalar implicature on stronger alternatives, how these results related to those of Ronai and Xiang (2023) and Lacina et al. (2023) will require further work to be done.

Mentioned Alternatives and Activation/Selection Mechanisms

Taken together, these and other studies have shown that unmentioned alternatives rely on activation from both marked constituents and more broadly sentence/situational context followed by a rapid selection process unfolding over a half a second or so which prunes activated candidates that do not fit as alternatives for the sentence context. This activation/selection mechanism leaves the comprehender with a set of appropriate alternatives that can be used to infer a speaker's intended meaning.

Table 3.2 summarizes the general state of play for unmentioned alternatives given the research conducted so far. While an activation/selection mechanism is broadly consistent with the empirical results thus far, clearly more research is needed to fill in empirical gaps. This is especially the case when the source for alternatives is situational or scalar in nature where fewer studies have been published. Initial activation is currently underexplored in these areas, though the evidence of activity post-selection requires that these have become active at some point in the time course. Additionally, it is not clear whether mere semantic associates of scalar items are filtered out of the alternative set during the calculation of scalar implicatures, though the priming results with antonyms reported in Lacina et al. (2023) suggest that they may not be.

Table 3.2 Summary of the time course of unmentioned alternatives given their relationship to marked constituents/contexts

		Initial Access (0 ms)	After Selection (~>500 ms)
True alternative	Semantic	Active	Active
	Situational	?	Active
	Scalemate	?	Active
Nonalternative	Semantic	Active	Deactivated
	Situational	?	Inhibited
	Scalemate	?	?

3.3.1.2 Retrieval of Mentioned Alternatives

As noted above, candidates for the alternative set need not only arise from implicit relationships to marked constituents. They can also be introduced overtly in the discourse as mentioned alternatives. While one might expect these to be treated similarly to unmentioned alternatives during language comprehension, research sometimes reveals differential behavior driven by their mentioned status.

Mentioned Focus Alternatives

Gotzner and Spalek (2019) used both lexical decision and probe recognition tasks to examine very early effects of mentioned alternatives on the processing of focus particles (SOA: 0 ms). As shown in (7), they constructed contexts to introduce three items and critical sentences with a contrastively pitch accented target word referring to one of them. The presence of a focus particle marking this target word in critical sentences was manipulated. Probe words were then either an alternative mentioned with the target word, an unmentioned alternative semantically related to the target word, or simply unrelated. In their lexical decision study, mentioned alternatives were facilitated more than unmentioned alternatives in conditions without a focus particle, though both showed facilitation overall. In conditions with a focus particle, both continued to show facilitation, with no difference between mentioned and unmentioned alternatives. The presence of a focus particle, therefore, slowed responses to mentioned alternatives, but did not affect unmentioned alternative response times. In their probe recognition study, mentioned and unmentioned alternatives were responded to equally more slowly than unrelated controls, but the presence of a focus particle had no significant effect.

(7) In der Obstschüssel liegen Pfirsiche, Kirschen und Bananen.
'In the fruit bowl, there are peaches, cherries and bananas.'
Ich wette, Carsten hat Kirschen und Bananen gegessen.
'I bet Carsten has eaten cherries and bananas.'
Nein, er hat (nur) Pfirsiche gegessen.
'No, he (only) ate peaches.'
Targets/Probes: Kirschen 'cherries' (Mentioned), Melonen 'melons' (Unmentioned), Keulen 'clubs' (Unrelated)

The lack of focus particle effect on lexical decisions to unmentioned alternatives is consistent with our general summary concerning activation/selection for unmentioned alternatives. Slower responses to mentioned alternatives, however, suggest that focus particles were able to affect their processing. Since mentioned alternatives are already available as a potential contrast, the presence of a focus particle may have acted as an early cue to retrieve them as potential candidates for the alternative set. This is distinct from unmentioned alternatives as these rely on activation by the target word and therefore were unaffected by the presence of the earlier focus particle cue. Why a similar pattern did not emerge in probe recognition is less clear, though the decision process to correctly recognize mentioned alternatives and to reject unmentioned alternatives may have played an intervening role. That both were slower than unrelated controls, however, suggests that comprehenders access mentioned and unmentioned alternatives very rapidly in early processing.

Gotzner et al. (2016) also investigated the same design exampled in (7) at a slightly longer SOA (main verb duration + 2,050 ms silence) again with both lexical decision and probe recognition tasks. In lexical decision, mentioned alternatives were now more facilitated than unmentioned alternatives, though both were primed relative to an unrelated baseline. The presence of a focus particle slowed response times equally for all probe word conditions as an independent effect. In their probe recognition study, the presence of a focus particle inhibited correct recognition of mentioned alternatives and rejection of unmentioned alternatives. No effects were found for unrelated controls.

A similar delay was examined in Gotzner et al. (2013). They used a probe recognition task to examine effects of mentioned alternatives on the processing of contrastive accents and focus particles. They examined contexts that introduced two individuals, followed by a critical sentence where one of those individuals was referred to again either with a neutral accent, a contrastive accent, or a focus particle plus a contrastive accent. For their experimental items, the probe word, presented 2,000 ms after the offset of the sentence, was the alternative individual. An example item is given in (8). Response times to these probe words revealed no sensitivity to their manipulations.

(8) Der Richter und der Zeuge verfolgten die Beweisführung.
'The judge and the witness followed the argument. '
Der Richter/Der RICHTER/(Nur) der RICHTER glaubte dem Angeklagten.
'The judge/The JUDGE/Only the JUDGE believed the defendant.'
Probe: Zeuge 'witness'

At this later processing time, around 2,000 ms post-target word, the general pattern for focus particles is slower processing in both lexical decision and probe recognition responses. In lexical decision, this slow down merely tempers what is otherwise a priming effect on mentioned and unmentioned alternatives, suggesting that both are affected by focus particle processing at this point. Similarly, in probe recognition, this slowdown is in addition to the already inhibited responses to mentioned and unmentioned alternatives. The main difference between tasks, however, is that unrelated controls show effects of focus particles in lexical decision, but not in probe recognition.

A further delay in time was also explored in Gotzner et al.'s (2013) probe recognition study. They added a filler sentence after the critical sentence (e.g., for (8): *Er verkündete das Urteil.* 'He announced the verdict.'), followed by 2,000 ms of silence. At this delay, responses to probes showed significant facilitation with contrastive pitch accents, and some facilitation with focus particles, though this was significantly slower than pitch accent-only conditions, suggesting continued interference effects on alternatives in the presence of focus particles.

Most studies investigating mentioned alternatives, including those above, have manipulated those alternatives to be semantically related to the focused constituent. Byram-Washburn et al. (2011), however, represent an early study that manipulated whether a mentioned alternative (*lock*) to be either semantically associated or unassociated to a word focused by *only* (in (9): *bolt* vs. *nails*). This design teases apart mentioned alternatives that must be retrieved solely from memory from those that could be activated, and thus possibly boosted, by their semantic association with the focused word. Using a lexical decision task (SOA: 250 ms), they found a priming effect for mentioned but unassociated targets when prime sentences included *only*, and a priming effect for mentioned and semantically associated targets with prime sentences without *only*. These differences again suggest that focus particles are early cues to retrieve candidates for the alternative set, though semantic association appeared to interfere with priming in a way that is not well understood.

(9) Christina wants to buy a lock, nails, and a bolt.
She needs these to fix her front entrance.
Two days ago, she went to a store that didn't have a wide selection.
At the store, she was able to buy (only) a $\text{bolt}_{\text{Associated}}$/$\text{nails}_{\text{Unassociated}}$/a $\text{lamp}_{\text{Unrelated}}$.
Target: lock

Mentioned Scalar Alternatives

Turning to scalar relations, there appears to be a significant gap in our understanding of how these are affected by mention. The closest cases come from untimed comprehension studies of scalar diversity reviewed above (Doran et al., 2009, 2012; Gotzner et al., 2018; van Tiel et al., 2016). In these studies, context sentences that contained the scalar item were presented simultaneously with comprehension questions that contained overt mention of an alternative. Comprehenders therefore were allowed to reread and compare context sentences and comprehension questions if they chose to do so, which may have allowed them to consider the scalar item in context sentences in the context of the alternative mentioned in the question prior to making a response. Future research controlling the timing and presentation of alternatives could clarify this.

Mentioned Alternatives and Retrieval Mechanisms

In general, evidence suggests that mentioned alternatives form part of the alternative set early on during language comprehension, especially when there is an early marker like a focus particle. As most of the studies on mentioned alternatives have investigated the role of focus particles and used probe recognition, these effects are generally inhibitory in early processing (Gotzner & Spalek, 2019). While this provides solid evidence that mentioned alternatives are recovered early in the comprehension process, suggesting that comprehenders can rapidly navigate discourse context to find them, the mechanisms that bring such alternatives into the alternative set have not been well explored.

One possibility is that comprehenders rely on a content-addressable memory architecture that otherwise supports many other language-related processes (Lewis & Vasishth, 2005; McElree, 2000; Van Dyke, 2007; Van Dyke & McElree, 2011; see Vasishth et al., 2019 for an overview). In this architecture, the processing of input that depends on other representations triggers the comprehension system to search its memory and retrieve the relevant representations that input depends on. This retrieval process is cue-based, in that search is guided by the content of the input representation, which is assumed to be bundles of features/cues. Search in memory happens in parallel; all representations that (partially) match the retrieval cues of the current input are potentially retrieved.

Content-addressable memory architectures have been supported by two key empirical signatures: First, the availability of a representation in memory is degraded by various forms of interference. Representations that share cues with the correct representation interfere with its retrieval, and the addition of intervening material also interferes with correct retrieval, either through temporal decay of the correct representation or an increase in interference from encoding new content. Second, access to a representation in memory is insensitive to the temporal or positional order in which that representation was encoded. These two signatures account for a speed-accuracy trade-off in processing. Access to representations in memory is insensitive to their distance, reflected in the same initial speed of retrieval regardless of the amount of intervening material, but that distance and the presence of similar representations lead to declines in the availability of relevant representations, reflected in lower accuracy with the more intervening material. This pattern of speed and accuracy has been found for several phenomena that are antecedent in nature, including filler-gap dependencies (McElree, 2000; McElree et al., 2003), pronominal reference (Foraker & McElree, 2007; Kush et al., 2015), verb-phrase ellipsis (Martin & McElree, 2008), slucing (Martin & McElree, 2011), and anaphoric presuppositions (Chen & Husband, 2018).

As another type of antecedent phenomenon, mentioned alternatives may also be recovered via content-addressable memory retrieval. Comprehenders are unlikely to have the capacity to maintain all previously mentioned discourse elements active in their focus of attention, and may not know which, if any, will be relevant for the current sentence. Therefore, they must rely on memory storage for maintenance. If access to this memory storage is content-addressable, we expect comprehenders to use cues from the focused constituent to directly access their memory representations of the prior discourse for possible mentioned alternatives to include in the alternative set. This direct access and retrieval of mentioned alternatives is predicted to display the characteristic empirical signatures of distance-insensitive accessibility to representations and distance-sensitive availability of representations.

Because this has not been investigated in the prior literature, we manipulated distance in a pilot probe recognition study based on 36 items from Fraundorf et al. (2013) (see Sect. 3.2). 36 participants recruited online first read an initial context, self-paced sentence-by-sentence, which introduced two sets with two alternatives each, with the relevant two alternatives always occurring in the last sentence of the initial context. In the long-distance condition, an additional one to four sentences, also read self-paced sentence-by-sentence, intervened between the initial context and a final sentence. The short distance condition did not include these intervening sentences. The final sentence, read self-paced word-by-word, included all capitals font emphasis on the last or second-to-last word ending the sentence, signaling focus. 2,000 ms after the last word of the final sentence, participants were presented with a probe word and were asked to say whether this word appeared in the last sentence they read. Initial contexts and final sentences were manipulated so that the same probe word (*playground*) was either the target word that was focused in the final sentence, or it was a mentioned alternative from the initial context (when *skateboard park* was emphasized) or an unmentioned semantically associated alternative to the focused word (when *dog park* replaced *playground* in the initial context and was emphasized). We also collected data from an additional 36 participants where we removed font emphasis from the stimuli. A sample item is given in (10).

(10) Initial Context: The local parks commission had a busy meeting on Wednesday to decide how to spend its money for the year. People disagreed on whether the commission should focus its resources on expanding the parks or tidying the existing parkland. The parents wanted a playground$_{\text{Target/Mentioned}}$/dog park$_{\text{Unmentioned}}$ and the teenagers wanted a skateboard park.
Distance: The meeting turned into a rather raucous affair. There were several incidents of shouting and some speakers were interrupted. It didn't seem like anyone was going to be very happy with the decision.
Critical Sentence: After a long debate, a compromise was worked out to tidy the parks and build a PLAYGROUND$_{\text{Target}}$/SKATEBOARD PARK$_{\text{Mentioned}}$/DOG PARK$_{\text{Unmentioned}}$.
Probe: playground

Accuracy, shown in Table 3.3, was very high. Focusing on contrasts where the probe word was an alternative, we found that mentioned probes were responded to less accurately than unmentioned probes ($z = 8.74$, $p < 0.001$); however, this did not interact with either distance or emphasis. Interestingly, distance did not hamper retrieval of mentioned alternatives; if anything, distance improved mentioned alternative rejection rates ($z = 1.67$, $p = 0.054$). Analysis of accurate trial response times, shown in Fig. 3.1, found that mentioned probes were slower than unmentioned

Table 3.3 Accuracy to probe type given emphasis and distance

	Emphasis		No Emphasis	
	Short (%)	Long (%)	Short (%)	Long (%)
Target	98.4	99.0	99.0	99.5
Mentioned	83.2	88.1	80.9	84.5
Unmentioned	96.8	97.8	97.5	98.0

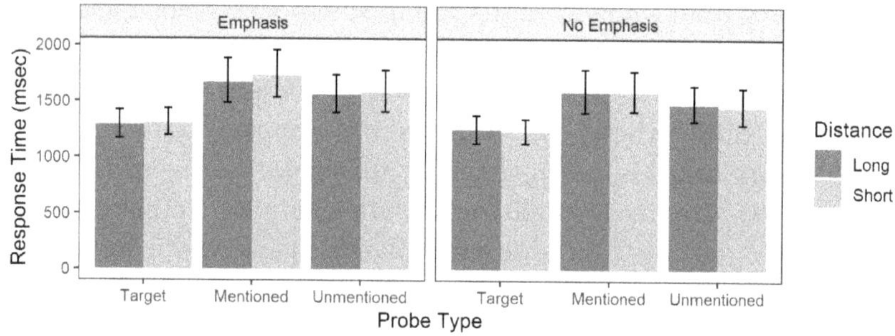

Fig. 3.1 Response times to correctly recognized/rejected probes by emphasis and distance. Error bars represent 95% confidence intervals

probes ($t = -4.01$, $p < 0.001$). However, neither distance nor emphasis had an effect.

The differences in response times between mentioned and unmentioned alternatives suggest that participants successfully retrieved an alternative when it was mentioned in the context and do not rely merely on semantic association. However, these effects appeared to be independent of whether focus was marked by emphasis or not and it did not interact with distance. This is consistent with a content-addressable memory architecture as accessibility was not affected by distance. Availability of mentioned alternatives was, however, affected by distance, though this effect appears to be inconsistent with the predicted degraded effect expected in content-addressable memory architectures as rejection rates improved in long distances. It may be that mentioned alternatives were still being held in active memory in short distance conditions and directly interfered with probe recognition accuracy, while long distance required mentioned alternative storage and retrieval. This may be related to Frazier and Duff's (2019) Activated

Syntactic Memory hypothesis which proposes that comprehenders hold the current sentence and the last potentially independent clause in active memory. However, it is unclear how these results bear on mentioned focus alternatives specifically since no differential effects of font emphasis were detected in either accuracy or response times. It may be that participants in the no emphasis study imposed implicit contrastive prosody during silent reading (Fodor, 2002; Speer & Foltz, 2015) since there was no font differentiation between focused and non-focused constituents, or that self-paced reading disrupted the font emphasis manipulation, possibilities that will require further investigation.

Summing up, psycholinguistic evidence has shown that mentioned alternatives are rapidly recovered for the alternative set during language comprehension. How comprehenders navigate discourse memory to retrieve these alternatives in real time, however, clearly will require further theorizing and research.

3.3.2 Longer-Term Maintenance and Encoding of Alternatives

Much of the experimental work on alternatives has focused on early processing. However, successful communication requires comprehenders to maintain alternatives in long-term memory over longer periods of time. Several studies have investigated whether mentioned alternatives are maintained during an experimental session (Calhoun et al., 2023; Fraundorf et al., 2010, 2013; Gotzner et al., 2013; Káldi et al., 2021; Koch & Spalek, 2021; Norberg & Fraundorf, 2021; Spalek et al., 2014; Tjuka et al., 2020).

Fraundorf et al. (2013) investigated the long-term maintenance of focus alternatives within an experimental session using font emphasis, mimicking contrastive pitch accents in spoken language. They had participants read short stories which introduced two pairs of referents and then mentioned one of the referents in each pair. Font emphasis was manipulated so that the first, second, both, or neither of the mentioned referents were contrastively focused. An example with contrast on the second referent is shown in (11).

(11) Originally, the space probe was designed to fly past Mars and Jupiter and send photographs and videos back to NASA from both planets. However, due to a glitch in the system, the photos from MARS were lost.

Probe: The photos from $\text{Mars}_{\text{Target}}$/$\text{Jupiter}_{\text{Mentioned}}$/$\text{Saturn}_{\text{Unmentioned}}$ were lost.

They found that contrastive focus improved participants' ability to recognize correct targets and reject mentioned alternatives on a memory task following a study phase where participants read all 36 stories. Unmentioned alternatives, however, were unaffected. This suggests that the contrastive focus led participants to better encode both the target and mentioned alternatives in long-term memory.

Spalek et al. (2014) found similar effects of focus particles on the memory of alternatives as Fraundorf and colleagues. Using the same stimuli as Gotzner and Spalek (2019) in (7), Spalek et al. manipulated the presence/absence of German focus particles *nur* 'only' /*auch* 'also' prior to the critical alternative. After a block of stimuli, participants were given a cued recall test in which they were asked to name the alternatives (e.g., *What was in the fruit bowl*?). They found that memory for the alternatives improved in the presence of a focus particle compared to a context in which there was no focus particle, suggesting that the focus particle enhanced the maintenance of alternatives along with the target word through the duration of the experiment regardless of the focus particle type.

This effect has been replicated in other languages and using other alternative producing constructions. Calhoun et al. (2023) found similar effects for cleft constructions in Samoan. Participants were given a probe recognition task after a set of six discourses. Focused mentioned alternatives were recognized faster than unmentioned and unrelated alternatives, suggesting that mentioned alternatives maintain activation, while unmentioned do not. Similarly, Káldi et al. (2021) used a change detection task to investigate the long-term activation of focus alternatives in Hungarian, which marks focus preverbally both prosodically and syntactically. In their study, participants heard short discourses as in (12).

(12) A házibuli után Annára és Mikire hárult az elpakolás feladata. Reneztek mindent, ami a kezük ügyébe kerüt. A konyhában is volt eendo elég.
'After the party Ann and Mike undertook the work of tidying up. They created order everywhere they went. There was a lot to do in the kitchen, as well.'
a. Miki [egy tányért]$_{FOCUS}$ rakott be a szekrénybe (Focus)
'Mike put [a plate]$_{FOCUS}$ in the cupboard.'
b. Miki rakott [egy tányért] be a szekrénybe. (No Focus)
'Mike put [a plate] in the cupboard.'

After hearing six discourses, participants played a virtual game for two minutes to prevent them from relying on working memory processes before doing a memory probe task. In the memory task, participants were asked to judge whether the probe was a sentence they heard in the previous part of the experiment. Probes were either the unchanged experimental sentence (*tányért* 'plate') or the critical noun was replaced with a semantically related word (*edényt* 'pot') or a contextually related word (*dobozt* 'box'). Káldi, et al.'s results were consistent with previous studies in which focus doesn't occur preverbally: When in the presence of a focused element, contextually suitable alternatives produced interference in the change detection task, suggesting alternatives remained active in long-term memory.

Interestingly, sex differences in alternative maintenance have been documented in the literature. Koch and Spalek (2021) again used the same stimuli described in (7). In this experiment, the cued recall task was given after 10 intervening trials to investigate long-term maintenance of alternatives. They found that recall for contextual alternatives was facilitated by contrastive focus. Interestingly, the observed benefit was predominantly driven by females. Tjuka et al. (2020) replicated this pattern of data, including the finding that the benefit of focus was driven by females, in Vietnamese, a tonal language. Finally, the advantage for focused alternatives disappears when working memory is taxed (Gotzner & Spalek, 2017), suggesting that the retrieval of alternatives requires working memory resources.

Taken together, these studies suggest that alternatives are maintained over the course of an experiment, but comprehension often requires language users to maintain meaning representations for much longer than the course of a single experimental session. To date, only a single study has investigated long-term maintenance of alternatives outside of a single experimental session. Fraundorf et al. (2010) tested memory representations for the alternatives after 24 hours. After listening to the experimental stories in (11) above on day 1, participants came back on day 2 and were given a true/false verification task, which contained either the target, mentioned alternative, or unmentioned alternative. As in previous studies, target words in the experimental discourses were either marked with a contrastive or neutral accent. Fraundorf et al. found that contrastive accents increased both the recognition for statements involving the focused target and correct rejections for mentioned alternatives. There was no increase in correct rejections for the unmentioned alternative. This suggests that both a focused constituent and an explicitly mentioned alternative are better represented in memory when contrastive accenting is used, and that this representation is maintained for at least 24 hours. However, the memory benefit does not extend to any possible alternative.

The studies above suggest that unmentioned alternatives are not encoded in long-term memory. However, this may be due to the fact that in these focus constructions, unmentioned alternatives may not be critically relevant for understanding the meaning of the discourse, which may explain why they are not maintained. In (11), used by Fraundorf et al. (2013), Mars and Jupiter were the only planets overtly mentioned in the space mission discourse. While the names of other planets, like Saturn, might be initially primed by mention of Mars, comprehenders have no compelling reason to encode Saturn as part of their long-term discourse representation as it is much less relevant and unlikely to be mentioned in subsequent discourse.

As these studies have exclusively examined focus alternatives that are derived from semantic associations, we do not know how other kinds of alternatives, such as those generated from scalar relationships or situational alternatives, are maintained in memory. There is reason to expect that long-term maintenance of these kinds of alternatives will be different. Consider scalar alternatives. Although they are frequently unmentioned, scalar alternatives are critically relevant to comprehension, as scalar implicatures derive strengthened meanings by negating the scalar alternative. For example, when comprehenders interpret the scalar quantifier *some*, with its lexical meaning 'at least some,' in upward-entailing contexts, they are often permitted to infer the negation of the stronger scalemate *all*, drawing the strengthened interpretation 'at least some, but not all.' Given the relevance of stronger scalemate alternatives for the comprehension of the strengthened interpretation of *some*, unmentioned scalar alternatives may be more robustly represented in intermediate and long-term memory compared to unmentioned focus alternatives.

To begin to understand how unmentioned scalemates may be maintained in memory, we conducted a in-person pilot study in the Language Lab at the Center for Science and Industry (COSi) in Columbus, OH. 41 participants read short vignettes in which the second sentence included either the scalar *some* or its alternative *all*, as in (13). Participants read 20 vignettes before seeing a memory probe. During the memory phase, participants saw a version of the second sentence in the vignette in the same order in which they were presented. Either they saw it exactly as it had appeared (correct), or the scalar term was replaced with its alternative (alternative scalemate change), or the scalar term was replaced with *none* (non-scalar alternative 'none' change). Participants were asked to judge whether the sentence was the exact sentence they had seen previously. Participants repeated the vignette/memory probe pairs six times for a total of 120 items (60 experimental, 60 fillers).

(13) Kaine was excited for the science fair.
He won some/all of the awards at the ceremony.
He was excited to share his work with everyone.
Probe: He won all/some/none of the awards at the ceremony.

We calculated *d'* scores for both critical sentence types as a measure of sensitivity (correct recognitions vs. false alarms). If the stronger scalemate is active in memory as an alternative due to scalar implicature, we expect to see a decrease in recognition sensitivity to probe change (e.g., *some* changed to *all* in probes) due to more failures to reject the stronger scalemate (i.e., more 'false alarms'). Recognition sensitivity for changes to weaker scalemates and non-scalemates should, however, be stronger as they are not relevant alternatives for scalar implicature. As Fig. 3.2 illustrates, this is what we found. Participants showed less sensitivity to changes from *some* to *all* than changes from *all* to *some* ($t = 2.053$, $p = 0.043$), but were not differentially sensitive to 'none' change given the original quantifier *some* or *all* ($t = 0.819$, $p = 0.415$). These data are interestingly different from previous studies showing that unmentioned alternatives seem to be deactivated when they are probed after a delay (Calhoun et al., 2023; Fraundorf et al., 2010, 2013). This suggests that unmentioned alternatives, when relevant for comprehension, are durably encoded by comprehenders.

Table 3.4 summarizes what is currently understood about the maintenance of alternatives in memory. Importantly, our understanding of the long-term maintenance is less well understood because fewer studies on this topic have been conducted with fewer manipulations compared to the number of studies on the early activation/selection of alternatives. However, we can currently say that within an experiment, mentioned alternatives to focused elements seem to be maintained in memory as they cause interference during memory probe tasks (Calhoun et al., 2023; Fraundorf et al., 2010, 2013; Gotzner et al., 2013; Káldi et al., 2021; Koch & Spalek, 2021; Spalek et al., 2014; Tjuka et al., 2020). Unmentioned alternatives do not seem to be retained in long-term memory when the alternatives are derived from semantic associations (Calhoun et al., 2023; Fraundorf et al., 2010, 2013). However, our pilot data investigating the activation of scalar alternatives suggests that

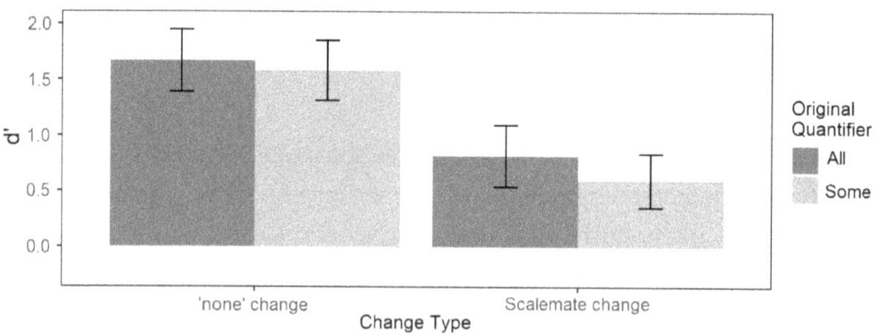

Fig. 3.2 Average *d'* score by original quantifier and recognition probe change type. Error bars represent 95% confidence intervals

Table 3.4 Summary of the time course of maintenance of alternatives in memory

	Early (0 ms)	Early (~>500 ms)	Late (same study)	Late (1 day)
Mentioned	Retrieved	Maintained	Maintained	Maintained
Unmentioned	Accessed	Maintained	Lost?	Lost?
Associates	Accessed	Suppressed	N/A	N/A

scalar alternatives may be retained in long-term memory even when they are unmentioned, perhaps because scalar alternatives are relevant for comprehension. Certainly more work must be done to better understand how different kinds of alternatives are differentially represented in memory. Additionally, these finds have been qualified by recent evidence that sex differences (Koch & Spalek, 2021; Tjuka et al., 2020) and working memory differences (Gotzner & Spalek, 2017) exist in alternative maintenance. These differences mirror the differences found in the scalar implicature processing literature showing that increasing demands on working memory decreases the likelihood that comprehenders make the implicature (De Neys & Schaeken, 2007; Marty & Chemla, 2013; see Nys et al. (2024) for review). Better understanding individual differences in the maintenance of alternatives may help elucidate individual differences in pragmatic processing, such as the finding that some comprehenders are 'pragmatic responders' (i.e., they more often compute the implicature than not) while other comprehenders are 'semantic responders' (i.e., they do not compute the implicature; Bott & Noveck, 2004; Noveck & Posada, 2003). Clearly, much more work must be done to understand the role of individual differences in the maintenance of alternatives and how this may be related to pragmatic processing.

3.4 Conclusion

Comprehenders are often faced with the task of inferring a speaker's meaning. One way they do this is by considering what *alternatives* the speaker could have said but did not. This chapter has explored what current empirical evidence suggests about the cognitive mechanisms that are used by comprehenders to generate a set of relevant alternatives and to understand whether different sources of information trigger different processes that may impact comprehension over time. We considered whether alternatives were explicitly mentioned in the discourse or unmentioned but implicitly related. We further considered whether alternatives were related by a semantic, situational, or scalar relationship to a marked utterance.

Evidence, predominantly from lexical decision tasks, suggests that comprehenders immediately activate a set of unmentioned candidates for the alternative set through their relationship to the marked constituent and its context and retrieve mentioned alternatives from discourse memory. This initial set of candidates includes both true alternatives and elements that are merely associated. Selection mechanisms, operating rapidly afterward (~500 ms), weed out mere associates, leaving only those true alternatives that are relevant for comprehension activated. Evidence from probe recognition tasks suggests that true alternatives are then maintained in memory, with mentioned alternatives showing the most success at long-term encoding, related perhaps to their relevance for successful comprehension.

This research has been important in establishing the time course of processing alternatives, but questions still remain and important theoretical work is still needed. One area that we have not emphasized so far is the linking hypothesis between how active an alternative is in a comprehender's mind and how that alternative is ultimately used for comprehension. Active alternatives affect response times, but it is unclear whether and how that activity is related to what a comprehender encodes as part of the durable mental representation of discourse. For example, Ronai and Xiang (2023) were unable to find evidence for a correlation between the amount of priming of the strong scalar terms and the rate of scalar implicature inferences. Indeed, the measures of other real-time sentence processing phenomena are known to not necessarily reflect comprehenders' sentence interpretations (see Ferreira & Patson, 2007, for a review). While clever theory and experimental design can link activity and use, further research is needed to make these links more direct and clearer in our theories of language comprehension, both concerning alternatives and in phenomena further afield.

References

Benz, A., Bombi, C., & Gotzner, N. (2018). Scalar diversity and negative strengthening. In U. Sauerland & S. Solt (Eds.), *Proceedings of Sinn und Bedeutung 22* (Vol. 1, pp. 191–204). ZAS.

Bott, L., & Frisson, S. (2022). Salient alternatives facilitate implicatures. *PLoS One, 17*(3), e0265781.

Bott, L., & Noveck, I. A. (2004). Some utterances are underinformative: The onset and time course of scalar inferences. *Journal of Memory and Language, 51*(3), 437–457.

Braun, B., & Tagliapietra, L. (2010). The role of contrastive intonation contours in the retrieval of contextual alternatives. *Language and Cognitive Processes, 25*(7–9), 1024–1043.

Byram-Washburn, M., Kaiser, E., & Zubizarreta, M. L. (2011). Focus facilitation and non-associative sets. In *SemDial 2011: Proceedings of the 15th workshop on the semantics and pragmatics of dialogue* (pp. 94–102).

Calhoun, S., Yan, M., Salanoa, H., Taupi, F., & Kruse Va'ai, E. (2023). Focus effects on immediate and delayed recognition of referents in Samoan. *Language and Speech, 66*(1), 175–201.

Chemla, E., & Singh, R. (2014). Remarks on the experimental turn in the study of scalar implicature, Part II. *Language and Linguistics Compass, 8*(9), 387–399.

Chen, S. Y., & Husband, E. M. (2018). Comprehending anaphoric presuppositions involves memory retrieval too. *Proceedings of the Linguistic Society of America, 3*(1), 44–51.

Chevallier, C., Noveck, I. A., Nazir, T., Bott, L., Lanzetti, V., & Sperber, D. (2008). Making disjunctions exclusive. *Quarterly Journal of Experimental Psychology, 61*(11), 1741–1760.

De Carvalho, A., Reboul, A. C., Van der Henst, J. B., Cheylus, A., & Nazir, T. (2016). Scalar implicatures: The psychological reality of scales. *Frontiers in Psychology, 7*, 1500.

De Neys, W., & Schaeken, W. (2007). When people are more logical under cognitive load: Dual task impact on scalar implicature. *Experimental Psychology, 54*(2), 128–133.

Doran, R., Baker, R. E., McNabb, Y., Larson, M., & Ward, G. (2009). On the non-unified nature of scalar implicature: An empirical investigation. *International Review of Pragmatics, 1*, 1–38.

Doran, R., Ward, G., Larson, M., McNabb, Y., & Baker, R. E. (2012). A novel experimental paradigm for distinguishing between what is said and what is implicated. *Language, 88*(1), 124–154.

Ferreira, F., & Patson, N. D. (2007). The 'good enough' approach to language comprehension. *Language and Linguistics Compass, 1*(1–2), 71–83.

Fodor, J. D. (2002). Psycholinguistics cannot escape prosody. In *Proceedings of the speech prosody 2002 conference* (pp. 83–90).

Foraker, S., & McElree, B. (2007). The role of prominence in pronoun resolution: Active versus passive representations. *Journal of Memory and Language, 56*(3), 357–383.

Fox, D., & Katzir, R. (2011). On the characterization of alternatives. *Natural Language Semantics, 19*, 87–107.

Fraundorf, S. H., Benjamin, A. S., & Watson, D. G. (2013). What happened (and what did not): Discourse constraints on encoding of plausible alternatives. *Journal of Memory and Language, 69*(3), 196–227. https://doi.org/10.1016/j.jml.2013.06.003

Fraundorf, S. H., Watson, D. G., & Benjamin, A. S. (2010). Recognition memory reveals just how CONTRASTIVE contrastive accenting really is. *Journal of Memory and Language, 63*(3), 367–386. https://doi.org/10.1016/j.jml.2010.06.004

Frazier, L., & Duff, J. (2019). Repair or accommodation? Split antecedent ellipsis and the limits of repair. *Glossa: A Journal of General Linguistics, 4*(1), 78. https://doi.org/10.5334/gjgl.728

Gotzner, N. (2017). *Alternative sets in language processing: How focus alternatives are represented in the mind*. Palgrave studies in Pragmatics, Language and Cognition, Palgrave Macmillan.

Gotzner, N. (2019). The role of focus intonation in implicature computation: A comparison with *only* and *also*. *Natural Language Semantics, 27*(3), 189–226. https://doi.org/10.1007/s11050-019-09154-7

Gotzner, N., & Romoli, R. (2022). Meaning and alternatives. *Annual Review of Linguistics, 8*(1), 213–234.

Gotzner, N., Solt, S., & Benz, A. (2018). Adjectival scales and three types of implicature. In *Semantics and linguistic theory* (Vol. 28, pp. 409–432).

Gotzner, N., & Spalek, K. (2016). The role of contrastive and non-contrastive associates in the interpretation of focus particles. *Discourse Processes, 8*(1), 59–95.

Gotzner, N., & Spalek, K. (2017). Role of contrastive and noncontrastive associates in the interpretation of focus particles. *Discourse Processes, 54*(8), 638–654.

Gotzner, N., & Spalek, K. (2019). The life and times of focus alternatives: Tracing the activation of alternatives to a focused constituent in language comprehension. *Language and Linguistics Compass, 13*(2), e12310.

Gotzner, N., Spalek, K., & Wartenburger, I. (2013). How pitch accents and focus particles affect the recognition of contextual alternatives. In M. Knauff, M. Pauen, N. Sebanz, & I. Wachsmuth (Eds.), *Proceedings of the 35th annual meeting of the cognitive science society* (pp. 2434–2440). Cognitive Science Society.

Gotzner, N., Wartenburger, I., & Spalek, K. (2016). The impact of focus particles on the recognition and rejection of contrastive alternatives. *Language and Cognition, 8*, 59–95. https://doi.org/10.1017/langcog.2015.25

Hirschberg, J. (1985). *A theory of scalar implicature.* Doctoral dissertation, University of Pennsylvania.

Horn, L. R. (1972). *On the semantic properties of logical operators in English* (PhD Thesis). University of California, Los Angeles.

Husband, E. M. (2015). *Inhibition in the computation of scalar implicature.* Poster given at the 28th CUNY Human Sentence Processing Conference, Los Angeles, CA.

Husband, E. M., & Ferreira, F. (2016). The role of selection in the comprehension of focus alternatives. *Language, Cognition and Neuroscience, 31*(2), 217–235.

Jördens, K. A., Gotzner, N., & Spalek, K. (2020). The role of non-categorical relations in establishing focus alternative sets. *Language and Cognition, 12*(4), 729–754.

Káldi, T., Szöllösi, Á., & Babarczy, A. (2021). Hungarian structural focus: Accessibility to focused elements and their alternatives in working memory and delayed recognition memory. *Frontiers in Psychology*, 1233.

Katzir, R. (2007). Structurally-defined alternatives. *Linguistics and Philosophy, 30*, 669–690.

Kennedy, C., & McNally, L. (2005). Scale structure, degree modification, and the semantics of gradable predicates. *Language, 81*(2), 345–381.

Kim, C. S., Gunlogson, C., Tanenhaus, M. K., & Runner, J. T. (2015). Context-driven expectations about focus alternatives. *Cognition, 139*, 28–49.

Koch, X., & Spalek, K. (2021). Contrastive intonation effects on word recall for information-structural alternatives across the sexes. *Memory & Cognition, 49*(7), 1312–1333.

Kush, D., Lidz, J., & Phillips, C. (2015). Relation-sensitive retrieval: Evidence from bound variable pronouns. *Journal of Memory and Language, 82*, 18–40.

Lacina, R., Alexandropoulou, S., Ronai, E., & Gotzner, N. (2023). Which alternatives are relevant in scalar implicature processing? A priming study with antonyms and negation. In M. Goldwater, F. K. Anggoro, B. K. Hayes, & D. C. Ong (Eds.), *Proceedings of the annual meeting of the cognitive science society*, 45.

Lewis, R. L., & Vasishth, S. (2005). An activation-based model of sentence processing as skilled memory retrieval. *Cognitive Science, 29*, 375–419.

Martin, A. E., & McElree, B. (2008). A content-addressable pointer mechanism underlies comprehension of verb-phrase ellipsis. *Journal of Memory and Language, 58*(3), 879–906.

Martin, A. E., & McElree, B. (2011). Direct-access retrieval during sentence comprehension: Evidence from sluicing. *Journal of Memory and Language, 64*(4), 327–343.

Marty, P. P., & Chemla, E. (2013). Scalar implicatures: Working memory and a comparison with *only*. *Frontiers in Psychology, 4*, 403.

McElree, B. (2000). Sentence comprehension is mediated by content-addressable memory structures. *Journal of Psycholinguistic Research, 29*, 111–123.

McElree, B., Foraker, S., & Dyer, L. (2003). Memory structures that subserve sentence comprehension. *Journal of Memory and Language, 48*(1), 67–91.

Morzycki, M. (2012). Adjectival extremeness: Degree modification and contextually restricted scales. *Natural Language and Linguistic Theory, 30*, 567–609. https://doi.org/10.1007/s11049-011-9162-0

Norberg, K. A., & Fraundorf, S. H. (2021). Memory benefits from contrastive focus truly require focus: Evidence from clefts and connectives. *Language, Cognition and Neuroscience, 36*(8), 1010–1037.

Noveck, I. A., & Posada, A. (2003). Characterizing the time course of an implicature: An evoked potentials study. *Brain and Language, 85*(2), 203–210.

Nys, B. L., Wong, W., & Schaeken, W. (2024). Some scales require cognitive effort: A systematic review on the role of working memory in scalar implicature derivation. *Cognition, 242*, 105623.

Repp, S., & Spalek, K. (2021). The role of alternatives in language. *Frontiers in Communication, 6*, 682009.

Rees, A., & Bott, L. (2018). The role of alternative salience in the derivation of scalar implicatures. *Cognition, 176*, 1–14.

Ronai, E., & Xiang, M. (2023). Tracking the activation of scalar alternatives with semantic priming. *Experiments in Linguistic Meaning, 2*, 229–240.

Rooth, M. (1992). A theory of focus interpretation. *Natural Language Semantics, 1*, 75–116. https://doi.org/10.1007/BF02342617

Schwarz, F., Clifton Jr, C., & Frazier, L. (2007). Strengthening 'or': Effects of focus and downward entailing contexts on scalar implicatures. In J. Anderssen, K. Moulton, F. Schwarz, & C. Ussery (Eds.), *University of Massachusetts occasional papers in linguistics* (Vol. 33, No. 1, p. 9).

Solt, S. (2015). Measurement scales in natural language. *Language and Linguistics Compass, 9*(1), 14–32. https://doi.org/10.1111/lnc3.v9.1; https://doi.org/10.1111/lnc3.12101

Spalek, K., Gotzner, N., & Wartenburger, I. (2014). Not only the apples. Focus-sensitive particles improve memory for information-structural alternatives. *Journal of Memory and Language, 70*, 68–84. https://doi.org/10.1016/j.jml.2013.09.001

Spalek, K., & Oganian, Y. (2019). The neurocognitive signature of focus alternatives. *Brain and Language, 194*, 98–108.

Speer, S., & Foltz, A. (2015). The implicit prosody of corrective contrast primes appropriately intonated primes (for some readers). In L. Frazier & E. Gibson (Eds.), *Explicit and implicit prosody in sentence processing: Studies in honor of Janet Dean Fodor* (Studies in Theoretical Psycholinguistics 46) (pp. 263–285). Springer. https://doi.org/10.1007/978-3-319-12961-7

Tjuka, A., et al. (2020). Foxes, deer, and hedgehogs: The recall of focus alternatives in Vietnamese. *Laboratory Phonology: Journal of the Association for Laboratory Phonology, 11*(1), 16, 1–29. https://doi.org/10.5334/labphon.253

Tomlinson, J. M., Jr., Gotzner, N., & Bott, L. (2017). Intonation and pragmatic enrichment: How intonation constrains ad hoc scalar inferences. *Language and Speech, 60*(2), 200–223.

Van Dyke, J. A. (2007). Interference effects from grammatically unavailable constituents during sentence processing. *Journal of Experimental Psychology: Learning, Memory, and Cognition, 33*(2), 407.

Van Dyke, J. A., & McElree, B. (2011). Cue-dependent interference in comprehension. *Journal of Memory and Language, 65*(3), 247–263.

Van Tiel, B., Van Miltenburg, E., Zevakhina, N., & Geurts, B. (2016). Scalar diversity. *Journal of Semantics, 33*(1), 137–175.

Vasishth, S., Nicenboim, B., Engelmann, F., & Burchert, F. (2019). Computational models of retrieval processes in sentence processing. *Trends in Cognitive Sciences, 23*(11), 968–982.

Waldon, B., & Degen J. (2020). Symmetric alternatives and semantic uncertainty modulate scalar inference. In S. Denison, M. Mack, Y. Xu, & B. C. Armstrong (Eds.), *Proceedings of the 42nd Annual Conference of the Cognitive Science Society (CogSci 2020)*, pp. 123–29. Cognitive Science Society.

Yan, M., Calhoun, S., & Warren, P. (2023). The role of prominence in activating focused words and their alternatives in Mandarin: Evidence from lexical priming and recognition memory. *Language and Speech, 66*(3), 678–705.

Yan, M., Calhoun, S., & Warren, P. (2019). The role of prosody in priming alternatives in Mandarin Chinese. In S. Calhoun, P. Escudero, M. Tabain, & P. Warren (Eds.), *Proceedings of the 19th international congress of phonetic sciences, Melbourne, Australia 2019* (pp. 437–441). Australasian Speech Science and Technology Association.

4

Constructing Alternatives: Evidence for the Early Availability of Contextually Relevant Focus Alternatives

Christian Muxica and Jesse A. Harris

4.1 Introduction

Determining the focus of an utterance is an essential component of sentence interpretation. In English and other languages, focus (indicated here with $[\cdot]_F$ brackets) contains a prominent element, signaled by morphosyntactic or suprasegmental reflexes such as pitch accent (marked by underlining here), though the scope of focus usually depends on the context of utterance (Jackendoff, 1972; Selkirk, 1984). Typically, theoretical accounts of focus emphasize that the focus of an utterance is interpreted against a contextually determined set of alternatives (Krifka, 1992; Rooth, 1985, 1992). For instance, the sentence in (1) not only conveys that the referent corresponding to the focused phrase *Merle*

C. Muxica (✉) · J. A. Harris
University of California, Los Angeles, Los Angeles, CA, USA
e-mail: cmuxica@g.ucla.edu

J. A. Harris
e-mail: jharris@humnet.ucla.edu

N. Gotzner et al. (eds.), *Alternatives in Grammar and Cognition*, Palgrave Studies in Pragmatics, Language and Cognition, https://doi.org/10.1007/978-3-031-76676-3_4

Haggard plays the fiddle, but also (by default) an implicature that there is some relevant set of individuals who do not play the fiddle.

(1) [Merle Haggard]$_F$ plays the fiddle.

Intuitively, membership to this set of alternatives is determined by the context. If the discourse concerns country singers, then the alternatives to *Merle Haggard* in (2) might include individuals such as *Willie Nelson* or *Dolly Parton*. Crucially, though, any individual could theoretically serve as an alternative to the name in focus, if warranted by the context.

Focus is realized in different ways, both across and within languages, and can be categorized into multiple types (Büring, 2009). A major distinction is between *bare* (or *free*) and *associated* focus. In bare focus, the focused element is not situated within the scope of a focus-sensitive operator. In general, the interpretive effect of excluding other salient possibilities in bare focus is considered an implicature and thus can be canceled by explicit denial (2)a. In instances of *associated* focus, focus-sensitive operators such as *only* and *also* are said to associate with focus to produce truth-conditional effects. For example, the effect of *only* (2)b is to exclude other contextually-salient possibilities not as an implicature, but as asserted or entailed content, and attempts to deny it are thus infelicitous.

(2) a. [Merle Haggard]$_F$ plays the fiddle.
Implicature: No other contextually-relevant individual plays fiddle
Denial: In fact, Dolly Parton plays the fiddle too.

b. Only [Merle Haggard]$_F$ plays the fiddle.
Entailment: No other contextually-relevant individual plays fiddle
Denial: # In fact, Dolly Parton plays the fiddle too.

In general, successful comprehension of an utterance containing focus requires inferring the set of alternatives intended on the part of the speaker. As (nearly) all sentences within a discourse contain focus, this inference process is likely an inescapable part of regular sentence comprehension. Yet, only recently has psycholinguistic research attempted to characterize how focus is processed in detail. This paper addresses how the alternative set required for focus interpretation is established and at what time point the language comprehension system has access to its members.

Early research from Cutler and Fodor 1979 using phoneme monitoring established that comprehenders are sensitive to the presence of focus during online comprehension, conclusions later supported by a host of reading studies (Beier & Ferreira, 2022; Benatar & Clifton, 2014; Birch & Rayner, 1997, 2010; Hoeks et al., 2023; Morris & Folk, 1998). Multiple visual-world studies have also established that comprehenders rapidly search for contextually relevant alternatives after encountering focus (Dahan et al., 2002; Ito & Speer, 2008; Kim et al., 2015; Watson et al., 2008; Weber et al., 2006). More recent research, using cross-modal forced-choice tasks, has investigated the cognitive mechanism used to identify alternatives and the time point at which those alternatives become available (Braun & Tagliapietra, 2010; Gotzner, 2017; Gotzner & Spalek, 2019; Gotzner et al., 2016; Husband & Ferreira, 2016; Jördens et al., 2020; Lacina et al., 2023).

Much of the recent literature has pursued a two-stage model which uses lexical activation to represent and select alternatives (Gotzner, 2017; Husband & Ferreira, 2016). After processing an element in focus, all of the words semantically related to that element will become highly activated through semantic priming. These highly activated words are often referred to as semantic *associates* and include potential alternatives to the relevant focus. In the second stage, a focus-sensitive mechanism selects the contextually relevant alternatives from among the associates and maintains their raised levels of activation. Eventually, only relevant alternatives will remain highly activated, yielding a representation of the appropriate alternative set.

The two-stage model presents a number of open issues regarding the role of semantic priming in alternative formation. The key feature of this model is that focus alternatives are first generated by a context-insensitive process, and then later *constrained* by the discourse. However, contextually relevant alternatives need not be semantically associated with the word in focus. To our knowledge, the case of semantically unrelated yet contextually relevant focus alternatives has not been directly investigated in experimental designs probing focus. This case is crucial to understanding the architecture of focus processing in a two-stage model, as the initial stage of semantic priming could not in principle provide these words with the increased activation necessary for inclusion in the initial focus alternative set.

To address these issues, we present the results of a cross-modal probe recognition task study. We employ discourses that make salient an *Associate alternative* (i.e., one which is semantically related to the focus) and another *Non-associate alternative* (i.e., one which is semantically unrelated to the focus). In doing so, we test the predictions of alternative models which emphasize the role of discourse representations over semantic priming in identifying alternatives. Counter to the predictions of a two-stage model, the results of our experiment suggest that both associate and non-associate alternatives are selected immediately upon encountering a focused element.

We first begin with a brief overview of the Alternative Semantics framework and survey the most directly relevant psycholinguistic research to date on focus alternatives. We then discuss the predictions of the two-stage model and its competitors with respect to the availability of focus alternatives during real-time comprehension. We conclude by arguing that the generation of focus alternatives is *constructive*, rather than *destructive* in nature, in that the set of focus alternatives is assembled according to contextual considerations in the earliest moments of focus processing.

4.1.1 Alternative Semantics

In formal semantics, syntactic constituents are associated with semantic values via an interpretation function (Heim & Kratzer, 1998). However, focus can enrich interpretation in multiple ways depending on the placement of focus, the focus structure, and the context. For example, both utterances in (3) consist of the same string and thus contribute the same core proposition: *Dolly likes Willie*, represented as $\text{LIKE}(w)(d)$. However, the different locations of focus result in different ways that the proposition is interpreted in the context.

We follow the Alternative Semantics framework developed by Rooth (1985, 1992), in which a focused element is interpreted against a set of alternatives, abbreviated as ALTS, consisting of semantic values that can be substituted for the element in focus, in this case, any individual in the context, e.g., *Merle Haggard*, *Johnny Cash*, *Loretta Lynn*, etc. Focusing *Dolly* in (3)a expresses that *Dolly* does not like any contextually relevant individual in ALTS, $\forall x \in \text{ALTS}.[\neg\text{LIKE}(x)(d)]$. In contrast, focus on *Willie* in (3)b expresses that no other contextually relevant individual in ALTS likes *Willie*, $\forall x \in \text{ALTS}.[\neg\text{LIKE}(w)(x)]$.

(3) a. [<u>Do</u>lly]$_F$ likes Willie
Assertion: $\text{LIKE}(w)(d)$
Implicature: $\forall x \in \text{ALTS}.[\neg\text{LIKE}(x)(d)]$
Dolly likes Willie and she doesn't like anyone else

b. Dolly likes [<u>Wil</u>lie]$_F$
Assertion: $\text{LIKE}(w)(d)$
Implicature: $\forall x \in \text{ALTS}.[\neg\text{LIKE}(w)(x)]$
Dolly likes Willie and no one else likes Willie

In Alternative Semantics, the interpretation of focus relies on a phonologically null anaphor *C*, which takes the contextually relevant set of alternatives as its referent.[1] For example, a highly plausible set of alternatives to *donuts* in (4) might be the class of other baked goods (5), e.g., *cookies*, *cupcakes*, etc.

(4) Willie eats only [<u>do</u>nuts]$_F \sim C$

In this case, *C* would take the form depicted in (5)b. Focus-sensitive operators such as *only* in (5)a quantify over *C* when computing the specific effect of focus on interpretation in context.

[1] There is considerable variation in how alternatives are modeled in the theoretical literature. For instance, *C* is often treated as referring to a set of alternative propositions rather than a set of alternative semantic values to the focus as described here. The difference is subtle and it is unclear whether a propositional treatment of alternatives would make any distinct predictions with respect to processing. For ease of presentation, we will continue to treat *C* and the related notion of the alternative set as non-propositional, but we are not committed to this view. In general, while we assume a roughly Roothian framework in what follows, we intend to remain agnostic with respect to the formal implementation of alternatives.

(5) a. $[\![(4)]\!] = \text{EATS}(d)(w) \wedge \forall x \in \text{ALT}_C.[\neg\text{EATS}(x)(w)]$

b. $C = \{[\![\text{cookies}]\!], [\![\text{cupcakes}]\!], \ldots\}$

Importantly, while the class of baked goods is a highly plausible alternative set, the actual set will depend almost entirely upon the particular discourse context. For example, one could certainly imagine a context in which Willie has especially selective culinary taste, eating donuts to the exclusion of all other food. In this case, C would range over all types of food, not just baked goods, e.g., $C = \{[\![\text{cookies}]\!], [\![\text{cupcakes}]\!], [\![\text{pasta}]\!], [\![\text{kale}]\!], ...\}$.

In fact, the only restriction (beyond contextual relevance) which Rooth (1985, 1992) places upon the referent of C is that the alternatives must be semantically (type-theoretically) intersubstitutable with the focus (following the assumption that $C \subseteq$ ALTS). For example, a property P cannot serve as an alternative to an entity such as *Willie* in (6), nor can an entity serve as an alternative to a property such as *likes Willie* in (6b), as they belong to different semantic types.

(6) a. Dolly likes [<u>Willie</u>]$_F \sim C$
$\text{LIKE}(d)(w) \wedge \forall x \in \text{ALT}_C.[\neg\text{LIKE}(d)(w)]$
Dolly likes Willie and she doesn't like anyone else relevant in the context

b. Dolly [likes <u>Willie</u>]$_F \sim C$
$\text{LIKE}(d)(w) \wedge \forall P \in \text{ALT}_C.[\neg P(d)]$
Dolly likesW illie and she has no other contextually relevant properties

Although we have concentrated on how Alternative Semantics captures the compositional contribution of focused material, other theories of focus (e.g., Büring, 2016b; Krifka, 1992; Schwarzschild, 1999; Von Stechow, 1991) also treat focus as a kind of context-dependent abstraction that enriches the meaning of an expression against a set of contextually relevant alternatives. Implementational details may vary, but these long-standing intuitions are generally preserved across approaches.

Thus, although much of this paper and much of the experimental literature are framed in terms of Alternative Semantics, the majority of the discussion should straightforwardly extend to other frameworks.

In short, focus is a complex interface-spanning phenomenon. It enriches the meaning an expression by establishing a variety of potential relationships (e.g., exclusive, additive, etc.) between the focus and its contextually determined set of alternatives. Interpreting focus online requires a comprehender to infer the contents of this set within strict time constraints. This raises a number of interesting psycholinguistic questions. Chiefly, to what extent is language processing sensitive to the presence of focus online? It is clear that focus is crucial to interpretation given theoretical intuitions, but how incremental is the process of generating this interpretation? In the following section, we review evidence that interpreting focus is achieved by incremental processes, not merely post-sentential ones.

4.1.2 The Processing of Focus

4.1.2.1 Incremental Focus Processing

A large body of psycholinguistic research has established that comprehenders are sensitive to focus during incremental sentence comprehension. In a phoneme monitoring task, Cutler and Fodor (1979) found that subjects were faster to identify a phoneme when the containing constituent was in focus. They argued that a focused constituent attracts attention, yielding faster response times when the target phoneme occurs within that constituent (see Beier & Ferreira, 2022, for replication). However, the results of later reading time studies have been more mixed. While some studies found that, in keeping with the interpretation of Cutler and Fodor (1979), focus increases reading times (Benatar & Clifton, 2014; Birch & Rayner, 1997), others reported a decrease in readings times (Birch & Rayner, 2010; Morris & Folk, 1998). As Hoeks et al. (2023) note, the different results could be on account of conflating focus with the related but independent notion of newness. Using a maze task (Forster et al., 2009), Hoeks et al. (2023) found that new foci elicited slower response times than given foci, but that the penalty was reduced when alternatives to new foci were contextually mentioned. Together, these studies indicate that focus demands additional processing resources, which prior mention can reduce.

Visual-world studies have provided further evidence for the rapid inference of alternatives. Ito and Speer (2008) recorded the eye movements of subjects hanging ornaments onto a holiday tree according to auditory instructions. The authors manipulated whether these instructions contained a contrastive L+H* pitch accent (a strong cue to the presence of focus) or an H* pitch accent (a weaker cue to the presence of focus). They found that L+H* pitch accents generated a higher percentage of early fixations toward ornaments contrasting with previously mentioned ones (i.e., contextually relevant alternatives) than H* pitch accents did. Other visual-world studies concerning focus have found similar results (Dahan et al., 2002; Kim et al., 2015; Watson et al., 2008; Weber et al., 2006). As in other studies using different methods, these results support the conclusion that the processing of focus is not post-sentential. Rather, comprehenders immediately identify the presence of focus and subsequently engage in a search for contextually relevant alternatives.

While there is clear evidence for selecting focus alternatives during comprehension, the nature of the selection process and the representation of alternatives involved are less certain, and numerous foundational questions remain. Under Alternative Semantics, a variable *C* has as its referent a set of contextually relevant alternatives. Is such a set represented during comprehension? And, if so, how closely does this representation resemble the offline judgments which motivated the *C* variable? In principle, it is possible that the alternative set is less constrained online, including both contextually relevant alternatives and a large set of possible but contextually irrelevant ones. Or perhaps, more in-line with offline judgments, only contextually relevant alternatives are ever represented. A plethora of factors determine which alternatives are relevant in any given context. How and when does this mechanism tap into each of these information sources? Now, we turn our attention to models that address these issues.

4.1.2.2 The Selection of Alternatives

A number of lexical decision and probe recognition experiments have further investigated the selection of alternatives. Here, the emerging picture is that in the earliest moments after encountering focus, contextually relevant alternatives are activated along with irrelevant alternatives and semantically associated non-alternatives. Over time, however, only contextually relevant alternatives remain activated. The delayed influence of context provides evidence for a two-stage model of alternative selection.

Fraundorf et al. (2010) investigated whether deriving an interpretation for contrastive focus strengthens the encoding of a focused element and its alternatives in memory. Subjects listened to short recorded dialogues which introduced two alternatives (e.g., *British* and *French* in 7a), followed by a continuation mentioning only one (e.g., *British* in 7b). The type of pitch accent (H* vs. L+H*) on the focus was manipulated in the continuation sentence. Twenty four hours after the initial test, subjects were given probe sentences in one of three conditions, depicted in (8) below, targeting memory for the focused continuation and indicated whether the sentence was accurate.

(7) *Sample discourse pair from Fraundorf et al. (2010)*

a. Both the British and the French scientists had been searching Malaysia and Indonesia for the endangered monkeys.

b. Finally, the [Br<u>it</u>ish]$_F$ spotted one of the monkeys in Malaysia and planted a radio tag on it.

(8) *Probe sentence*

a. *Focus:* The British scientists found the endangered monkey.

b. *Alternative:* The French scientists found the endangered monkey.

c. *Unmentioned:* The Portuguese scientists found the endangered monkey.

Contrastive focus helped subjects correctly accept the probe sentences that contained foci and correctly reject probe sentences that contained mentioned alternatives. This suggests that contrastive focus not only creates the need to represent contextual alternatives, but to negate them during processing, possibly producing a stronger memory trace.

However, contrastive focus did not help subjects to correctly reject probe sentence containing unmentioned alternative (e.g., *Portuguese*). One possible explanation is that unmentioned alternatives are not represented in the alternative set and so are not explicitly negated, making it harder for subjects to correctly reject them later on. This result provides some evidence for a contextually restricted representation of the alternative set in processing, one which excludes unmentioned alternatives, at least in long-term memory.

Braun and Tagliapietra (2010) hypothesized that the alternative set is realized online through lexical activation. Under this view, alternatives are words which become activated from semantic association with the focused word. The authors presented subjects with recorded sentences in Dutch containing or lacking contrastive focus as indicated by pitch accent. In their study, immediately after the hearing the sentence, subjects performed a cross-modal lexical decision task on written target words. The targets were either plausible alternatives semantically associated with the focus (e.g., *hiking tour*), non-alternatives semantically associated with the focus (e.g., *jungle*), or non-alternative controls not semantically associated with the focus (e.g., *karate*).

(9) *Sample sentence targets from Braun and Tagliapietra (2010)*

a. *Contrastive focus:* In the spring, they went on $[\text{sa}\underline{\text{fa}}\text{ri}]_F$

b. *No contrastive focus:* In the spring, they went on safari

(10) *Target word*

a. *Alternative*: HIKING TOUR (TREKTOCHT in Dutch)

b. *Associate Non-alternative*: JUNGLE

c. *Control:* KARATE

In two experiments, Braun and Tagliapietra (2010) found that alternatives were accepted faster than controls, but only when the critical word was presented with contrastive pitch accent (i.e., L+H*). Braun and Tagliapietra (2010) also found a weak priming effect for associate non-alternatives, which was not influenced by the presence of focus. The authors argue that alternatives receive increased activation after encountering focus which distinguishes them from non-alternatives during processing. This difference in lexical activation between alternatives and non-alternatives can be thought of as instantiating the alternative set.

In order to investigate how the representation of alternatives evolves over time, Husband and Ferreira (2016) varied the point at which the lexical decision task was administered. They hypothesized that alternatives are selected online in a process similar to two-stage models of ambiguity resolution, in which context-appropriate senses are selected only after an initial context-insensitive stage (Swinney, 1979). In their model, all words that are semantically primed by the focus, including potential focus alternatives, are automatically activated, regardless of context. After a delay in which contextual information is accessed, only focus alternatives remain activated.

Husband and Ferreira (2016) ran a cross-modal lexical decision experiment with a between-subjects stimulus onset asynchrony (SOA) manipulation. In one experiment, a lexical decision task was administered immediately (i.e., 0 ms) after a potentially focused word in the prime (e.g., *sculptor*). In the other experiment, a lexical decision task was administered after a 750 ms delay.

(11) *Sample materials from Husband and Ferreira (2016)*

  a. *Focused:* The museum thrilled the [sculptor]$_F$ ...

  b. *Unfocused:* The museum thrilled the sculptor ...

(12) *Lexical decision targets*

  a. *Alternative:* PAINTER

  b. *Associate Non-alternative*: STATUE

  c. *Control*: REGISTER

Without a delay, there was a priming effect, in which alternatives (e.g., *painter*) and associate non-alternatives (e.g., *statue*) were accepted faster than non-associate controls (e.g., *register*) independent of the pitch accent manipulation. However, after a 750 ms delay, an effect of focus was observed such that alternatives were accepted faster than either associate non-alternatives or controls, but only in the presence of a contrastive pitch accent.

The results clearly support a two-stage model for alternative selection. In the first stage, words which are semantically associated with the word in focus receive increased activation from semantic priming. Crucially, the first stage is not sensitive to context, in that semantic associates depend on the lexical-level properties of the item, not the discourse context. However, in the second stage, a focus-sensitive mechanism selects the set of contextually relevant alternatives, maintaining their activation, while the activation of non-alternatives decreases.[2] The two-stage model can explain both the observed effect of semantic priming and the delayed influence of focus in the lexical decision task.

All of the previous studies tested instances of *bare* focus which lacked a focus-sensitive operator. Recall that bare focus contrasts with instances of *associated* focus in which operators such as *only* and *also* interact with focus with truth-conditional effects. Addressing this gap in the literature, Gotzner et al. (2016) performed a cross-modal probe recognition experiment in German comparing *bare* and *associated* focus. The authors hypothesized that the truth-conditional nature of *associated* focus might encode alternatives more strongly in memory yielding different behavior from *bare* focus.

Subjects were presented with short two speaker discourses. Speaker A introduced a set of three alternatives (e.g., *peaches*, *cherries*, and *bananas*) and Speaker B selected one (e.g., *peaches*) using bare or associated contrastive focus. Roughly two seconds (2050 ms) after hearing the focus, subjects were presented with a written word and asked to indicate as quickly as possible whether or not that word had occurred anywhere in the audio. These probe words came in one of three conditions: mentioned alternatives (e.g., *cherries*), unmentioned but plausible alternatives (e.g., *melons*), and unmentioned non-alternative controls (e.g., *clubs*).

---

[2] Husband and Ferreira (2016) remain agnostic as to whether or the decreased activation of non-alternatives stems from an active process of suppression or a passive process of decay.

(13) *Sample discourse from Gotzner et al. (2016)*

a. **Speaker A:** In the fruit bowl, there are peaches, cherries, and bananas I bet Carsten has eaten cherries and bananas

b. **Speaker B:** No, he (only) ate [peaches]$_F$

(14) *Probe words*

a. *Mentioned*: CHERRIES

b. *Unmentioned*: MELONS

c. *Control*: CLUBS

Correct rejection of controls was fastest, followed by correct rejection of unmentioned alternatives, and lastly correct recognition of mentioned alternatives. The addition of a focus particle *only* increased average response times, but did not interact with the probe type. The authors argued that the increased response times reflect greater competition between elements for membership in the alternative set. In a follow-up, Gotzner and Spalek (2019) performed the same experiment with an SOA of 0 ms instead. Here, the authors found that controls were correctly rejected faster than the other two conditions were accepted, which did not significantly differ from one another. Again, the addition of the focus particle increased average response times across each condition.

While the results from these probe recognition tasks are highly informative, the fact that different response types correspond to different conditions presents some challenges for interpretation. To correctly respond to the different probe types, subjects would have to *accept* probes that occurred in the discourse, but would have had to *reject* probes that did not appear in the discourse. Consequently, the correct response to a mentioned alternative is a *Yes*, whereas the correct response to an unmentioned alternative is a *No*. However, it is difficult to directly compare behavior across these conditions as accepting and rejecting probes is known to engage different kinds of processing biases (Rotello & Macmillan, 2007). This is not to say that the results from these studies are invalid, but rather that some caution should be taken in interpreting them. To preview, the issue of mixed response types is addressed in the study we present below in that all correct responses are of the same type.

Taken together, these studies paint a cohesive picture in which processing focus occurs in two stages. First, an unrestricted alternative set is formed from lexical-level associative priming from the word in focus. This unrestricted set contains (i) mentioned alternatives, (ii) unmentioned yet plausible alternatives, and (iii) non-alternatives semantically associated with the focus. Soon after, contextual information is used to restrict the alternative set to mentioned alternatives, as well as unmentioned (but still plausible) alternatives. It appears that this restricted representation is the set according to which contrastive focus is interpreted and stored in long-term memory. Nonetheless, we note a number of questions and open issues with a two-stage view of focus alternative selection in the following section.

4.1.2.3 Limitations of Semantic Priming in Selecting Alternatives

While the experimental literature appears to support a two-stage model for selecting alternatives, numerous questions of implementation remain. In particular, the two-stage model emphasizes the role of automatic lexical-level associative priming in the early stages of processing focus. This choice appears to overlook evidence for the highly flexible and context-sensitive nature of focus. There are a number of examples which the two-stage model seemingly cannot capture and which the experimental literature has not previously tested. We discuss these concerns below.

Certain aspects of the two-stage model are undoubtedly attractive. As Gotzner and Spalek (2019) argued, the two-stage model shares a basic pattern with the Alternative Semantics framework: focus evokes a large initial set of alternatives which pragmatic processes then constrain. The large initial set can be thought of as the focus-semantic value in Alternative Semantics and the first stage of the two-stage model. The pragmatic processes of selecting alternatives in the second stage could correspond to resolution of the *C* variable in Alternative Semantics. In this sense, the two-stage model creates an attractive correspondence between theories of competence and performance.

However, as others before us have emphasized, Alternative Semantics was not intended as a psycholinguistic theory, and there remain multiple ways in which the central insights of the framework might be realized within the sentence or discourse processing system. To this point, we discuss two important differences between Alternative Semantics and the two-stage model: the contextual flexibility of alternatives and the scopal flexibility of focus projection.

In Alternative Semantics, the unrestricted set of alternatives initially evoked by focus is defined type-theoretically, rather than by the semantic priming that is assumed in the two-stage model. Consequently, in Alternative Semantics, almost any element which can replace the focus is capable of serving as an alternative given the proper pragmatic support. As we understand it, a two-stage model in which alternatives are defined solely through associative priming lacks sufficient contextual flexibility.

Imagine a context in which a group of artists has painted a mural that depicts a tank driving through a meadow. In such a context, *tank* is a likely alternative to *flowers* in (15) despite the fact that these words presumably do not prime one another.

(15) Simon only painted the [flowers]$_F$ on the mural

As the second stage selects the relevant alternatives from semantic associates, it is not clear how contextually relevant yet lexically unrelated words like *tank* could ever enter the alternative set. While contextually relevant alternatives are often associates of the focused word, examples like (15) show that this relationship is not strictly necessary. For instance, *Pete* is clearly the relevant alternative to *Linda* in (16), but it is unlikely that names in general would be semantic associates of one another.[3]

(16) a. **Speaker A:** Pete didn't like the borscht I made yesterday

b. **Speaker B:** Well, only [Linda]$_F$ likes borscht

---

[3] However, certain strongly associated names such as *Jack* and *Jill* might be potential exceptions.

Jördens et al. (2020) addressed a similar but crucially different case of semantically related alternatives of a different taxonomic category than the focus (e.g., *straw*—FEED vs. *cow*—ANIMAL). In a cross-modal probe recognition experiment, the authors found a response time advantage for semantically related alternatives over non-alternatives that were also associates of the focus. These results do provide some important evidence for the presence of contextual flexibility in the real-time processing of focus. However, they do not address the more extreme case of alternatives which are not semantic associates of the focus and thus lack the initial boost in activation from semantic priming.

Similarly, although the experimental literature has predominantly investigated the processing of individually focused words, larger elements can be focused as well. Theoretically, at least, constituents of any size can be put into focus (17). It not clear how complex constituents would generate the initial alternative set under the two-stage model, as associative priming is typically understood with respect to individual lexical items (Neely, 2012).

(17) a. **Speaker A:** I went to the gym and made borscht yesterday

b. **Speaker B:** I only [played video games]$_F$ yesterday

Lacina et al. (2023) is the only experimental study we are aware of which has investigated the representation of alternatives under broad focus. Across three probe recognition experiments, the authors find mixed evidence for the representation of associate alternatives (nouns, verbs, and entire VPs) given broad VP focus. Thus, the extent to which alternatives under broad focus are represented during real-time language processing remains uncertain. However, certainly on the basis of Alternative Semantics and pre-experimental intuitions, such examples seem to present a conceptual challenge for the two-stage model.

The central observation that a two-stage model must contend with is that the contents of the focus alternative set are highly flexible with respect to context and scope. These properties constitute fundamental aspects of focus and are part of what makes it such a rich phenomenon for linguistic inquiry. For these reasons, constraining the mechanism responsible for alternative selection to a context-independent stage of semantic priming appears untenable to us. In the following section, we briefly sketch a number of alternative approaches. In particular, these alternative models, and our experiments testing them, address the contextual flexibility of focus rather than that of scope. We leave such further refinements to future research.

4.1.3 Alternative Models of Alternative Selection

There are many possible ways that the focus-alternative set could be formed during processing. Evidence from Fraundorf et al. (2010) suggests that the end product is restrictive in nature, in that the set of alternatives is eventually limited to those that are relevant given the context. The immediate question then is what mechanism generates the contextually constrained set of alternatives.

We contend that the formation of focus alternatives (at least those which are not semantically primed by their focus) must derive from some source other than semantic association. We do not attempt to characterize the precise nature of this source here. Rather, we consider the point at which such information becomes available after encountering focus. We consider two broad possibilities: (i) a *delayed-access model*, in which alternatives require cognitive resources (and thus time) to be established, and (ii) an *immediate-access model*, in which alternatives are established immediately upon encountering focus. See Table 4.1 for comparison.

Despite open conceptual issues with the two-stage model discussed above, selecting alternatives could nonetheless proceed in two stages. For example, contextual information required for identifying relevant alternatives may not be available during the initial moments of focus processing. Instead, the early advantage observed for words that are semantically associated with the focused word (including alternatives and non-alternatives) would be due to an independent process of associative priming, without feeding into the set of focus alternatives. The alternative set would then be formed at a later stage, including contextually relevant alternatives as well as semantic associates, provided that they too are relevant focus alternatives. Only at this later stage would the processor access the full set of alternatives. We call this the *delayed-access model*.

Table 4.1 Schema of the information available and predicted behavior at potential probe points for the original two-stage model, the delayed-access-focus model, and the immediate-access model

Model	Probe point	Information utilized	Increased activation for ...
Two-stage	Early	Semantic association	Words primed by the focus
	Late	Discourse information	Relevant associate alternatives
Delayed-access	Early	Semantic association	Words primed by the focus
	Late	Discourse information	All relevant alternatives
Immediate-access	Early/late	Discourse information	All relevant alternatives

While there are technically two stages in this model, it differs from previous versions of the two-stage model in that the stages are independent from one another. Crucially, the second stage of the delayed-access model does not rely upon the first stage to generate the alternative set. Instead, an independent focus-sensitive mechanism utilizes the available contextual information to identify and activate relevant alternatives; priming and the selection of focus alternatives remain wholly independent processes. Consequently, the delayed-focus model is not necessarily a serial model in the classic sense, in which one process feeds another. That is, there are not two stages comprising a single process, but rather, two independent processes with different time courses that both influence lexical activation.

Selecting alternatives could also proceed in a single focus-sensitive stage independent from semantic priming. Under such a model, the contextual information identifying relevant alternatives would be available from the earliest moment of processing focus. Thus, immediately after encountering focus, both associate and non-associate alternatives would be highly activated. Non-alternatives that are semantically associated with the focus will be activated as well, but this fact simply reflects independent semantic priming rather than the mechanism responsible for generating the alternative set. We call this model the *immediate-access model*.

At first glance, the immediate-access model appears to be incompatible with results from the previously discussed forced-choice task experiments. Husband and Ferreira (2016) found that alternatives were not distinguished from associate non-alternatives immediately after the presentation of focus. Similarly, Gotzner and Spalek (2019) found that mentioned alternatives were not distinguished from unmentioned alternatives immediately after the presentation of focus. However, these studies only tested *associate* alternatives. Consequently, it is impossible to disentangle the influence of semantic priming from that of contextual relevance.

Associate non-alternatives might yield similar response times to associate alternatives at early SOAs on account of semantic priming, but this does not necessarily mean that the mechanism responsible for generating the alternative set depends upon semantic priming or that the contextual information identifying relevant alternatives is unavailable. Instead, semantic priming and the selection of alternatives might be independent processes. However, having limited the scope of investigation to associate alternatives, the prior literature would not disentangle these processes.

In order to determine whether early moments of focus processing are truly insensitive to context, we must also consider contextually relevant alternatives which are semantically primed by their focus. We refer to such alternatives as *non-associate* alternatives in order to contrast them with *associate* alternatives. Take the example discourse in (18) below.

(18) a. **Speaker A:** Andy used a muffin and a pistol as props in an independent movie that he was directing

b. **Speaker B:** No, he only used a [cake]$_F$

In this example, the focused word (*cake*) has two salient contextually relevant alternatives. One of these is an associate of the focus (*muffin*) and the other is not (*pistol*). We test such examples experimentally to tease apart the role of contextual information from semantic priming in selecting alternatives.

If the earliest moments of processing focus purely reflect semantic priming as the two-stage and delayed-access models predict, then associate alternatives should be highly activated immediately after encountering focus. On the other hand, if the earliest moments of processing focus are context sensitive, as predicted by the immediate-access model, then both associate and non-associate alternatives should be highly activated immediately after encountering focus.

In order to test these possibilities, we conducted two cross-modal probe recognition task experiments. We probed subjects' recall on associate alternatives, non-associate alternatives, and non-associate non-alternative controls. Each of these probe words was mentioned in a previous discourse. This design ensured that the conditions did not engage different response biases or processing strategies, allowing for clear comparison across conditions (Table 4.2).

We utilized probe recognition as our forced-choice task rather than lexical decision for two main reasons. One, the vast majority of experimental work concerning the representation of alternatives has utilized probe recognition (e.g., Fraundorf et al., 2010; Gotzner, 2017; Gotzner & Spalek, 2019; Gotzner et al., 2016; Jördens et al., 2020; Lacina et al., 2023, etc.). We aimed to build upon this literature and facilitate comparison with our results by means of methodological consistency. Two, as Gotzner et al. (2016) discussed, a correct response in a lexical decision task only requires low-level orthographic information that is largely irrelevant to the interpretation of focus. On the other hand, a correct response in a probe recognition task requires a subject to access

Table 4.2 Schema of the probe task response time predictions made at an early SOA by the original two-stage model, the delayed-access model, and the immediate-access model. The Non-associate condition is crucial to these predictions (hence the bold and underline). In particular, these predictions differ as to whether Non-associate alternatives will have a response time advantage like Associate alternatives or a response time penalty like Non-associate non-alternative controls

Model	Predictions by condition
Two-stage	Associate faster than <u>**Non-associate**</u> and control
Delayed-access	Associate faster than <u>**Non-associate**</u> and control
Immediate-access	Associate and <u>**Non-associate**</u> faster than control

some mental representation of the discourse. This is not to say that a lexical decision task will never reflect the presence of alternatives, but rather, that a probe recognition task might more deeply engage the kind of high-level pragmatic processing that is of interest here.

To preview our results, we found that, even at a 0 ms SOA, subjects were faster to correctly accept associate and non-associate alternatives than non-alternative controls. Further, we find evidence that the *Associate* and *Non-associate* alternative conditions failed to elicit different response times from one another. The overall results of our study provide evidence in favor of an immediate-access model for selecting alternatives and experimental evidence against models in which the access of contextual information is delayed.

4.2 Experiment

4.2.1 Materials and Method

Thirty short dialogues were constructed as in (19). Dialogues were immediately followed by a probe word after the final, focused word (*cake*) in B's utterance. Probe words were drawn from one of three conditions (20). In two conditions, the probe word was a discourse alternative to the focused word, but was differentiated by whether they were semantically associated with the focused word (Associate: *muffin*) or not (Non-associate: *pistol*). The third condition provided an experimental control (Control: *movie*), in which the probe appeared in the prior utterance context but did not present a focus alternative given the target sentence and the discourse context.

(19) *Sample dialogue*

a. **Speaker A:** Andy used a muffin and a pistol as props in an independent movie that he was directing.

b. **Speaker B:** No, he only used a $[\underline{\text{cake}}]_F$.

(20) *Probe words*

a. *Associate*: MUFFIN

b. *Non-associate*: PISTOL

c. *Control*: MOVIE

In the first utterance, Speaker A described a situation using the Associate alternative, the Non-associate alternative, and the Control. The alternatives were always conjoined arguments of a main verb.[4] The control always appeared within an adjunct which occurred utterance initial in half of the items and utterance final in the other half. This between-items control ensured that neither condition was more active or prominent in memory across the experiment purely on account of recency.[5] In the second utterance, Speaker B contradicted Speaker A's statement with *No*, followed by the focus particle *only* with an utterance final noun in corrective contrastive focus. All of the material in Speaker B's utterance was discourse-given except for the focus, which was always discourse-new.

Speaker B was a male speaker trained in the Tones and Breaks Indices intonational system (ToBI; Pierrehumbert & Hirschberg, 1990) and was instructed to produce the focus with an L+H* pitch accent—the canonical prosodic marking for focus in English (Büring, 2016a). See Figure 4.1 for an example L+H* accent produced for the stimuli. It is important to note that the focus was always the final word in Speaker B's utterance. As a result, the L+H* pitch accent was technically ambiguous between marking focus and English's default Intonation Phrase (IP) final placement of Nuclear Pitch Accent (NPA). However, due to the presence of *only* and the givenness of the non-focused material in Speaker B's

[4] It is possible that in using conjunction, rather than say disjunction, the associate and non-associate words are treated as a single conjoined alternative (e.g., ALTS = {[pistol and muffin]} rather than ALTS = {pistol, muffin}). However, given that both words would still be present in the alternative set, we do not consider this to be a confound of our design. That being said, disjunction itself has been proposed to introduce alternatives (Alonso-Ovalle, 2006; Harris, 2019), so an experimental comparison of these two operators could prove fruitful.

[5] We did not explicitly control for the order of the alternatives in the conjunct, however. The Associate alternative was first in 29 of the 30 critical items, but we have no reason to believe that this asymmetry could explain our results. See Husband & Patson in this volume for relevant discussion of how distance interacts with the recognition of focus alternatives.

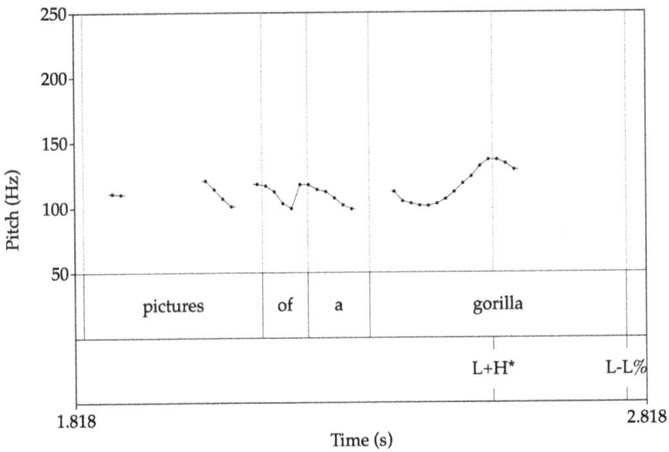

Fig. 4.1 Example pitch track including the final focused word; ToBI transcription is provided in the bottom tier

utterance, the focus structure was in fact unambiguous. Thus, the pitch accent served more to generate perceptual salience for the word in focus, rather than to determine focus structure itself. Before each of Speaker B's recordings, another speaker produced Speaker A's corresponding utterance to license the use of corrective focus and make production more natural. Speaker A was a female speaker who had received formal voice training, though not familiar with ToBI, and was instructed to produce the items naturally rather than with a specific contour.

In addition to the 30 critical items, another 60 filler items were written and recorded as well. These followed the same two utterance two speaker structure as the critical items. Speaker B's responses were of a similar length to the critical items, but never involved negation. Unlike the critical items where the probe words were all mentioned nouns, the probe words in the fillers were of various parts of speech and the majority were not mentioned in the audio dialogue. Of the 60 filler items, 30 had a probe word which was not a noun (predominately adjectives, verbs, and prepositions) and 45 had a probe word which not mentioned. Across the full set of items 2/3 of probes were nouns and 1/2 of probes were mentioned. In five of the filler items, the probe word was identical to the final word in Speaker B's utterance. These fillers acted as catch trials.

The speakers were not instructed to produce any of the filler items with a specific contour.

The three sets of probe words (Associate, Non-associate, and Control) were controlled for length, frequency, number of morphemes, and orthographic neighborhood size, as these factors are known to influence the speed and accuracy of written word recognition (Balota et al., 2007), summarized in Table 4.3. Pairwise differences between each of the conditions were evaluated with a Bayesian t-test. No reliable differences in length or orthographic neighbors were observed, as the 89% credible interval of all pairwise comparisons contained 0 with a BF < 1 for each comparison. Frequency of each probe word was estimated with the SUBTLEX_US English subtitle corpus (Brysbaert & New, 2009). There was no evidence that the frequency of the Associate word was different than Non-associate or Control words. While there was weak evidence that the Control was more frequent than the Non-associate word (Med $= 0.34$, $CrI_{89\%} = [0.03, 0.64]$, BF $= 2.12$), the direction of the difference crucially goes against the hypothesis that Non-associate probe words will be recognized faster than Control probe words. Lastly, probe words for a given item were controlled such that each word had the same number of morphemes (max: 2, min: 1) within an experimental triplet.

We used Latent Semantic Analysis (LSA; Landauer & Dumais, 1997) to estimate the expected semantic association from the focused word to each probe word. Probe words were compared against the focused word using a one-to-many comparison with the "General Reading up to 1st year college" embedding space. Mean and standard error cosine similarity

Table 4.3 Means and standard errors in parentheses of lexical factors (length, number of morphemes, orthographic neighborhood size, log frequency according to SUBTLEX_US, cosine similarity with focused word according to latent semantic analysis, and semantic similarity with focused word rating from online norming study) by probe word condition

Condition	Length	Orth. neighbors	Frequency	LSA sim.	Likert rating
Associate	5.80 (0.18)	3.37 (0.70)	2.87 (0.11)	0.59 (0.02)	5.65 (0.08)
Non-associate	5.77 (0.21)	4.30 (0.86)	2.83 (0.12)	0.09 (0.01)	2.67 (0.09)
Control	5.77 (0.20)	4.13 (0.93)	3.20 (0.12)	0.08 (0.01)	2.17 (0.09)

values by condition are shown in Table 4.3. In keeping with the design requirements, words from the Associate condition were more strongly associated with the focused word than those from the Control (Med = −0.51, $CrI_{89\%}$ = [−0.55, −0.47], BF > 1000) and Non-associate (Med = 0.5, $CrI_{89\%}$ = [0.45, 0.54], BF > 1000) condition. There was no evidence that words from the Control and Non-associate conditions differed in this respect (Med = −0.01, $CrI_{89\%}$ = [−0.03, 0.01], BF = 0.41).

We also performed an online norming study to further estimate the expected semantic association from the focus word to each probe word. This study was performed after our probe recognition experiments. In exchange for course credit, twenty-eight self-reported native English-speaking undergraduates from the University of California Los Angeles Psychology Department subject pool rated the semantic similarity of 60 word pairs on a 7-point Likert scale. Half of these word pairs were taken from the thirty foci and probe words used in our stimuli and the other half were fillers which varied in expected semantic association. Word pairs were presented in three counterbalanced conditions such that each subject rated each foci with one of the three possible probe words. This provided us with an estimate of semantic association which was more specific to the population used in the main experiment. These similarity ratings are shown in Table 4.3.

The results show that words from the Associate condition were more strongly associated with the focused word than those from the Control (Med = −3.47, $CrI_{89\%}$ = [−3.70, −3.22], BF >1000) and the Non-associate (Med = 2.98, $CrI_{89\%}$ = [2.75, 3.20], BF > 1000) condition. There was also evidence that words from the Control and Non-associate condition differed with respect to similarity ratings, but this effect was far smaller (Med = −0.49, $CrI_{89\%}$ = [−0.71, −0.27], BF > 100). This might suggest that LSA is a coarser evaluation of semantic association, or at least a less accurate one with respect to our experimental population. Importantly though, when LSA and relatedness norming measures were added as predictors in Bayesian mixed effects models, the overall patterns reported below remained the same.

4.2.2 Analysis

Data from the two studies were analyzed as Bayesian mixed effects models using `brms` (Bürkner, 2017) in R (R Core Team, 2023) with full by-subject and by-item random slopes and intercepts. In the main study, all models were computed on 4 parallel chains sampling from 12,000 iterations with a 2000 iteration burn in. The pilot required fewer iterations. Accuracy was treated as a binary response and modeled as a Bayesian regression (link logit) model. Response times above 2500 ms were removed as we were crucially interested in the earliest moments of focus processing. Similarly, response times below 200 ms were not taken to involve sufficient processing of the stimulus and thus were removed as well. Response times were then log transformed and subjected to a Bayesian linear mixed effects model. As the distribution still showed a rightward skew even after log transformation, the model was specified with a log-normal distribution. No divergent chains were observed and all models converged with $\hat{R} \approx 1$ and sufficient Effective Sample Sizes for each parameter. Posterior predictive checks graphically confirmed that the model was an appropriate fit of the response variable.

We were primarily interested in the effects that alternative status and semantic associate with focus would have on response times. To this end, the contrasts of fixed effects were coded as user-defined to compare (i) alternatives vs non-alternatives (Associate $= 0.5$, Non-associate$= 0.5$, Control $= -1$) and (ii) associate alternatives vs non-associate alternatives ignoring the control (Associate$= -0.5$, Non-associate$= 0.5$, Control $=$ 0).[6] The first comparison allowed us to investigate the effect of alternative status, while the second allowed us to investigate the effect of semantic relatedness among alternatives.

Bayesian models were chosen for numerous reasons. First, models with random slopes tended not to converge in comparable frequentist linear mixed effects models, despite the relatively large number of observations per condition per participant. Second, the non-normal distribution of scores could be better captured with the log-normal distribution available

[6] A more standard sum-coded model was also computed for the online pilot and the main in-person study. The results support the same conclusions, as they mirror the pairwise comparison reported in the text, but are not discussed in detail for sake of brevity.

in Bayesian approaches. Third, a Bayesian approach allowed us to model the effects with a prior obtained from the online pilot study conducted with a subset of items and different subjects, resulting in more powerful inferences. Fourth, and most importantly, the Bayesian approach allowed us to quantify evidence in favor of the null hypothesis. As the immediate-access model predicted a crucial lack of a difference between the Associate and Non-associate focus-alternative conditions, we used Bayes Factors to investigate the extent to which the data provided positive evidence for the lack of a difference between these conditions.

That said, frequentist models were also fit to the data. When the model did not converge, we simplified the random effect structure until convergence was obtained. In all cases, the qualitative findings match those observed under the Bayesian approach. Parameter estimates for models are provided in footnotes. As mentioned, a pilot study was conducted over the internet. We present the results of the pilot before turning to the main experiment. Unless otherwise noted, the analysis in the internet pilot followed the same principles as the main in-person study.

4.2.3 Internet Pilot Study

Prior to the in-person experiment, a pilot study was conducted with a subset of the critical items over the internet. The pilot served two central purposes. First, it allowed us to compare the general effect with different subjects on an alternate experimental platform. Second, it allowed us to extract an informative prior from the posterior distribution for the central study.

Subjects ($N = 47$) were sampled from the same population as the main experiment (undergraduate students at UCLA). Three lists from 12 of the 30 critical items were created in a counterbalanced design. Eighteen of the 60 filler items from the experiment were added to each of these lists resulting in a total of 30 trials. Each participant saw only one list. As in the full experiment, subjects correctly identified the probe with over 75% accuracy and in the analysis of response times, only correct responses were considered.

The pilot was administered over the internet with PCIbex (Zehr & Schwarz, 2018). After reading the instructions, subjects were tested on their understanding of the task. Subjects were instructed to complete the experiment using wired headphones in a quiet distraction-free environment. On each trial, participants listened to the audio dialogue while presented with a fixation cross in the center of the computer screen. Immediately after the audio completed, a written probe word appeared in the center of the screen. Subjects were instructed to provide their responses as quickly as possible without sacrificing accuracy. There was no explicit timeout for long responses. After every trial, participants were presented with a blank screen and an opportunity to take a self-paced break. The pilot took approximately 12 minutes to complete on average.

Accuracy in the probe task was high in the Associate (M = 92%, SE = 1.93%) and Non-associate (M = 90%, SE = 2.15%) conditions, and was lower in the Control condition (M = 80%,SE = 3.09%). However, in a Bayesian logistic regression analysis, there was no evidence that the Control probes reliably differed from the Associate or Non-associate probes.

Mean response times supported the predictions of the immediate-access model. Subjects were faster to correctly recognize the probe word in the Associate (M = 1130 ms, SE = 42 ms) and Non-associate (M = 1134 ms, SE = 43 ms) conditions, compared to the Control condition (M = 1335 ms, SE = 50 ms). Response times were subjected to a Bayesian linear mixed effects model with the same model specifications as the main experiment with a few exceptions. First, the data were fit using a uniform (flat) prior for the purposes of extracting an informative prior for the main study. Second, the models in the main study were specified with a high number of iterations in order to compute Bayes Factors for the parameters. Bayes Factors cannot be computed with flat priors, and fewer iterations were needed to analyze data from the pilot.

As shown in Table 4.4, the combined focus conditions (Associate and Non-associate) elicited faster response times than the Control, but there was no evidence that the two focus conditions differed from one

Table 4.4 Pilot study. Results from Bayesian linear mixed effects regression model with full random effect structure. Uninformative (flat) priors were used, and so no Bayes Factor could be computed. Contrasts were user-coded to establish the comparisons of interest. The model was run with 5000 iterations and a 1000 iteration warm up, and converged with $\hat{R} = 1$ and at least an 2500 Effective Sample Size per parameter

Parameter	Median	89% CrI
Intercept	1.944	[1.930, 1.957]
Control vs. focus	−0.025	[−0.040, −0.011]
Associate vs. non-associate	0.003	[−0.012, 0.016]

another.[7] The estimated marginal means of the model indicated that response times in the Control condition were slower compared to the Associate, Median = 0.026, HPD = [0.010, 0.042], and Non-associate, Median = 0.024, HPD = [0.007, 0.040], conditions, whereas the focus-alternative conditions did not reliably differ from one another, Median = −0.003, HPD = [−0.016, 0.012].

Our model indicates that non-alternative and alternative probe words elicited distinct response time patterns. Probe words that are focus alternatives (the Associate and Non-associate conditions combined) were associated with lower response times compared to probe words that were simply mentioned (the Control condition). However, the distinction *within* focus alternatives (Associate versus Non-associate probe words) did not produce different response time patterns, indicating that focus alternatives, regardless of semantic association, were equally accessible at the probe point.

Results from the pilot study already lend initial support in favor of the immediate-access model. We observed faster response times for probe words corresponding to focus alternatives, regardless of semantic association, over the Control word. Crucially, the priming effect for focus alternatives that are semantically unrelated to the probe word appeared immediately, rather than at a delay. This finding suggests that discourse-relevant focus alternatives are immediately available in the calculation of

[7] A similar pattern was observed in a frequentist linear mixed effects regression model. Combined focus conditions elicited faster response times than the Control, $\beta = -0.15$, SE = 0.04, $t = -4.06$, $p < .001$, but did not differ from each other, $\beta = 0.02$, SE = 0.03, $t = 0.58$.

the alternative set. We now turn to the main study, where a larger version of the experiment will be presented.

4.2.4 In-Person Experiment

The main experiment was conducted in-person using the full set of items with the addition of comprehension questions. In all other respects, the design was identical to that of the pilot.

4.2.4.1 Participants

Sixty-one self-reported native English-speaking undergraduates from the University of California Los Angeles Psychology Department subject pool participated in this study. All subjects were given course credit in exchange for participation.[8]

4.2.4.2 Method

During the experiment, participants sat in front of a desktop computer in a sound-attenuated booth wearing a pair of Sennheiser HD280 Pro wired headphones. A researcher initiated a Linger script for the experiment and then briefly explained the procedure (Rhode, 2001). Under the supervision of the researcher, participants read through a series of instructions and completed three practice trials which were not related to the manipulation. After answering any questions, the researcher left the subject to complete the experiment alone.

[8] Ninety-nine subjects were recruited, and 61 were used in the final analysis. Although the number of excluded subjects seems high, we have previously observed comparable exclusion rates in studies across multiple experimental paradigms from our population. The 39 excluded subjects were rejected on the basis of accuracy in the probe task and with the comprehension questions on both critical and filler trials. Subjects with less than a mean accuracy of 75% in the probe task were excluded. For the filler trials this resulted in the exclusion of 1 subject, and for the critical trial this resulted in the exclusion of 5 subjects. Most participants were removed on the basis of comprehension question performance. Subjects with less than a mean accuracy of 75% on these questions were excluded. For the filler trials, this resulted in the exclusion of 17 subjects and for the critical trial this resulted in the exclusion of 16 subjects.

On each trial, participants listened to the audio dialogue through the headphones while presented with a fixation cross in the center of the computer screen. Immediately after the audio completed, a written probe word appeared in the center of the screen. Participants then indicated using a PS/2 keyboard whether or not this probe word occurred or did not occur anywhere in the preceding audio. Participants were instructed to provide this response as quickly as possible without sacrificing accuracy. As in the pilot, there was no explicit timeout for long responses.

On a third of the trials, participants were presented with a comprehension question. Subjects were instructed to prioritize accuracy over speed in responding to these comprehension questions. After every trial, participants were presented with a blank screen and an opportunity to take a self-paced break. Once the participant pressed the spacebar, the next trial would begin. The experiment took approximately 30 minutes to complete on average.

4.2.4.3 Results

Accuracy in the probe task corroborated the results from the pilot experiment. Subjects correctly identified the probe in Associate (M = 94%, SE = 0.86%) and Non-associate (M = 91%, SE = 1.03%) conditions with comparable accuracy, whereas the Control condition elicited lower accuracy rates (M = 86%, SE = 1.49%). However, in a Bayesian logistic regression model with user coding, no reliable differences were observed between the Control condition and the combined focus-alternative conditions, Median = 1.25, $CrI_{89\%} = [-0.01, 2.57]$, which also did not reliably differ from each other, Median = 0.53, $CrI_{89\%} = [-0.21, 1.38]$. Pairwise comparisons of the marginal means also failed to provide reliable evidence for a difference in accuracy between any of the conditions.

Response times over 2500 ms were removed from the analysis, resulting in less than 10% data loss across conditions.[9] As in the pilot

[9] Similar results were obtained for various cutoffs, in particular at 5000 ms and for no threshold, i.e., when all response time scores were used in the analysis.

Table 4.5 Response times. Results from the Bayesian linear mixed effects regression model on log response times with full random effect structure and a log-normal distribution. Informative priors from the pilot study were used. Contrasts were user-coded to establish the contrasts of interest. The model was run with 12,000 iterations and a 2000 iteration warm up, and converged with $\hat{R} = 1$ and an Effective Sample Size ≥4000 per parameter. Bayes Factor (BF) was computed over a null point estimate using the Savage-Dickey density ratio

Parameter	Median	89% CrI	BF
Intercept	1.943	[1.937, 1.948]	>1000
Control vs. focus	−0.024	[−0.028, −0.019]	>1000
Associate vs. non-associate	0.002	[−0.002, 0.006]	0.584

study, subjects were, on average, faster to correctly recognize the probe words in the Associate (M = 1077 ms, SE = 17 ms) and Non-associate (M = 1085 ms, SE = 17 ms) conditions, and were slower in the Control condition (M = 1258 ms, SE = 19 ms). As before, a Bayesian linear mixed effects regression model was computed on log response times with user-defined contrast coding. Results of the model are provided in Table 4.5.

The Bayesian model indicates that the focus-alternative conditions elicited reliably faster response times than the Control.[10] Plots of the posterior distributions of the fixed-effect parameters, excluding the intercept, are shown in Fig. 4.2a.

The Bayes Factor for the intercept is >1000 which is interpreted as extreme evidence supporting a difference between levels (Jeffreys, 1998). The model also fails to find reliable support for a difference between the two focus-alternative conditions. The Bayes Factor of 0.58 further indicates that there is weak evidence in favor of the hypothesis that the two conditions do not, in fact, differ.[11]

[10] A qualitatively similar pattern was observed in a frequentist linear mixed effects regression model. Combined focus conditions elicited faster response times than the Control, $\beta = -0.16$, SE = 0.01, $t = -10.38$, $p < .001$, but did not differ from each other, $\beta = 0.01$, SE = 0.02, $t = 0.88$.

[11] In lieu of a formal sensitivity analysis, two additional Bayesian models were fit with uninformative prior and a weakly informative prior. All models tested showed the same pattern reported here, except that the informative prior model presented in main text yielded higher Bayes Factor values. The informative prior model was preferred in model comparison, BFs > 30.

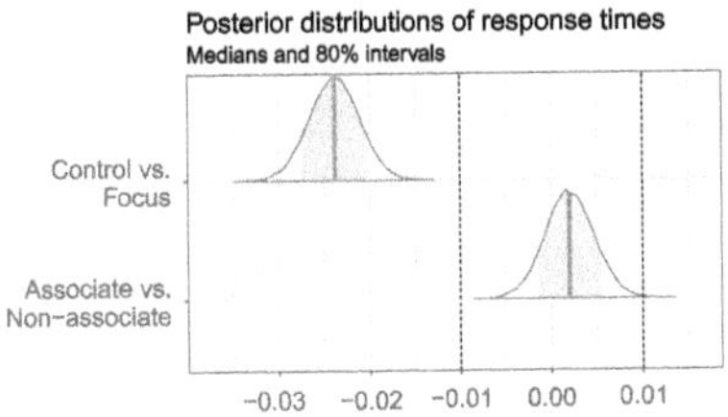

(a) Posterior distribution of Bayesian model computed with an informative prior. While there was reliable evidence of an advantage for the two focus-alternative conditions over the Control, there was no evidence supporting a distinction within the focus-alternative conditions themselves.

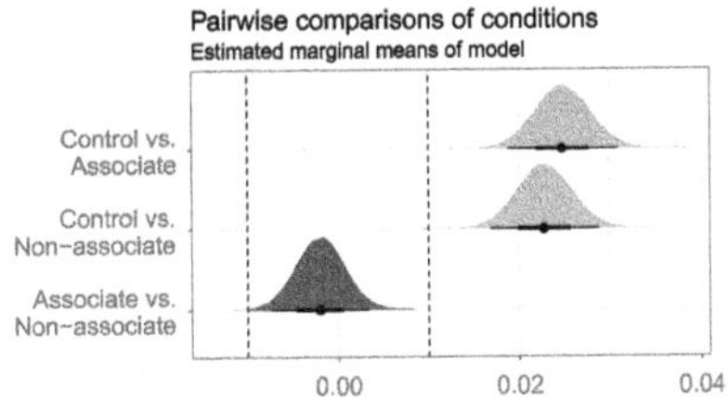

(b) Pairwise comparisons of the posterior distributions obtained from the estimated marginal means of the response time model. The dark gray color indicates that the contrast between Associate and Non-associate did not meet the criteria for a reliable difference, as the mass of the distribution is centered close to zero.

Fig. 4.2 Posterior distributions associated with a Bayesian model of log-transformed response times obtained in the in-person study

Pairwise comparisons of the estimated marginal means obtained from the model revealed that the Control probe word elicited slower response times than the Associate, $\beta = 0.023$, HPD = [0.017, 0.030], and Non-associate, $\beta = 0.021$, HPD = [0.015, 0.028], probe word conditions. Response times collected from Associate and Non-associate conditions did not reliably differ from one another, β −0.002, HPD = [−0.008, 0.004]. Estimates from the marginal means are depicted in Fig. 4.2b.

4.2.4.4 Discussion

On the whole, the results of the second experiment closely follow the pilot. In both cases, we observed a reliable advantage for focus-alternative probes over Control words in the probe recognition task. In contrast, there was no evidence, in either study, that the Associate and Non-associate focus-alternative conditions elicited different response times. A Bayes Factor analysis of the main study provided positive, though weak, evidence that the two focus-alternative conditions truly did not differ from one another.

That the effect of alternatives status manifests immediately after the offset of the focused word indicates that the earliest stages of processing focus do not purely reflect semantic priming and are sensitive to the presence of contextually relevant focus alternatives, as defined by the discourse. The overall finding is compatible with the immediate-access model, in which members of the focus-alternative set are immediately activated during the processing of focus.

Although the advantage for Associate focus-alternative probe words over Controls conceptually replicates previous studies, it is unclear how the delayed-access model or the two-stage model could explain the advantage for Non-associate focus-alternative probe words. If the earliest stages of focus processing reflects semantic priming, unconstrained by the context, then the recognition of Non-associate alternatives would have been delayed. We further elaborate on the theoretical significance of the main findings in the section below, offering a number of speculations and directions for further research.

4.3 Conclusion

Using the cross-modal probe recognition paradigm, we found that two focus-alternative conditions collectively elicited faster response times than non-alternative controls. Further, we found no evidence that response times to the focus-alternative (Associate and Non-associate) conditions differed from one another. Lastly, these results were observed immediately after the presentation of focus. It is unclear how a two-stage model in which focus alternatives are formed from a subset of semantic associates could explain the observed advantage for Non-associate focus alternatives. It is also unclear how a delayed-access model which requires time to access contextual information for selecting alternatives could be compatible with the early time course of the advantage. At present, it appears that only an immediate-access model, in which focus alternatives are immediately determined from the context, is fully compatible with our results.

As discussed in the introduction, the original two-stage model is *destructive* in nature. Under this model, a large set of semantic associates containing both alternatives and non-alternatives is initially activated. Over time, members are removed from this set through a combination of decreased activation and focus-sensitive selection, eventually yielding a restricted set of alternatives consisting of just the relevant mentioned alternatives (Gotzner & Spalek, 2019; Gotzner et al., 2016) or possible alternatives when no alternatives are provided (Husband & Ferreira, 2016).

In some sense, Alternative Semantics is similarly destructive in nature. A large initial set of possible alternatives is generated in a context insensitive fashion and subsequently restricted by context to just the set of relevant alternatives. However, the initial set in Alternative Semantics is the focus-semantic value ($[\![\cdot]\!]^f$) of an expression and it is generated with respect to semantic type rather than semantic priming. Consequently, Alternative Semantics permits far more flexibility with respect to contextually relevant alternatives than the two-stage model would. Given that unrelated words can serve as alternatives according to theoretical intuitions, the strictest conception of such a priming-dependent destructive model is not supported by our study.

We proposed two *constructive* models as alternatives to the two-stage model, in which the formation of the alternative set is driven by the discourse rather than semantic association. In these models, semantic priming and alternative selection are independent processes. While behavior in a forced-choice task might be influenced by both semantic priming and alternative selection, these processes might not be cognitively intertwined. Prior forced-choice task studies have exclusively tested related alternatives. Our results suggest that this comparison has possibly obscured the independence of semantic priming and alternative selection.

While we have argued in favor of a constructive model throughout this chapter, it may still be possible to maintain a destructive model. For example, if both lexical-level associative priming and discourse relevance can influence lexical activation during the initial stage, then the activation for non-associate alternatives could be increased. In other words, the initial stage of alternative set formation could then reflect a mixture of processes from diverse information sources. As in the constructive models, alternatives would be limited to discourse relevant alternatives in the second stage of such a destructive model.

This model is possible in principle, but arguably suffers with respect to parsimony. Under such a destructive model, the discourse representations necessary to increase activation of non-associate alternatives must be immediately accessible. Crucially, to account for our results, discourse representations would have to privilege non-associate alternatives that are mentioned in the discourse over non-associate non-alternatives mentioned in the discourse.

However, if the required discourse information is already available, it is unclear why semantic priming would be necessary to the establish associates as alternatives. A constructive model is arguably more parsimonious in that the selection of associate and non-associate words as alternatives would derive from a single source (discourse representations) rather than multiples sources (discourse representations and semantic priming).

Many discourse-intentional factors (e.g., topicality) determine whether a possible alternative is a relevant one within a given context. However, there is no theory, to our knowledge, in which lexical-level semantic association to the constituent in focus is one of these factors. To be clear, we think it is entirely plausible that there is an early effect of semantic priming on responses; what's far less certain is whether semantic priming serves to generate the set of alternatives. In other words, the priming effect observed in prior studies may simply reflect an independent advantage for related word forms. Nonetheless, it is possible that future results may necessitate some more nuanced compromise between the roles of semantic priming and discourse relevance in the selection of focus alternatives.

We have been intentionally vague in describing the discourse representations utilized by our constructive model to identify contextually relevant alternatives. There are many possibilities and our design largely does not help to distinguish them. Undoubtedly, focus is a context-sensitive phenomenon and our results do suggest that the early processing of focus is similarly context sensitive in nature. Importantly, the probe words in each condition were previously mentioned in our design. Despite this fact, we observe faster response times for Non-associate alternatives than Controls. Thus, the representations involved must distinguish previously mentioned entities with respect to their ability to serve as alternatives for potential foci.

One promising candidate for a discourse representation comes from the Question Under Discussion (QUD) approach to information structure (Roberts, 1996). A great deal of theoretical research has argued that questions, and consequently focus, guide much of discourse organization: some shared line of inquiry between interlocutors introduces a set of alternatives and a focus selects one of these as a possible answer (Beaver & Clark, 2009). Previous experimental work has already demonstrated that both implicit and explicit QUDs can influence incremental processing (Clifton & Frazier, 2018). Perhaps comprehenders are predicting possible QUDs and organizing mentioned entities with respect to their ability to serve as possible answers/foci.

There are a number open question with respect to semantic priming, timing, structural position, and associated focus. Starting with semantic priming, we did not include a condition for non-alternatives semantically related to the focus in our design. This condition was not included in order to improve statistical power and to preserve the naturalness of the sentences. As there was no evidence that Associate alternatives and Non-associate alternatives elicited different response patterns, it is unclear whether the effect of such Associate non-alternatives would pattern like that of alternatives, non-alternatives, or somewhere in-between. Given the possibility that semantic association influences the availability of a related lexical item, independently from its status as a focus alternative, testing such a condition would provide further insight into how semantic priming and alternative status independently influence response times in probe recognition tasks.

Regarding timing, we only investigated response times immediately after the focused word. Prior forced-choice task studies in this literature have explored both early and late probe points (Gotzner & Spalek, 2019; Gotzner et al., 2016; Husband & Ferreira, 2016). Given prior studies, as well as theoretical intuitions, we predict that both Associate and Non-associate alternatives maintain their activation over time. Although investigating the accessibility of alternatives over time is an important task, the central question of this study is whether the Non-associate alternatives are available as early as Associate alternatives in focus processing. The evidence we presented indicates that they are.

Across all of our items, alternatives were conjoined arguments of a main verb while non-alternatives appeared within an adjunct. The use of adjuncts allowed us to easily control for memory effects on account of recency (see Sect. 4.2.1 for discussion). However, recent research by Chromý and Vojvodić (2023) suggests that recall for information conveyed by adjuncts might be worse than that conveyed by arguments. Interestingly, Chromý and Vojvodić (2023) found that this penalty was reduced when the adjunct was put into focus.[12] We cannot rule out the possibility that such structural factors were (at least partially) responsible for the slower response times observed for non-alternatives. However, given that we found no reliable difference in accuracy between alternatives and non-alternatives, we believe that any effects of structure are likely minimal. Further, this difference would not address our core finding: the lack of any reliable differences between the Associate and Non-associate alternatives. That being said, future work should address the undoubtedly complex relationship between memory, structural position, and information structure.

Lastly, there are some open questions with respect to the effect of associated focus on the results. Focus was always associated with a specific focus-sensitive particle (*only*) in our study. We had two motivations for this design. First, the particle *only* provided subjects with a strong cue to the presence of focus in addition to prosodic cues. Second, the particle *only* strengthens the interpretative effect of focus from an implicature to a truth-conditional entailment. We imagined that strengthening the role of focus in this way might further entice subjects to generate a representation of the alternative set for interpretation. Gotzner et al. (2016) and Gotzner and Spalek (2019) found that sentences with associated focus elicited longer response times in a memory probe task. The authors argued that the truth-conditional effect of associated focus triggered increased competition between potential members of the alternative set generating a penalty in response time. Our design does not provide any

[12] We thank Radim Lacima for bringing this paper to our attention.

evidence for or against this analysis, but further comparisons of bare and associated focus using our design could prove informative.

Relatedly, Gotzner et al. (2016) did not find any evidence for response time differences between *only* and *even* in German. Still, the unique interpretive effects of different focus-sensitive particles might induce different relations to the alternative set. For instance, compare the two uses of associated focus given the same context in (21).

(21) a. **Speaker A:** Andy used a muffin and a pistol as props in an independent movie that he was directing.

b. **Speaker B:** No, he only used a [cake]$_F$.

c. **Speaker B':** Well, he also used a [cake]$_F$.

The relevant alternatives (*muffin* and *pistol*) can each felicitously replace the focus (*cake*) in (21B) but not in (21B'). Perhaps given an exclusive focus particle like *only* in (21B), the parser anticipates that one or more of the relevant alternatives will occupy the position of the focus, a prediction which would be inappropriate for an additive particle like *also* in (21B'), cf. *# Well, he also used a muffin.* The initial activation generated for relevant alternatives might well be influenced by whether the focus particle indicates that the item in focus will be added to the items in the focus-alternative set or induce a contrast with those elements.

At various points in this paper, we have described the immediate-access model as a one-stage model of selecting alternatives. We have adopted this terminology in order to contrast the immediate-access model with the delayed-access and two-stage models. However, in doing so, we also evoke many classic debates of the sentence processing literature, particularly those concerning the timing of context (see Altmann & Steedman, 1988; Crain, 1985; Frazier, 1979; Frazier & Fodor, 1978, among others). Historically, one-stage models have been associated with a number of architectural commitments such as interactivity, parallelism, and certain reanalysis strategies. It is not our intention to invoke any of these commitments here. In particular, we are not committed to a processing model under which all forms of contextual information are immediately available and, for example, utilized in early parsing decisions. Rather, we view the early availability of focus alternatives as emerging from the *grammatical* necessity to identify focus alternatives for interpretation (see, Frazier, 1999, chap. 4). In general, we consider these broad architectural considerations, such as interactive parsing, to remain open possibilities.

To conclude, results from a cross-modal probe recognition task indicate that the initial moments of processing focus reflect the selection of contextually relevant focus alternatives, regardless of how semantically related they are to the focus. It remains unclear how a two-stage model or delayed-access model could explain this result. While much more work needs to be done to clarify the representations involved, our results support an immediate-access model where discourse information is utilized to select alternatives immediately upon encountering the focus.

Focus is a pervasive phenomenon in natural language. Naturally, the field is obligated to characterize the inference processes involved in comprehending focus. Further, focus is a fundamentally context-dependent affair. Thus, studying the selection of alternatives will not only serve to better our understanding of focus, but also our understanding of context in language processing at large.

Acknowledgements We'd like to thank Jake Aziz and Neeti Badve for helping to record materials and the RAs of the UCLA Language Processing Lab past and present (Joseph Alamo, Jacob Bower, Dhanya Charan, Katie Chung, Lionel Hu, Iwanka Iwanojko, Jiachen Jin, Ryan Kien, Madeline Kim, Audrey Laun, Iris Shi, Eva Speiser, Marina Suh, Jessica Ti, Amaia Villegas, and Anna Walburger) for helping to run subjects. We'd also like to thank Dylan Bumford, Chuck Clifton, Lyn Frazier, Nicole Gotzner, Tim Hunter, Radim Lacina, Thomas Bye, as well as audiences at XPrag X and the UCLA Psycholinguistics / Computational Linguistics seminar for helpful discussion. All of our data, materials, and analysis are available on the following OSF page: https://osf.io/mctxg/?view_only=664b673f2abf40f6b833e9fddc2931af.

References

Alonso-Ovalle, L. (2006). *Disjunction in alternative semantics*. PhD thesis, University of Massachusetts Amherst.

Altmann, G., & Steedman, M. (1988). Interaction with context during human sentence processing. *Cognition, 30*(3), 191–238.

Balota, D. A., Yap, M. J., Hutchison, K. A., Cortese, M. J., Kessler, B., Loftis, B., Neely, J. H., Nelson, D. L., Simpson, G. B., & Treiman, R. (2007). The English Lexicon Project. *Behavior Research Methods, 39*, 445–459.

Beaver, D. I., & Clark, B. Z. (2009). *Sense and sensitivity: How focus determines meaning*. Wiley.

Beier, E. J., & Ferreira, F. (2022). Replication of Cutler, A., and Fodor, J. A. (1979). Semantic focus and sentence comprehension. Cognition, 7(1), 49–59. *Journal of Memory and Language, 126*, 104339.

Benatar, A., & Clifton, C., Jr. (2014). Newness, givenness and discourse updating: Evidence from eye movements. *Journal of Memory and Language, 71*(1), 1–16.

Birch, S., & Rayner, K. (1997). Linguistic focus affects eye movements during reading. *Memory & Cognition, 25*, 653–660.

Birch, S., & Rayner, K. (2010). Effects of syntactic prominence on eye movements during reading. *Memory & Cognition, 38*(6), 740–752.

Braun, B., & Tagliapietra, L. (2010). The role of contrastive intonation contours in the retrieval of contextual alternatives. *Language and Cognitive Processes, 25*(7–9), 1024–1043.

Brysbaert, M., & New, B. (2009). Moving beyond Kučera and Francis: A critical evaluation of current word frequency norms and the introduction of a new and improved word frequency measure for American English. *Behavior Research Methods, 41*(4), 977–990.

Büring, D. (2009). Towards a typology of focus realization. In M. Zimmermann & C. Féry (Eds.), *Information structure: Theoretical, typological, and experimental perspectives* (pp. 177–205). Oxford: Oxford University Press.

Büring, D. (2016a). *Intonation and meaning*. Oxford University Press.

Büring, D. (2016b). Unalternative semantics. *Semantics and Linguistic Theory, 25*, 550–575.

Bürkner, P.-C. (2017). brms: An R package for Bayesian multilevel models using Stan. *Journal of Statistical Software, 80*(1), 1–28.

Chromý, J., & Vojvodić, S. (2023). When and where did it happen? systematic differences in recall of core and optional sentence information. *Quarterly Journal of Experimental Psychology, 77*, 111–132.

Clifton, C., Jr., & Frazier, L. (2018). Context effects in discourse: The question under discussion. *Discourse Processes, 55*(2), 105–112.

Crain, S. (1985). On not being led up the garden path. In *Natural language parsing* (pp. 320–358). Cambridge University Press.

Cutler, A., & Fodor, J. A. (1979). Semantic focus and sentence comprehension. *Cognition, 7*(1), 49–59.

Dahan, D., Tanenhaus, M. K., & Chambers, C. G. (2002). Accent and reference resolution in spoken-language comprehension. *Journal of Memory and Language, 47*, 292–314.

Forster, K. I., Guerrera, C., & Elliot, L. (2009). The maze task: Measuring forced incremental sentence processing time. *Behavior Research Methods, 41*, 163–171.

Fraundorf, S. H., Watson, D. G., & Benjamin, A. S. (2010). Recognition memory reveals just how CONTRASTIVE contrastive accenting really is. *Journal of Memory and Language, 63*(3), 367–386.

Frazier, L. (1979). *On comprehending sentences: Syntactic parsing strategies.* PhD thesis, University of Connecticut.

Frazier, L. (1999). *On sentence interpretation* (Vol. 22). Springer Science & Business Media.

Frazier, L., & Fodor, J. D. (1978). The sausage machine: A new two-stage parsing model. *Cognition, 6*(4), 291–325.

Gotzner, N. (2017). *Alternative sets in language processing: How focus alternatives are represented in the mind*. Springer.

Gotzner, N., & Spalek, K. (2019). The life and times of focus alternatives: Tracing the activation of alternatives to a focused constituent in language comprehension. *Language and Linguistics Compass, 13*(2), e12310.

Gotzner, N., Wartenburger, I., & Spalek, K. (2016). The impact of focus particles on the recognition and rejection of contrastive alternatives. *Language and Cognition, 8*, 59–95.

Harris, J. A. (2019). *Alternatives on demand and locality: Resolving discourse-linked wh-phrases in sluiced structures.* Springer.

Heim, I., & Kratzer, A. (1998). *Semantics in generative grammar*. Blackwell.

Hoeks, M., Toosarvandani, M., & Rysling, A. (2023). Processing of linguistic focus depends on contrastive alternatives. *Journal of Memory and Language, 132*, 104444.

Husband, M., & Ferreira, F. (2016). The role of selection in the comprehension of focus alternatives. *Language, Cognition and Neuroscience, 31*(2), 217–235.
Ito, K., & Speer, S. R. (2008). Anticipatory effects of intonation: Eye movements during instructed visual search. *Journal of Memory and Language, 58*(2), 541–573.
Jackendoff, R. (1972). *Semantic interpretation in generative grammar*. MIT Press.
Jeffreys, H. (1998). *Theory of probability*. Oxford University Press.
Jördens, K. A., Gotzner, N., & Spalek, K. (2020). The role of non-categorical relations in establishing focus alternative sets. *Language and Cognition, 12*(4), 729–754.
Kim, C. S., Gunlogson, C., Tanenhaus, M. K., & Runner, J. T. (2015). Context-driven expectations about focus alternatives. *Cognition, 139*, 28–49.
Krifka, M. (1992). A framework for focus-sensitive quantification. *Semantics and Linguistic Theory, 2*, 215–236.
Lacina, R., Sturt, P., & Gotzner, N. (2023). The comprehension of broad focus: Probing alternatives to verb phrases. In *Information structure—Theory: How and why discourse limits the way we express what we express*. Language Science Press.
Landauer, T. K., & Dumais, S. T. (1997). A solution to Plato's problem: The latent semantic analysis theory of acquisition, induction, and representation of knowledge. *Psychological Review, 104*(2), 211.
Morris, R. K., & Folk, J. R. (1998). Focus as a contextual priming mechanism in reading. *Memory & Cognition, 26*(6), 1313–1322.
Neely, J. H. (2012). Semantic priming effects in visual word recognition: A selective review of current findings and theories. In *Basic processes in reading* (pp. 264–336). Routledge.
Pierrehumbert, J., & Hirschberg, J. (1990). The meaning of intonational contours in the interpretation of discourse. In *Intentions in communication* (pp. 271–311). MIT Press.
R Core Team. (2023). *R: A language and environment for statistical computing*. R Foundation for Statistical Computing.
Rhode, D. (2001). *Linger. A flexible platform for language processing experiments*.
Roberts, C. (1996). Information structure in discourse: Towards an integrated formal theory of pragmatics. In *Ohio State University working papers in linguistics* (Vol. 49). Ohio State University.
Rooth, M. E. (1985). *Association with focus (montague grammar, semantics, only, even)*. PhD thesis, University of Massachusetts Amherst.

Rooth, M. E. (1992). A theory of focus interpretation. *Natural Language Semantics, 1*(1), 75–116.

Rotello, C. M., & Macmillan, N. A. (2007). Response bias in recognition memory. In *Psychology of learning and motivation* (pp. 61–94). Elsevier.

Schwarzschild, R. (1999). GIVENness, avoidF, and other constraints on the placement of accent. *Natural Language Semantics, 7*, 141–177.

Selkirk, E. (1984). *Phonology and syntax: The relation between sound and structure*. MIT Press.

Swinney, D. (1979). Lexical access during sentence comprehension: (Re)Consideration of context effects. *Journal of Verbal Learning and Verbal Behavior, 18*, 645–659.

Von Stechow, A. (1991). Focusing and backgrounding operators. *Discourse Particles, 6*, 37–84.

Watson, D. G., Tanenhaus, M. K., & Gunlogson, C. A. (2008). Interpreting pitch accents in online comprehension: H* vs. L+H. *Cognitive Science, 32*(7), 1232–1244.

Weber, A., Braun, B., & Crocker, M. W. (2006). Finding referents in time: Eye-tracking evidence for the role of contrastive accents. *Language and Speech, 49*(3), 367–392.

Zehr, J., & Schwarz, F. (2018). *Penncontroller for Internet Based Experiments (IBEX).*

Part III

Operations on Salient Alternatives

5

Probing the Probe: Why Inference Tasks May Inflate Response Rates for Scalar Implicature

Paul Marty, Jacopo Romoli, Yasutada Sudo, and Richard Breheny

5.1 Introduction

A speaker who utters a sentence like (1) often implies that (2) is not true. This pattern of implication-by-exclusion is labelled Scalar Implicature (SI).

(1) Some of the horses jumped over the fence.

(2) All of the horses jumped over the fence.

SI is widely attested across different expressions of English. For example, sentences involving *or* are often understood to be implying that a similarly constructed alternative sentence with *and* is not true. Likewise, SIs are observed with *possible*/*certain*, *warm*/*hot* and many other scalar

We would like to thank Jinnan Guo, Márti Nagy and Zsófia Varga for their help with the materials. This research was supported by the Leverhulme Trust grant RPG-2018-425. Materials, data and scripts of analyses are available open access on the OSF Platform: https://osf.io/cmjg2/.

P. Marty (✉)
Centro de Linguística, Universidade de Lisboa, Lisbon, Portugal
e-mail: pmarty@edu.ulisboa.pt

N. Gotzner et al. (eds.), *Alternatives in Grammar and Cognition*, Palgrave Studies in Pragmatics, Language and Cognition, https://doi.org/10.1007/978-3-031-76676-3_5

terms. The fact that the same observations can be made across the world's languages has led to theoretical accounts that are based on some basic universal properties of language and its use (Chierchia et al., 2012; Grice, 1975).

Theories of SI overwhelmingly proceed from considerations of alternatives (Chierchia et al., 2012; Frank & Goodman, 2012; Gazdar, 1979; Horn, 1972). One key question for these theories is about which alternatives can be involved in this kind of strengthening process. In particular, it has been observed that related symmetric alternatives are seemingly never excluded in language interpretation (Breheny et al., 2018; Horn, 1972; Katzir, 2007; Kroch, 1972). To illustrate, consider the symmetric alternative for (1) given in (3). If we could strengthen what is expressed by (1) with the negation of (3), we would arrive at a meaning which corresponds to the one expressed by (2), but this is not an available interpretation for (1).

(3) Some but not all of the horses jumped over the fence.

Popular solutions to the so-called *symmetry problem* are based on the idea that the relative complexity or costs of competing alternatives are key. Among these, some proposals refer strictly to linguistic forms (Bergen et al., 2016) or their underlying structural representations (Fox & Katzir, 2011; Katzir, 2007), while for others, conceptual simplicity is more fundamental (Buccola et al., 2022).

Theories of SI are also bound to account for the fact that, while SI may often be available, sentences such as (1) may also be understood

---

J. Romoli
Heinrich Heine Universität Düsseldorf, Düsseldorf, Germany
e-mail: jacopo.romoli@hhu.de

Y. Sudo · R. Breheny
University College London, London, UK
e-mail: y.sudo@ucl.ac.uk

R. Breheny
e-mail: r.breheny@ucl.ac.uk

to not carry any SI. On this question of variability, there is widespread agreement that such sentences have a basic, literal meaning that is consistent with both SI and its absence, while contextual factors are decisive in whether scalar strengthening occurs (Bergen & Grodner, 2012; Breheny et al., 2006; Fox & Katzir, 2011; Geurts, 2010). In particular, although the notion of relevance can be understood in many different ways (Carnap, 1962; Grice, 1975; Roberts, 2012; Pankratz & Van Tiel, 2021; Sperber & Wilson, 1986), it is widely assumed that the contextual relevance of the alternative is an important factor (Fox & Katzir, 2011; Geurts, 2010). Thus, theories of SI hold that the right kind of alternative needs to be available and that contextual relevance of that alternative is an important factor for scalar strengthening to occur.

From its inception, experimental research on SI has demonstrated variability in all conceivable ways: between groups (Noveck, 2001; Papafragou & Musolino, 2003), between individuals (Bott & Noveck, 2004; Van Tiel & Schaeken, 2017), between experimental contexts (Breheny et al., 2006; Bott & Noveck, 2004; Papafragou & Musolino, 2003), across corpus contexts (Degen, 2015; Sun & Breheny, 2024) and between different scalar expressions (Baker et al., 2009; Sun et al., 2018; van Tiel et al., 2016, 2019). Most theoretical discussion of this variability has been cast in terms of theorists' proposed computation of SIs. In this paper, we focus on a different kind of variation—one between different experimental tasks. In particular, we focus on the fact that, at least for many commonly discussed scalar expressions, when participants perform an inference task, their responses indicate that SI is available to a greater extent than when they perform other commonly administered tasks, in particular those which involve sentence (or sentence-picture) verification.

To illustrate using an early demonstration of this phenomenon, Geurts and Pouscoulous (2009) presented the same sentential stimuli in an inference task and a sentence-picture verification task. In an inference task, participants are typically presented with a linguistic stimulus and asked about a potential implication of that stimulus. In this case, Geurts & Pouscoulous simply asked participants to indicate whether or not sentences like *Some of the B's are in the box on the left* implied that not all of the B's are in the box on the left. In their verification task, they presented such sentences alongside a picture and asked participants to

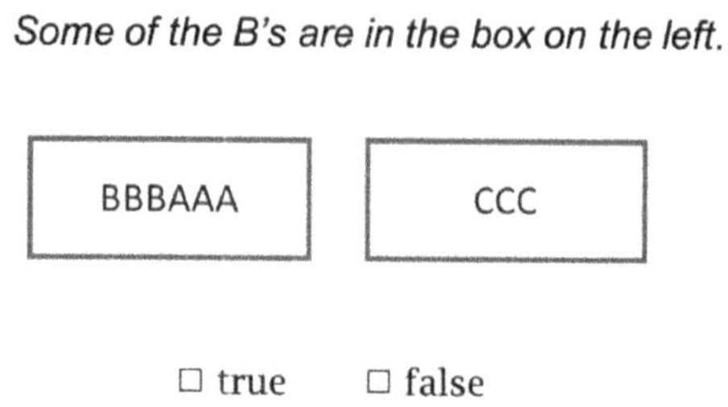

Fig. 5.1 Example test item in Geurts & Pouscoulous's verification task (Experiment 2). No reference is made to the canonical alternative. A negative response is indicative of an SI response

indicate whether the sentence was true or false, as shown in Fig. 5.1. A Yes-response in the inference task and a False-response in the verification task are assumed to result from the participant accessing the SI and integrating it into their overall understanding of the stimulus. Geurts and Pouscoulous (2009) report with-SI responses at nearly twice the rate in the inference task, compared to the verification task (62% vs. 34%).

A wider range of scalar expressions were studied in van Tiel et al. (2016), where SI rates for more than 40 expressions were elicited via an inference task of the sort illustrated in Fig. 5.2. Five of these scalar expressions were subsequently investigated in van Tiel et al. (2019) using a sentence-picture verification task. Looking across the results of the two studies, we can see, here again, a consistently wide gap between with-SI responses: 29% vs. 71% for *low*, 46% vs. 62% for *scarce*, 50% vs. 87% for *may/might*,[1] 62% vs. 96% for *some* and 56% vs. 62% for *try*.

Geurts and Pouscoulous (2009) attribute the higher SI rate in inference tasks to the experimental probe typically employed in inference tasks (but not in verification tasks) somehow promoting the contextual relevance of the alternative. To motivate this account, consider for instance the probe question in Fig. 5.2. We will refer to this type of probe, where the alternative of interest is embedded under negation, as a NOT-ALT probe. In this case, the participant is explicitly being asked whether they would exclude the alternative; this probe question is quite

[1] Epistemic *may* was used in the inference task, while *might* was used in the sentence-picture verification task; nouns and other predicates differed across tasks.

Mary says:

Some of the questions are easy.

Would you conclude from this that, according to Mary,
not all of the questions are easy?

☐ Yes ☐ No

Fig. 5.2 Example test item in a standard inference task à la van Tiel et al. (2016). The probe question references the negation of the canonical alternative. A positive response is indicative of an SI response

suggestive that the alternative would have been relevant in the context of the speaker's utterance, a piece of information which is otherwise absent from the stimulus. While this seems a plausible enough account, we note however that such inference task probes do not universally raise the SI rate across scalar expressions. Indeed, it is an important result of van Tiel et al. (2016) that, notwithstanding the potential boost for SI rates from the probe, inference task rates are still quite variable across scalar expressions, sometimes being very low. We return to this point in our discussion below. For now, we shall focus on what can account for the potential boost that the inference task appears to provide.

Sun and Breheny (2022) provide some support for Geurts and Pouscoulous's conjecture by manipulating whether the probe is likely to suggest the contextual relevance of the alternative for two scalar expressions, *some* and *possible*. In one condition, they used a NOT-ALT probe as in van Tiel et al. (2016), which they assume is suggestive that the sentence context is one in which the alternative is relevant. In another condition, they used a COULD-ALT probe—e.g., *Would you conclude that, it could be that Mary thinks that all of the questions are easy?*—which they hypothesise would provide a cue to contexts in which the alternative is not relevant, hence reducing with-SI responses. Their results provide evidence for the conjecture that the type of probe used is a factor and that COULD-ALT probes have the expected effect. However, they also report high rates of with-SI responses for the COULD-ALT probe. Sun & Breheny attribute this effect to the fact that their COULD-ALT probe still mentions the alternative expression and they speculate that mention of the alternative is a second factor in increased SI rates in the inference task. To the extent that this is true, there are two kinds of motivation in the literature as to why.

First, as already discussed in Geurts and Pouscoulous (2009), the presence of the alternative itself contributes to the impression of its relevance simply by making the form salient (see Pankratz and Van Tiel [2021] for a related notion of relevance). A second kind of motivation comes from priming research where it is found that SI rates are boosted by a prime containing the alternative (Marty et al., 2024; Rees & Bott, 2018; Skordos & Papafragou, 2016). Rees and Bott (2018) argue for the Salience Hypothesis, which states that simple salience of alternative is a necessary step in implicature computation. This view is aligned with the theory of alternatives, mentioned above, which sees salience of linguistic form as a factor in which an alternative is considered to be available. However, the Salience Hypothesis has been challenged on the basis that it makes incorrect predictions concerning a wider range of priming facts (Marty et al., 2024). In fact Marty et al. (2024), in the spirit of Geurts and Pouscoulous (2009) and Skordos and Papafragou (2016), argue that priming effects due to explicitly mentioned alternatives are the result of context adaptation effects. From this perspective, any effect of the presence of alternative in a probe question could result from it being a cue to the underlying relevance of the alternative.

Thus, we were motivated to further investigate whether mention of alternative plays an independent role in promoting with-SI responses in inference tasks. In order to achieve this, we set out to compare outcomes on inference tasks which probe directly for the SI, as in the standard inference task. Additionally, in order to explore more thoroughly the extent to which alternative salience affects SI availability, we operationalised two of the notions of alternative mentioned above. Recall that some theories of SI refer either to alternative forms (Bergen et al., 2016), or to more abstract underlying linguistic representations (Fox & Katzir, 2011; Katzir, 2007). In the study presented below, we manipulated whether the alternative was explicitly mentioned in the experimental probe, whether it was implicit in the probe, or entirely absent. Thus, what was held constant across the different probe conditions we tested was the meaning of the question asked in the probe and thereby the relevance of the alternative. To do so, we exploited the fact that for many scalar expressions, with-SI interpretations can be paraphrased with an antonymic predicate. To consider (1) again, the negation of (2) in the context of an assertion of (1) can be paraphrased as *Some horses did not jump over the fence*. Such paraphrases, which do not mention the alternative, were used to construe novel ways to probe for the SI.

To round out our exploration of variability in SI and the differences between experimental tasks, we conducted a post-hoc analysis of inference tasks response times. The context of this analysis is the widely replicated finding in Bott and Noveck (2004) that, in verification tasks, participants who respond based on the SI-strengthened interpretation take longer to respond than participants who do not. Several accounts of this response-time difference have been offered to date without a definitive agreement (Bott & Noveck, 2004; Bott et al., 2012; Huang & Snedeker, 2018; Van Tiel & Pankratz, 2021; van Tiel et al., 2019). Thus, we were motivated to see whether there is also a delay for with-SI responses in inference tasks and, more generally, what light this investigation may shed on the response-time results of different tasks.

5.2 Experiment

The experiment employed a standard inference task à la van Tiel et al. (2016) (see also Geurts & Pouscoulous, 2009; Gotzner et al. 2018; Sun & Breheny, 2022; Sun et al., 2018). Example items are shown in Fig. 5.3. In each trial, participants were presented with a de-contextualised statement uttered by a random speaker (henceforth, the source statement) and a probe question featuring another statement related to the one that the speaker made (henceforth, the target statement). Participants had to decide whether or not they could conclude from the source statement that the speaker also believes the target statement to be true.

In the test trials, the source statement involved a scalar term and the target statement associated with it expressed a proposition implying, directly or indirectly, the falsity of its canonical alternative. The lexical content of the target statement was experimentally manipulated to test whether raising the salience level of the alternative has any effect on

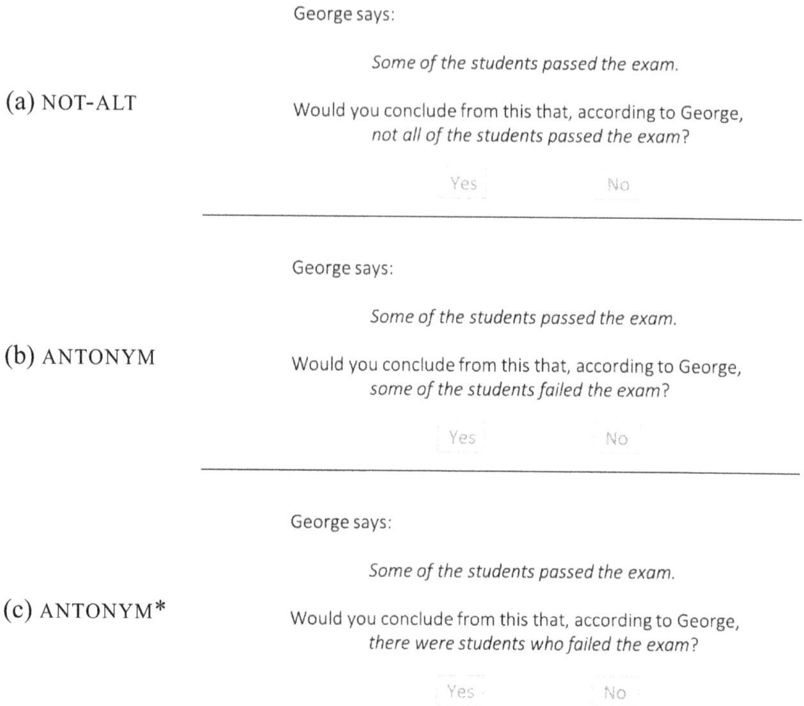

Fig. 5.3 Example trials illustrating the items' general layout. These examples correspond to test trials for the ⟨some, all⟩-scale in the (a) NOT-ALT, (b) ANTONYM and (c) ANTONYM* conditions. A positive response in the test trials indicates that an SI is drawn

SI rates above that of making the proposition expressed by the alternative contextually relevant. For these purposes, we introduced three types of probe: the NOT-ALT probe, used in previous inference task studies, and two novel ANTONYM probes, illustrated in Fig. 5.3b and c. As in the NOT-ALT probe, the target statement in ANTONYM probes had the potential to bias the participants to think that the context in which the source statement was made is one in which it is relevant to know whether its alternative is true. Crucially, unlike in the NOT-ALT probe, the target statement in these probes expressed the falsity of the alternative by other linguistic means than explicitly referencing the stronger alternative and embedding it under negation. Moreover, we distinguished between ANTONYM probe and ANTONYM* in order to detect if implicit activation of the alternative promotes SI. This is possible since in the former, as opposed to the latter, the scalar expression is employed in the probe and this itself may have tended to trigger a scalar implicature, involving a representation of the alternative in its derivation.

We hypothesised that if raising the salience of the alternative has a boosting effect on SI rates above that of raising its relevance, the proportions of 'Yes' responses in the test trials—our proxy measure for SI rates—should be higher in the NOT-ALT than in either of the ANTONYM conditions, or at least the ANTONYM* condition. Alternatively, if alternative salience boosts SI rates insofar as it provides a contextual cue that the alternative is more likely to be relevant than otherwise, the proportions of 'Yes' responses in the test trials should be comparable across all probe conditions. Specifically, the Salience Hypothesis predicts that SI responses should be higher in the NOT-ALT than in the ANTONYM* condition. In addition, depending on whether the Salience Hypothesis applies additionally to activated abstract linguistic representations, we may also see more SI rates in the ANTONYM than in the ANTONYM* condition. If only explicit discourse salience is relevant to activating SI computation, then it is predicted that SI rates should be higher in the NOT-ALT than either ANTONYM conditions.

5.2.1 Participants

164 native speakers of English took part in this experiment. Participants were recruited on Prolific (Palan & Schitter, 2018) using pre-screen criteria for first language (English), country of birth (UK) and prior approval rate (≥90%). Participants were paid £1.20 and average completion time was about 7 minutes (hourly rate: £10/hr). All participants gave written informed consent to participate in the study. The study was approved by the Research Ethics Committee at UCL. Data were collected and stored in accordance with the provisions of Data Protection Act 2018.

5.2.2 Stimuli Design

All test items involved a source statement, made by a character, and a probe question, directed to the participants. The source statement was introduced by the phrase '[Name] says:', where [Name] was the character's name. The value of [Name] was varied from item to item, without any repetition, to avoid that participants form speaker-related expectations. The source statement contained a weak scalar expression corresponding to the weaker member of one of 12 lexical scales. The list of scales tested in the experiment is given in Table 5.1. This list was devised by selecting a representative sample of scales among those most commonly discussed in the literature; it consisted of determiners (2 scales), verbs (5 scales), adverbs (1 scale), adjectives (3 scales) and connectives (1 scale). For each scale, three statements were constructed, applying two constraints. First, to ensure sufficient variation for each scalar expression, all three statements involved different content and/or function words except for the weak scalar term of interest. Second, the lexical content of these statements was selected so that the falsity of their stronger alternative could easily be expressed without mentioning the stronger scale-mate. This was mainly done by using predicates such as *pass the exam*, *be married* or *leave*, for which an antonym expression is readily available, e.g., *fail the exam*, *be single*, *stay*.

The probe question was displayed right below the source statement and it was of the form 'Would you conclude from this that, according to [Name], [Target]?', where [Name] was the character's name and [Target] was the target statement, that is, the statement expressing the targeted implication. The target statement always implied the falsity of the canonical alternative to the source statement; crucially, the wording of that statement was manipulated so that, depending on the probe condition, the relevant implication was conveyed by different linguistic means.

In the NOT-ALT conditions, the relevant implication was directly expressed by embedding the canonical alternative to the source statement under negation. Thus, for a sentence like *Some of the students passed the exam*, the target statement was *Not all of the students passed the exam* (see Fig. 5.3a). By contrast, in the ANTONYM and ANTONYM* conditions, this same implication was conveyed without referencing the canonical alternative. In the ANTONYM conditions, the target statement was obtained by minimally modifying the source statement so as to keep the weak scalar expression as is. For two-thirds of the items, this was done by replacing one of the predicates in the source statement with an antonym expression, e.g., *Some of the students failed the exam* (see Fig. 5.3b); in cases where such a replacement could not be done without affecting the weak scalar expression itself, the target statement was obtained by expanding on the intended meaning of that expression, e.g., expanding *try* as *try in vain*, *participate* as *participate without defeating the opponent*, etc. Finally, the target statements in the ANTONYM* conditions were variants of those used in the ANTONYM conditions in which neither the weak scalar expression, nor its stronger scale-mate appeared. This was done mainly by using a blank paraphrase of the weak scalar expression, e.g., *There are students who failed the exam* (see Fig. 5.3c), or else by replacing that expression with a lexical antonym, e.g., replacing *tried to help* with *failed to help*, *participated in the game* with *lost the game*, etc.

The scale factor was manipulated within subjects as in previous studies on scalar diversity. The probe factor, on the other hand, was manipulated between subjects to avoid potential carryover effects from one probe condition to another. Crossing both factors yielded 3 lists of 12(scales) $\times$ 3(instances) $=$ 36 test items. 10 control items were added to each list, yielding a total of 46 items per list. The layout of the control items was similar to that of the test items in all regards. Half of the control items involved a target statement that contextually entailed the source statement (e.g., inferring that *John owns a pet* from *John has a cat*); the other half involved a target statement that was in direct conflict with the source statement (e.g., inferring *Lisa loves golfing* from *Lisa hates golfing*). Control items were the same in all three lists. These items were included to identify low-effort responses (see 5.2.6).

5.2.3 Procedure

At the start of the study, participants were provided with the following instructions:

Table 5.1 List of scales tested in the experiment by grammatical category

Category	Scales
Adjective	⟨possible, certain⟩, ⟨good, excellent⟩, ⟨difficult, impossible⟩
Adverb	⟨sometimes, always⟩
Connective	⟨or, and⟩
Determiner	⟨some, all⟩, ⟨a few, a lot⟩
Verb	⟨allow, require⟩, ⟨may, have to⟩, ⟨permit, require⟩, ⟨try, succeed⟩, ⟨participate, win⟩

> In this study, you will be presented with sentences uttered by various people. After each utterance, we will ask you whether that utterance allows you to draw a certain conclusion from it. We want to know whether, assuming that the speaker spoke truthfully, you think that the proposed conclusion is likely to be intended by the speaker.

Participants were then presented with two practice trials, one in which the targeted implication was a valid conclusion (inferring *Tom has a brother or a sister* from *Tom's sibling is in town*) and one in which it was an unrealistic extrapolation (inferring *Albert is an athlete* from *Albert likes to swim*). These trials only served to familiarise participants with the display and were not included in the analysis. Following these trials, participants were pseudo-randomly assigned one of the three list of items so as to reach an even number of participants per probe condition. The experiment continued with 46 trials corresponding to the 46 items from the list assigned to them. Trials were presented in random order with a 500ms ISI. Participants reported their responses by clicking one of two response buttons labelled 'Yes' and 'No', respectively. Items remained on the screen until participants provided their responses. Responses and response times were recorded on each trial.

5.2.4 Data Availability

The full list of materials along with the raw data code files for result analysis can be found on the OSF Platform at https://osf.io/cmjg2/.

5.2.5 Software

Data treatment and analysis were carried out in the R statistical environment (R Core Team, 2023) using mainly the `Hmisc` (Harrell, 2023), `Rmisc` (Hope, 2022), `ggstatsplot` (Patil, 2021), `ggplot2` (Wickham, 2016), `brms` (Bürkner, 2017; Bürkner, 2018; Bürkner, 2021), `lme4` (Bates et al., 2015), `car` (Fox & Weisberg, 2019) `outliers` (Komsta, 2022) and `emmeans` (Lenth, 2023) packages for the R statistics program.

5.2.6 Analysis of Responses

Four participants were excluded from the analysis for making mistakes in more than two of the control items. The remaining subjects ($n = 160$) were relatively evenly distributed across all three probe conditions (NOT-ALT: $n = 55$, ANTONYM: $n = 55$, ANTONYM*: $n = 50$). Control items were answered correctly on 94.6% of the trials with a mean acceptance rate for supported and unsupported inferences of 94.5% (95% CI[92.6, 95.8]) and 5.1% (95% CI[3.8, 6.8]), respectively.

5.2.6.1 Probe Effect

Figure 5.4 shows the mean acceptance rates to the test items by Probe type. Overall, the distribution of by-participant mean rates was very similar in all three probe conditions with a grand mean rate of acceptance of 69.1% for the NOT-ALT probe (95% CI[67,71.1]), 68.6% for the ANTONYM probe (95% CI[66.6,70.6]) and 70.1% for the ANTONYM* probe (95% CI[67.9,72.1]).

To analyse the effects of Probe type, we fitted a Bayesian mixed-effects logistic regression model to the data using the `brms` package in R. The model predicted responses in the test trials on the basis of the probe factor. The three-level categorical predictor was treatment coded, with NOT-ALT serving as the reference group. The mixed-effects structure of the model consisted of by-participant and by-item random intercepts. We used weakly informative priors, as recommended by McElreath

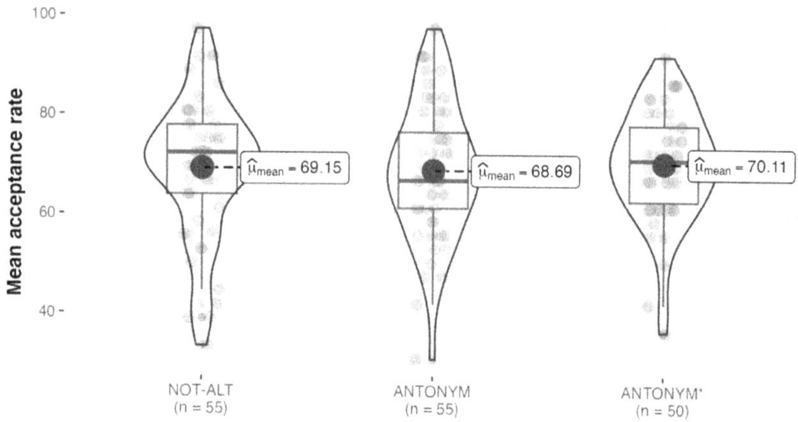

Fig. 5.4 Mean acceptance rate (i.e., percentage of 'Yes' responses) to the test items by probe condition. For each condition, the grand mean is visualised by a red dot, with its value on the right, and the distribution of by-participant mean rates by smaller, vertically-aligned dots and by a violin plot displaying the five-number summary of the variable's values and the kernel density estimate of its underlying distribution

(2020) and Nicenboim et al. (2023), among others. Specifically, for the intercept of the model, corresponding to the NOT-ALT group, we assumed a relatively broad prior distribution $N(0.7, 0.5)$. This prior distribution was weakly based on the results of van Tiel et al.'s Exp.2, which tested the NOT-ALT probe questions with linguistic stimuli similar to ours.[2] The prior distributions for the non-reference groups were set to $N(0, 0.3)$ so as to keep the same estimate as above for the μ-parameter $(0 + 0.7 = 0.7)$ while slightly increasing the σ-parameter $(0.5 + 0.3 = 0.8)$, reflecting our greater uncertainty regarding this parameter for these

[2] van Tiel et al.'s (2016) survey included 43 scales. Among those, 11 were either identical or closely related to the 12 scales tested in our study, the main exception being ⟨or, and⟩, which van Tiel et al. did not include. Thus, the results from van Tiel et al. (2016) allowed us to form clear expectations about the distribution of the responses in the NOT-ALT conditions of our experiment. In particular, the results from their Experiment 2 show that the probability of 'Yes' responses for these 11 scales was 0.69 ($SD = 0.25$), which is substantially above the one observed for the whole set of 43 scales ($M = 0.43$, $SD = 0.28$). This difference can be accounted for by the fact that 90% of these scales are bounded lexical scales, which have been found to license higher rates of SIs than non-bounded ones (50% of the scales in their set). Bounded scales represented 92% of the scales in our sample.

Table 5.2 Estimate, standard error, 95% credible interval and $\hat{R}$ statistic for each parameter of the model (varying intercept by subject and by item)

Parameter	Estimate	SE	Lower	Upper	Rhat
Intercept	1.25	0.22	0.82	1.69	1.00
ANTONYM	0.00	0.25	−0.49	0.48	1.00
ANTONYM*	0.04	0.25	−0.45	0.53	1.00
$\sigma_{subject}$	0.93	0.07	0.80	1.08	1.00
σ_{item}	1.85	0.14	1.60	2.15	1.00

groups. For random effects, the standard deviations were all assumed to come from the Half-Cauchy distribution with $\sigma = 1$. The posterior distributions reported below were estimated using four Hamilton Monte Carlo Markov Chains implemented in Stan. Each of these chains consisted of 11,000 samples, of which 1000 were used for warm-up. Both the trace plots (omitted here) and the Rhatt values (the potential scale reduction factor $\hat{R}$) indicated convergence. The output of the model is shown in Table 5.2.

The hypothesis that NOT-ALT should yield higher rates of acceptance than the other Probe levels was tested by determining if, compared to the NOT-ALT probe, either of the ANTONYM probes gave rise to reliably lower rates of acceptance, using the `hypothesis` function of `brms`. The posterior probability of ANTONYM yielding lower rates of acceptance than NOT-ALT was 51% with an evidence ratio of 1.03, and the difference was estimated to be 0 with 90% quantiles being $[-0.41, 0.40]$. For ANTONYM*, the posterior probability was 43% with an evidence ratio of 0.75, and the difference was estimated to be 0.04 with 90% quantiles being $[-0.37, 0.45]$.

In sum, our results show that SI rates are much the same across all three probe conditions and they provide evidence against the hypothesis that making the alternative contextually salient, as in the NOT-ALT probe, has a boosting effect on SI rates above that of merely raising the relevance of that alternative, as in the ANTONYM and ANTONYM* probes. These findings are consistent with the idea that the probe question generally biases participants to think that, in the context of the source statement, it is relevant to decide whether or not the alternative is true, enhancing the likelihood that the SI reading be endorsed and accounting in turn for the inflated rates of SIs yielded by the inferential paradigm.

5.2.6.2 Scalar Diversity

Figure 5.5 shows the mean acceptance rates for each scale by Probe type. There was substantial variation among scales, with positive responses ranging from 23% to 96% in the NOT-ALT condition, from 15% to 94% in the ANTONYM condition and from 10% to 93% in the ANTONYM* conditions. To further control for the reliability of our data, the NOT-ALT results were compared to those from van Tiel et al.'s Exp.1 & Exp.2 for 11 scales whose weaker member was tested in both studies (see also fn.2). Kendall's tau correlation tests were performed to determine if, for these scalar expressions, there was a correlation between the SI rates observed in our study and in van Tiel et al.'s. The results showed that there was a moderate to strong, positive correlation between them (comparison with Exp.1: $\tau = 0.78$, $p < 0.001$; comparison with Exp.2: $\tau = 0.5$, $p < 0.05$). Hence, the present results align with and replicate in part van Tiel et al.'s results in showing that the scalar expressions in our sample yielded widely different rates of SIs.[3] In addition, they show that, for the expressions we tested, scalar diversity is observed using different probe questions.

The effect of Probe type on each scale was also analysed to check for potential discrepancies with the results of the global analysis above. For each scale, we fitted a generalised linear mixed-effect regression (GLMER) model with a logit link function, predicting participants' responses from the fixed effect of Probe (treatment coded). All models included by-participant and by-item random intercepts. Each model was compared to a null model missing the fixed effect of interest, but with the same random effect structure. The results of the model comparison tests, synthesised in Table 5.3, showed that including Probe as a

[3] We note that, for the NOT-ALT conditions, the variations in SI rates were slightly less severe in our study than in van Tiel et al.'s study, in which positive responses ranged from 4% to 100%. The reason is simply that our sample did not include unbounded adjectival scales like ⟨content, happy⟩ or ⟨intelligent, brilliant⟩, which gave rise to the lowest rates of SIs (below 10%) in van Tiel et al.'s study.

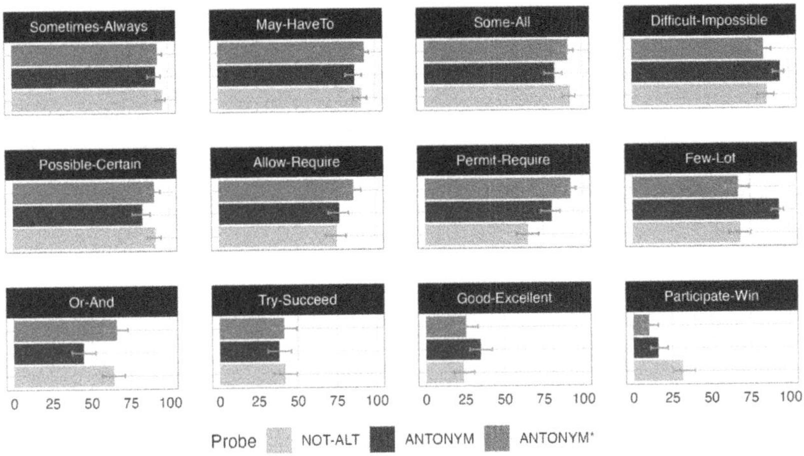

Fig. 5.5 Mean acceptance rate to the test items by scale and probe condition. Error bars represent the 95% CIs of the mean values

predictor led to a significantly improved fit over the null model for only two scales, ⟨permit, require⟩ and ⟨few, lot⟩. For both these scales, the estimated marginal means were found to be significantly lower in the NOT-ALT condition than in the ANTONYM or ANTONYM* conditions. Thus, we conclude that the by-scale rates of SIs were largely unaffected by the Probe manipulation, consistent with the results of the global analysis.

5.2.7 Analysis of Response Times

To the best of our knowledge, previous studies investigating SIs using the inferential paradigm did not look at responses times (RTs). One reason for this is simply that the primary focus of these studies has been on gauging the frequency at which various scalar terms yield SIs and identifying the factors explaining the variability observed. In the context of our research, however, RTs provide us with another behavioural measure which we can use to assess the extent to which results from inference and verification tasks may differ. For these purposes, we set out to explore the RTs collected in our study by considering three broad hypotheses:

Table 5.3 Chi-squared statistics, naïve and adjusted *p*-value from the model comparison tests. *p*-values were adjusted for multiple testing using a Bonferroni correction, yielding a significance threshold of 0.004

Scale	χ^2	Naïve *p*-value	Adjusted *p*-value
⟨sometimes, always⟩	0.27	0.87	1
⟨may, have to⟩	1.64	0.43	1
⟨some, all⟩	2.03	0.36	1
⟨difficult, impossible⟩	4.80	0.09	0.81
⟨possible, certain⟩	2.56	0.27	1
⟨allow, require⟩	2.15	0.34	1
⟨permit, require⟩	13.95	0.0009**	0.01*
⟨few, lot⟩	12.16	0.002**	0.02*
⟨or, and⟩	6.89	0.03*	0.3
⟨try, succeed⟩	0.26	0.87	1
⟨good, excellent⟩	2.03	0.36	1
⟨participate, win⟩	2.61	0.27	1

i. There are response delay effects similar to those commonly found in verification tasks, on which responses consistent with the SI being derived take more time than those that are not (Bott & Noveck, 2004). In the data, this would be verified if Yes-responses are associated with higher RTs than No-responses.
ii. There is a general effect of the task, on which endorsing the proposed implication is faster than rejecting it, e.g., because accepting a contextually salient conclusion is less demanding. In the data, this would be verified if Yes-response are associated with lower RTs than No-responses.
iii. The strength and direction of the RT contrasts between response types depend on participants' response preferences. In the data, this would be verified if the differences in RTs between Yes-responses and No-responses positively or negatively correlate with the rates of SI responses.

We used these hypotheses as reference points to guide our analysis of the data and refine our expectations stepwise. In effect, the plausibility of each hypothesis was initially evaluated through data summaries so as to first identify the most promising one(s) and then decide on the set of statistical hypotheses to be tested.

5.2.7.1 Data Treatment

Prior to analysing response latency, the distribution of RTs was inspected to determine whether further data treatment was needed. The distribution was positively skewed (skewness= 22), with a small amount of very low and very high RTs. To exclude these extreme values, we opted for the exclusion method based on the outer 10% quantiles of the distribution. That is, we excluded RTs smaller than the 0.05 quantile and larger than the 0.95 quantile, excluding in effect 10% of the trials from the RT analysis. Grubb's tests were performed on the resulting data set: neither the highest value in the set (15s), nor the lowest one (2.5s) was found to be an outlier. RTs were log-transformed to further reduce positive skewness. The log-transformed values were approximately normally distributed (skewness= 0.15).

5.2.7.2 RTs and Scalar Diversity

Figure 5.6 shows the mean logarithmised RTs (Log RTs) for all scales by probe conditions (top) and for all probe conditions by scale (bottom). These graphs allow us to illustrate two noticeable features of the RT data set. First, at the level of the whole study, Yes-responses were overall faster than No-responses: the mean Log RT was 8.67 for all Yes-responses (95% CI[8.66,8.69]) contra 8.73 for all No-responses (95% CI[8.71,8.73]), corresponding to a difference of about 350 ms in the original unit of measurement. Second, there were substantial variations in the expression of this overall tendency both across probe conditions and across scales. Starting with the by-probe summary, Yes-responses were overall faster than No-responses in the NOT-ALT and ANTONYM conditions, but not in the ANTONYM* conditions, where no reliable difference in the distribution of RTs was found between the two response types. Next, the by-scale summary shows further variations in the strength and direction of the Yes-No contrasts, with a spectrum

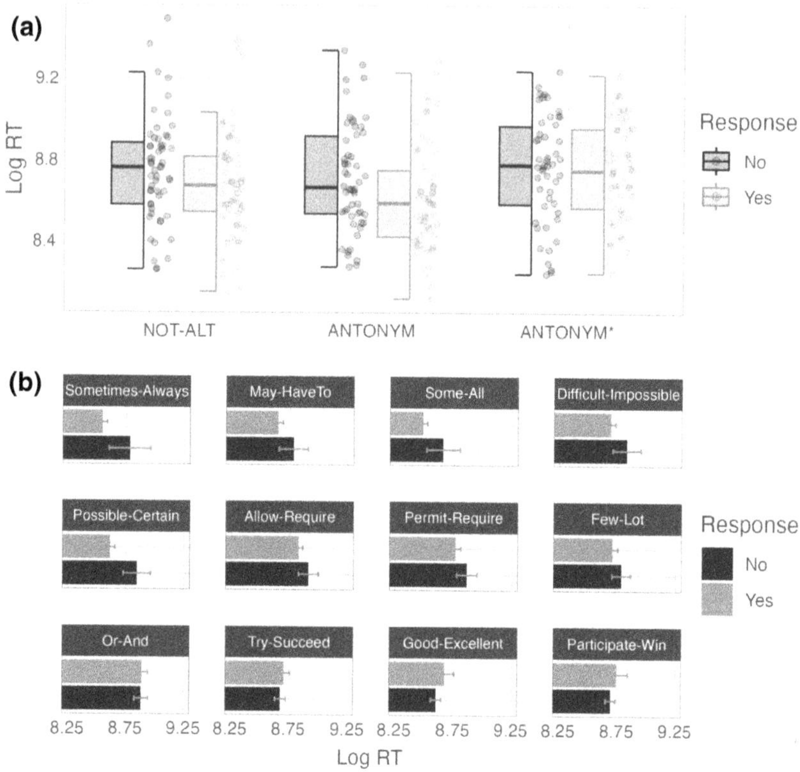

Fig. 5.6 (A) Distribution of the by-participant mean Log RTs for all scales by probe conditions. (B) Mean Log RTs for all probe conditions by scale (error bars represent the 95% CIs of the mean values)

of RT differences going from −1600 ms to +600 ms (from −0.23 to 0.07 on the log scale). Concretely, while the results for scales like ⟨sometimes, always⟩ aligned with the overall tendency (RTs Yes < RTs No), some scales like ⟨or, and⟩ showed no such contrasts while others, like ⟨good, excellent⟩, showed a trend in the opposite direction (RTs Yes > RTs No).

These initial observations suggest that, in our study, the magnitude and direction of the RT differences between response types varied as a function of the scalar expression involved, in a way reminiscent of the variability observed for SI rates. In the light of the three hypotheses we envisioned, these observations are inconsistent with the first one and only partly aligned with the predictions of the second, making the third hypothesis the most promising candidate. Thus, in our statistical analyses, we tested the prediction that the RT difference between response types for a given scalar expression is a covariate of speakers' response preference for that expression. To test this prediction, the two variables of interest were operationalised as follows. For the RT variable, we calculated the difference between the mean Log RT for Yes-responses and No-responses for each scale (henceforth, ΔLogRT). For the response variable, we calculated the mean acceptance rate for each scale in the RT data set, i.e., the data set post-RT treatment (see 5.2.7.1). Acceptance rates were squared transformed to reduce negative skewness and facilitate data visualisation. The scatter-plots in Fig. 5.7 depict the linear relationships between these two variables across all probe conditions (top) and for each probe condition separately (bottom).

Kendall's correlation tests were performed to determine the strength of association and direction of the relationship between acceptance rates and ΔLogRT among the scales tested in our study ($N = 12$). There was a strong, negative correlation between both measures aggregated across all probe conditions ($\tau_b = -0.79$, $p < 0.001$) and in each probe condition considered separately (all τ_bs< -0.47, all ps< 0.05). These results tell us that (i) the stronger the preference for one response type over the other, the greater the magnitude of the RT difference between them, and (ii) the stronger the preference for one response type, the shorter the RTs associated with that response type compared to the other one. These findings support the view that the variability observed between scales in participants' responses and response times is closely related, consistent with the third hypothesis.

5.3 General Discussion

Two plausible explanations, which are not mutually exclusive, are available as to why standard inference tasks tend to yield more with-SI responses than other paradigms, like verification tasks. On one explanation, the kind of probe used in inference tasks raises the contextual

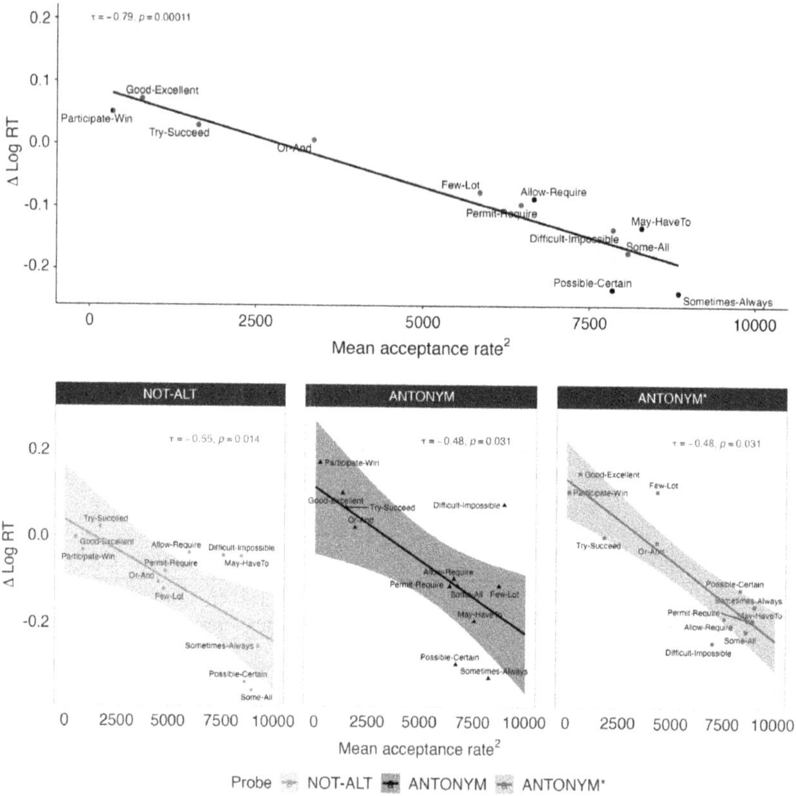

Fig. 5.7 Linear relationships between acceptance rates and ΔLogRT (A) across all probe conditions and (B) for each probe condition separately. Each point represents one of the 12 scales tested in our study, the *x*-value represents the squared-transformed mean acceptance rate, and the *y*-value represents the difference between the mean Log RTs for 'Yes' and 'No' responses. The line is the line of best fit for the relationship between scales along both variables of interest, with 95% CIs

salience of the alternative expression by virtue of mentioning it, and this alone can boost the rate of implicature response. This Salience Hypothesis has been developed to explain priming of SIs by alternative sentences (Rees & Bott, 2018) and is in line with theoretical proposals that count discourse salience as an important factor in choosing alternatives (Fox & Katzir, 2011). A second explanation would hold that the set-up of the inference task promotes the contextual relevance of the proposition expressed by the alternative. As discussed, both potential factors similarly account for the inflated rates of SIs observed in previous inference tasks, the design of which does not distinguish simple salience from relevance.

Our primary goal in this paper was to determine the relative strength of these two factors by testing whether mention of the alternative plays an independent role in promoting SI responses in the inference task. For these purposes, we designed an experiment manipulating the wording of the probe for 12 scalar expressions. We compared the classical NOT-ALT probe to novel ANTONYM probes in which the linguistic form of the alternative was absent. We hypothesised that if making the alternative contextually salient has a boosting effect on with-SI responses above that of raising its relevance, participants should give more with-SI responses in the NOT-ALT than in the ANTONYM conditions. In addition, we were interested in finding out what response latencies can teach us about decision making in inference tasks and, in particular, whether SI responses in such tasks show the classical delay effects commonly found in verification tasks for positive scalar terms.

The analysis of the response data yielded two main findings. First, in line with the findings from van Tiel et al. (2016), the scalar expressions in our sample yielded widely different rates of SI responses, ranging from 10% to 96%, independently of the probe condition in which they were tested. Second, and more importantly for us, the rates of SI responses were effectively the same across all probe conditions, except for two scales for which they were reliably lower in the NOT-ALT than with the ANTONYM conditions. In this regard, our analysis of the response data provides evidence against the hypothesis that the SI rates would be higher in the NOT-ALT than in the ANTONYM conditions. We take these findings to show that referencing the alternative in the probe had no remarkable boosting effect on SI rates over and above raising its relevance without mentioning it. Thus, we conclude that it is not the specific wording of the probe, but its very presence which, by raising the relevance of the targeted implication, promotes SI responses. These findings are consistent with those reported in Marty et al. (2024), who find that, in fact, mere salience of alternative expression is not an independent factor in priming SI responses in a covered card task, over and above contextual relevance.

Turning now to the RT data, our results unveil another aspect of scalar diversity in showing that the contrasts between SI and non-SI responses substantially varied from one scalar expression to another, with mean RT differences going from −1600 ms to +600 ms. Our exploration of these data suggests that these variations in response latency are not random, but closely relate to participants' response preferences. Specifically, our analysis shows that the more participants favoured one response type for a given expression, the longer the RTs associated with the least favoured response for that expression and the greater the mean RT difference between the two response types. This relationship between response frequency and response latency suggests that RTs in inference tasks reflect the degree of confidence that people have in their responses, and points to another critical difference with verification tasks, where SI responses associated with scalar terms like *some*, *or*, *might*, *possible*, have been found to be delayed relative to non-SI responses regardless of participants' response preferences (Marty et al., 2020; van Tiel et al., 2019).

Two limitations to the present study should be noted. The first pertains to the sample of expressions we tested. Compared to the sample in van Tiel et al.'s and subsequent studies documenting scalar diversity, our sample was relatively small ($N = 12$ contra $N = 43$ in van Tiel et al.) and included a higher proportion of bounded scales (92% contra 50% in van Tiel et al.), which have been found to yield higher rates of SI responses than non-bounded ones. One consequence is that, for about half of the expressions we tested, the rates of SI responses were at or near ceiling across all three probe conditions, resulting in less variability between scales than observed in previous studies. We note, however, that this aspect of our data, if anything, should have played in favour of the hypothesis that our data disproved: since most of the scales we tested yielded high to very high acceptance rates with the NOT-ALT probe, there was in principle more room for a decrease in acceptance to be observed with the ANTONYM probes for such scales than for unbounded adjectival scales like ⟨ugly, hideous⟩ or ⟨tired, exhausted⟩, for which the rates of SI responses have been found to be already very low with the NOT-ALT probe. Thus, the fact that the results for these scales were near ceiling across the board also speaks against the idea that mention of alternative played any particular role in this outcome.

The second limitation relates to our analysis and interpretation of the RT data. As discussed previously, we analysed RTs by considering a dedicated set of possible outcomes which we had identified as most likely. As such, our analysis was exploratory in nature and should be thus regarded as a preliminary step towards a more thorough investigation of RT data in inference tasks. We note, for instance, that our results do not formally rule out the possibility of a general task effect along the lines we outlined. That is, it is possible that the inference task makes it so that endorsing the proposed implication is somewhat less time-consuming than rejecting it. For now, we shall simply observe that aspects of our data suggestive of such an effect can also be explained in reference to participants' response preferences. Thus for instance, the observation that Yes-responses were overall faster than No-responses can be explained by the higher frequency of Yes-responses in our study, an outcome possibly driven by our selection of scales, as discussed above. Similarly, the fact that greater differences in ΔLogRT were observed for scalar terms associated with high rates of Yes-responses (e.g., *sometimes, may, some*) than for those associated with low rates (e.g., *try, good, participate*) can be accounted for by the fact that the former yielded more extreme rates than the latter. Thus, it remains an open question whether the inference task directly reduces RTs associated with Yes-responses or only indirectly, by facilitating SI responses at some general level.

Overall, it seems that a key difference between inference tasks and other experimental tasks used to study SIs lies in the fact that, in probing for whether an SI is available to participants, one makes that same SI more available by suggesting its relevance. Let us now consider how our results may shed light on some open issues that have emerged from research involving the inference task. The discussion that follows here is somewhat speculative and will require further research to substantiate.

Firstly, as mentioned in the introduction, Sun and Breheny (2022) developed a version of the inference task in which the probe was intended to suggest that the alternative is not relevant. They did this by asking questions of the form 'Would you conclude that, it could be that

[Name] thinks [Alternative]?', considering scalar expressions like *some* and *possible*. Sun & Breheny found that with-SI response rates were lower for this COULD-ALT probe than for the standard NOT-ALT probe but still higher than expected. They attribute this outcome to the fact that the COULD-ALT probe mentions the alternative. We believe that this explanation should be clarified since we now understand that simple mention of the alternative expression has no discernible effect on inference task responses, over and above suggesting its relevance. We may conjecture here that one reason why the COULD-ALT probe was only partially successful in suppressing SI responses has to do with the fact that, in attempting to suggest the irrelevance of the alternative, the experimental design succeeds in drawing participants' attention to the underlying order of entailments on which the scalar expressions and their alternatives sit. This may have had an unintended effect on many participants who otherwise might not automatically associate expressions like *some* or *possible* with contexts in which QuDs live on such orders. It is sometimes observed that common scalar expressions such as *some* and *possible*, when employed in tasks other than the inference task, give rise to something of a bimodal distribution in responses (Bott & Noveck, 2004; Guasti et al., 2005; Hunt et al., 2013; Marty et al., 2024; Noveck & Posada, 2003). Marty et al. (2024) provide evidence that such a contrasting set of responses reflects an underlying distribution of prior association between the scalar term and the relevant QuD, and they account for SI priming effects in terms of the primes acting on those priors. Similarly, we might say that even an inference task probe designed to suggest the *irrelevance* of the alternative may have the opposite effect on those participants whose priors on the strong QuD are low.

A second, related, open question arises from recent research in which the inference task involves the presentation of the utterance in a context. Ronai and Xiang (2021) adapt the standard NOT-ALT probe by adding information about which type of question the utterance is a response to. In a STRONG context condition, the speaker is asked if the alternative is true. For example, if the target utterance is *The student is intelligent*, the prompt question is, *Is the student brilliant?*. The probe is otherwise the same and the participant is asked to judge if, according to the speaker, the student is not brilliant. In a WEAK context condition, the question is simply *Is the student intelligent?*. Rather as with Sun and Breheny (2022), although Ronai and Xiang (2021) found a clear effect of condition in the expected direction, rates of SI response were unexpectedly high in the WEAK condition in many cases, including for commonly discussed scalar expressions such as quantifiers like, *some*, and modal expressions. Here we might explain the unexpected effect of WEAK questions by considering the dispositions of that part of the participant population which associates a high prior on strong contexts with these commonly discussed scalar expressions. Such participants may see that a hearer interested in whether *some* would typically be interested in whether *all* and that a cooperative answer to even the WEAK question would be to provide further information about *all*. The result is that, participants may perceive even WEAK questions as implicitly raising further STRONG questions, which a cooperative speaker would be expected to address.

Finally, we turn to the question of why many scalar expressions, especially adjectival scales, result in very low SI rates, if inference task probes so strongly promote the right kind of context to induce a SI response. We believe that the answer to this question lies in various factors that have been discussed previously. Among these factors, Gotzner et al. (2018) highlight that many adjective scales are susceptible to negative strengthening, which can result in lower SI rates in the inference task. Likewise, Sun and Breheny (2024) note that many adjectives are particularly susceptible to a type of pragmatic strengthening which raises the standard of application and that this type of strengthening results in the opposite of SI-strengthening. We also note that the particularly high and particularly low rates of SI recorded in van Tiel et al. (2016) and elsewhere are not reported when participants are asked to register responses on a graded scale, such as a Likert scale. Sun and Breheny (2024) demonstrate that variation in SI rates in the inference task is much greater when participants make a binary judgement, compared to graded responses.

5.4 Conclusion

At least since Geurts and Pouscoulous (2009), there has been speculation as to what is responsible for the inflated SI rates observed in inference tasks. Our study examined potential factors related to the form of inference task probes in promoting SI responses. Our finding is that mere salience of alternative expression does not contribute to increased rates, over and above the suggestion by the inference task probe that the alternative is relevant. Our results line up with findings in Marty et al. (2024) which, likewise, suggest that mere salience of linguistic alternatives is not a factor in computations that determine the availability of an SI.

References

Baker, R., Doran, R., McNabb, Y., Larson, M., & Ward, G. (2009). On the non-unified nature of scalar implicature: An empirical investigation. *International Review of Pragmatics, 1*(2), 211–248.

Bates, D., Mächler, M., Bolker, B., & Walker, S. (2015). Fitting linear mixed-effects models using lme4. *Journal of Statistical Software, 67*(1), 1–48. https://doi.org/10.18637/jss.v067.i01

Bergen, L., & Grodner, D. J. (2012). Speaker knowledge influences the comprehension of pragmatic inferences. *Journal of Experimental Psychology: Learning, Memory, and Cognition, 38*(5), 1450.

Bergen, L., Levy, R., & Goodman, N. (2016). Pragmatic reasoning through semantic inference. *Semantics & Pragmatics, 9*, 20.

Bott, L., Bailey, T. M., & Grodner, D. (2012). Distinguishing speed from accuracy in scalar implicatures. *Journal of Memory and Language, 66*(1), 123–142.

Bott, L., & Noveck, I. A. (2004). Some utterances are underinformative: The onset and time course of scalar inferences. *Journal of memory and language, 51*(3), 437–457.

Breheny, R., Katsos, N., & Williams, J. (2006). Are generalised scalar implicatures generated by default? An on-line investigation into the role of context in generating pragmatic inferences. *Cognition, 100*(3), 434–463.

Breheny, R., Klinedinst, N., Romoli, J., & Sudo, Y. (2018). The symmetry problem: Current theories and prospects. *Natural Language Semantics, 26*, 85–110.

Buccola, B., Križ, M., & Chemla, E. (2022). Conceptual alternatives: Competition in language and beyond. *Linguistics and Philosophy, 45*(2), 265–291.

Bürkner, P.-C. (2017). `brms`: An R package for Bayesian multilevel models using Stan. *Journal of Statistical Software, 80*(1), 1–28. https://doi.org/10.18637/jss.v080.i01

Bürkner, P.-C. (2018). Advanced Bayesian multilevel modeling with the R package `brms`. *The R Journal, 10*(1), 395–411. https://doi.org/10.32614/RJ-2018-017

Bürkner, P.-C. (2021). Bayesian item response modeling in R with `brms` and Stan. *Journal of Statistical Software, 100*(5), 1–54. https://doi.org/10.18637/jss.v100.i05

Carnap, R. (1962). *Logical foundations of probability*. University of Chicago Press.

Chierchia, G., Fox, D., & Spector, B. (2012). Scalar implicature as a grammatical phenomenon. In P. Portner, C. Maienborn, & K. von Heusinger (Eds.), *Semantics: An international handbook of natural language meaning* (Vol. 31, pp. 2297–2331). Mouton de Gruyter.

Degen, J. (2015). Investigating the distribution of some (but not all) implicatures using corpora and web-based methods. *Semantics and Pragmatics, 8*(11), 1–55.

Fox, D., & Katzir, R. (2011). On the characterization of alternatives. *Natural Language Semantics, 19*, 87–107.

Fox, J., & Weisberg, S. (2019). *An R companion to applied regression* (3rd ed.). Sage. https://socialsciences.mcmaster.ca/jfox/Books/Companion/

Frank, M. C., & Goodman, N. D. (2012). Predicting pragmatic reasoning in language games. *Science, 336*(6084), 998.

Gazdar, G. (1979). *Pragmatics: Implicature, presupposition, and logical form.* Academic Press.

Geurts, B. (2010). *Quantity implicatures*. Cambridge University Press.

Geurts, B., & Pouscoulous, N. (2009). Embedded implicatures?!? *Semantics and Pragmatics, 2*(4), 1–34.

Gotzner, N., Solt, S., & Benz, A. (2018). Scalar diversity, negative strengthening, and adjectival semantics. *Frontiers in Psychology, 9*, 1659.

Grice, H. P. (1975). Logic and conversation. In *Speech acts* (pp. 41–58). Brill.

Guasti, M. T., Chierchia, G., Crain, S., Foppolo, F., Gualmini, A., & Meroni, L. (2005). Why children and adults sometimes (but not always) compute implicatures. *Language and Cognitive Processes, 20*(5), 667–696.

Harrell, F. (2023). *Package 'Hmisc'*. https://CRAN.R-project.org/package=Hmisc. R package version 5.1-0.

Hope, R. (2022). *Package 'Rmisc'*. https://CRAN.R-project.org/package=Rmisc. R package version 1.5.1.

Horn, L. R. (1972). *On the semantic properties of logical operators in English* (Los Angeles Dissertation). University of California.

Huang, Y. T., & Snedeker, J. (2018). Some inferences still take time: Prosody, predictability, and the speed of scalar implicatures. *Cognitive Psychology, 102*, 105–126.

Hunt, L., Politzer-Ahles, S., Gibson, L., Minai, U., & Fiorentino, R. (2013). Pragmatic inferences modulate n400 during sentence comprehension: Evidence from picture-sentence verification. *Neuroscience Letters, 534*, 246–251.

Katzir, R. (2007). Structurally-defined alternatives. *Linguistics and Philosophy, 30*, 669–690.

Komsta, L. (2022). *Outliers: Tests for outliers*. https://CRAN.R-project.org/package=outliers. R package version 0.15.

Kroch, A. (1972). Lexical and inferred meanings for some time adverbs. *Quarterly Progress Reports of the Research Laboratory of Electronics, 104*, 260–267.

Lenth, R. (2023). *'emmeans': Estimated Marginal Means, aka Least-Squares Means*. https://CRAN.R-project.org/package=emmeans. R package version 1.8.7.

Marty, P., Romoli, J., Sudo, Y., & Breheny, R. (2024). Implicature priming, salience, and context adaptation. *Cognition, 244*, 105667. 10.1016/j.cognition.2023.105667. https://www.sciencedirect.com/science/article/pii/S0010027723003013

Marty, P., Romoli, J., Sudo, Y., van Tiel, B., & Breheny, R. (2020). *Processing implicatures: A comparison between direct and indirect SIs*. Oral presentation at Experiments in Linguistic Meaning (ELM), Philadelphia, PA.

McElreath, R. (2020). *Statistical rethinking: A Bayesian course with examples in R and STAN* (2nd ed.). Chapman and Hall/CRC. https://doi.org/10.1201/9780429029608

Nicenboim, B., Schad, D., & Vasishth, S. (2023). An introduction to Bayesian data analysis for cognitive science. Ms., University of Potsdam. https://vasishth.github.io/bayescogsci/book/

Noveck, I. A. (2001). When children are more logical than adults: Experimental investigations of scalar implicature. *Cognition, 78*(2), 165–188.

Noveck, I. A., & Posada, A. (2003). Characterizing the time course of an implicature: An evoked potentials study. *Brain and Language, 85*(2), 203–210.

Palan, S., & Schitter, C. (2018). Prolific.ac—A subject pool for online experiments. *Journal of Behavioral and Experimental Finance, 17*, 22–27.

Pankratz, E., & Van Tiel, B. (2021). The role of relevance for scalar diversity: A usage-based approach. *Language and Cognition, 13*(4), 562–594.

Papafragou, A., & Musolino, J. (2003). Scalar implicatures: Experiments at the semantics-pragmatics interface. *Cognition, 86*(3), 253–282.

Patil, I. (2021). Visualizations with statistical details: The 'ggstatsplot' approach. *Journal of Open Source Software, 6*(61), 3167. https://doi.org/10.21105/joss.03167. https://doi.org/10.21105/joss.03167

R Core Team. (2023). *R: A language and environment for statistical computing*. R Foundation for Statistical Computing Vienna, Austria. https://www.R-project.org/

Rees, A., & Bott, L. (2018). The role of alternative salience in the derivation of scalar implicatures. *Cognition, 176*, 1–14.

Roberts, C. (2012). Information structure: Towards an integrated formal theory of pragmatics. *Semantics and Pragmatics, 5*(6), 1–69.

Ronai, E., & Xiang, M. (2021). Exploring the connection between question under discussion and scalar diversity. *Proceedings of the Linguistic Society of America, 6*(1), 649–662.

Skordos, D., & Papafragou, A. (2016). Children's derivation of scalar implicatures: Alternatives and relevance. *Cognition, 153*, 6–18.

Sperber, D., & Wilson, D. (1986). *Relevance: Communication and cognition.* Blackwell.

Sun, C., & Breheny, R. (2022). The role of alternatives in the interpretation of scalars and numbers: Insights insights from the inference task. *Semantics and Pragmatics*, 15.

Sun, C., & Breheny, R. (2024). A corpus-based examination of scalar diversity. *Journal of Experimental Psychology: Learning, Memory, and Cognition.*

Sun, C., Tian, Y., & Breheny, R. (2018). A link between local enrichment and scalar diversity. *Frontiers in Psychology, 9*, 2092.

Van Tiel, B., & Pankratz, E. (2021). Adjectival polarity and the processing of scalar inferences. *Glossa: A Journal of General Linguistics, 6*(1).

van Tiel, B., Pankratz, E., & Sun, C. (2019). Scales and scalarity: Processing scalar inferences. *Journal of Memory and Language, 105*, 93–107.

Van Tiel, B., & Schaeken, W. (2017). Processing conversational implicatures: Alternatives and counterfactual reasoning. *Cognitive Science, 41*, 1119–1154.
van Tiel, B., van Miltenburg, E., Zevakhina, N., & Geurts, B. (2016). Scalar diversity. *Journal of Semantics, 33*(1), 137–175.
Wickham, H. (2016). *ggplot2: Elegant graphics for data analysis*. Springer-Verlag New York. https://ggplot2.tidyverse.org

6

How to Operate Over Alternatives: The Place of the L*+H Pitch Accent Among Possible Focus Meanings

Alexander Göbel

6.1 Introduction

One phenomenon for which the notion of alternatives has played an important—and often defining—role is that of Focus. On Rooth's (1985, 1992) influential account, the meaning of Focus corresponds to a semantic operator that evokes a set of alternatives and puts restrictions on the content of this set. For instance in the case of question-answer dialogues like (1a), the evoked set only contains propositions that vary with respect to the position of Focus (1b).

This paper is an extension of Göbel and Wagner (2023, Proceedings of Sinn und Bedeutung 27). I am first and foremost indebted to Michael Wagner, without whom this research would have never gotten off the ground. Next, I want to thank Emma Nguyen, Katy Carlson, and Byron Ahn for contributing the audio recordings for the experimental stimuli. I am also grateful to audiences at XPrag 2022 at the IUSS Pavia, Rutgers, Northwestern, and Edinburgh for feedback. Lastly, infinite thanks to Jesse Harris for suggestions on an initial draft of this manuscript and the opportunity to be a part of this edited volume. All errors, as always, are on me.

A. Göbel (✉)
University of Manchester, Manchester, UK
e-mail: alandergoebel@gmail.com

N. Gotzner et al. (eds.), *Alternatives in Grammar and Cognition*, Palgrave Studies in Pragmatics, Language and Cognition, https://doi.org/10.1007/978-3-031-76676-3_6

(1) a. A: Who makes a tremendous risotto?
B: [Sydney]$_F$ makes a tremendous risotto.
b. [[[Sydney]$_F$ makes a tremendous risotto.]]^f) =
{Sydney makes a tremendous risotto,
Carmy makes a tremendous risotto,
Tina makes a tremendous risotto}

A major advantage of this account is that it easily allows the extension to particles like *only* and *even* that conventionally associate with Focus. Such Focus-particles operate over the alternative set and modify it in specific ways. For example, the (simplified) at-issue contribution of *only* in B's response in (2a) is to exclude all other alternatives, illustrated in (2b).[1]

(2) a. A: Are there many people who make a tremendous risotto?
B: No, **only** [Sydney]$_F$ makes a tremendous risotto.
b. [[Only]] ([[[Sydney]$_F$ makes a tremendous risotto.]]^f) =
{Sydney makes a tremendous risotto,
~~Carmy makes a tremendous risotto~~,
~~Tina makes a tremendous risotto~~}

From the perspective of linguistic theory, an important question arising from this account is what operations of the alternative set are possible and how they are expressed in the grammar. The present paper examines (Mainstream American) English intonation—and more specifically differences in the type of pitch accent—with respect to this question. Pitch accents are the default way to express Focus in intonational languages like English, as implicitly communicated through the use of small capitals in (1a). However, theories of intonational phonology argue for the existence of different categories of pitch accents in English. For instance, the widely adopted ToBI system (Beckman et al., 2005) distinguishes between at least four different types for categorizing pitch accents in our case: H*, L*, L*+H, and L+H*.[2] Based on this array of

[1] Note that the contribution of bare Focus (i.e., Focus without an overt Focus-particle) in cases like (1a) is also frequently associated with such an exhaustive interpretation, see, e.g., Zondervan (2010) and Gotzner (2019).

[2] Note that ToBI is a framework for describing intonation based on certain theoretical assumptions but may differ in the specific phonological inventory depending on the language.

options, we may ask whether all pitch accents correspond to marking Focus and evoking alternatives. A glance at prior research on intonational meaning provides a clear negative answer to this question. The most notable instances to consider here concern research on contrastive topics (e.g., Büring, 1997; Lee, 1999) as well as psycholinguistic work on so-called contrastive accents (e.g., Ito & Speer, 2008; Watson et al., 2008). Pitch accents thus constitute a highly relevant domain of research when examining the role of alternatives in language.

The present work aims to extend this research by investigating the meaning contribution of the L*+H pitch accent, which has received less attention thus far. The two starting points for the investigation are Pierrehumbert and Hirschberg (1990)'s proposal that L*+H evokes a scale and the intuition that L*+H affects the interpretation of *at least*. In three auditory rating experiments, it is shown that the pitch accent contributes a meaning similar to—and still distinct from— concessive *at least*. These findings thus make an empirical contribution in broadening our understanding of the range of meanings expressed by pitch accents as well as provide a connection to psycholinguistic work in this area, which will be discussed at the end of the paper.

6.2 Background

This section reviews relevant prior research on meaning differences of pitch accents in English 6.2.1 and then sets up the background directly pertaining to the first experiment 6.2.2.

6.2.1 Prior Research on Pitch Accent Differences

As noted above, the question about how pitch accents in English may have different semantic and pragmatic effects is not novel, going back at least to the distinction between A-accents and B-accents by Bolinger (1965) and Jackendoff (1972) and their correspondence with Contrastive Topics (CTs, Büring, 1997). Prosodically, CTs have been argued to be marked by a fall-rise accent—L+H* in ToBI terms—rather than the simple falling accent used for Focus. Although formal details vary across accounts (e.g., Büring, 2003; Constant, 2014; Wagner, 2012), one shared analysis component concerns how the interaction of CT and Focus results in a hierarchically structured discourse: CTs are taken to indicate strategies of approaching an issue by dividing the discourse into super- and subquestions, as made explicit in (3).[3] As a result, dialogues lacking the need or possibility for such a strategy are restricted to Focus-accents, see (4).

(3) A: What about Fred? What did he eat?
B: $[\text{Fred}]_{CT}$ ate $[\text{the beans}]_{F}$. [audio]

(4) A: Did Knut break up with Allessa? (Buring, 2003: 32)
a. B: No, Allessa_{F} broke up with Knut_{F}. [audio]
b. B: #No, Allessa_{CT} broke up with Knut_{F}. [audio]

However, recent research by Martens (2022) raises doubt about the validity of some of the prior characterizations of CTs as a concept distinct from Focus. For instance, production data show qualitatively indistinguishable results for classic CT cases like (3) compared to multiple Focus questions (e.g., *Who ate what?*). While other sources of evidence such as the contrast in (4) may require further investigation, the experiments presented in Section 6.3 crucially make a clearer case for pitch accent differences correlating with a difference in meaning.

A different source of data that support the necessity to distinguish different pitch accents comes from psycholinguistic research on the activation of alternatives by so-called contrastive accents (see also Sedivy

[3] Here, audio recordings of relevant sentences are provided and semantic labels indicated, rather than prosodic labels. The issue with prosodic labels such as ToBI is that there may still be some underspecification of relevant properties and more crucially that they require additional background knowledge, whereas we hope that audio recordings can make relevant intuitions more accessible to naive readers. However, the frequent prior practice of only providing prosodic labels without audio recordings means that recordings are our rendition of what we think how examples from prior papers were intended, which may be inaccurate. We hope that providing audio recordings where relevant becomes a more common practice to avoid such issues of interpretation in the future. All audio recordings are also accessible at the OSF repository associated with this publication: https://osf.io/3dtpx.

et al., 1999 for the influence of contrastive accents on implicature calculation). For example, Watson et al. (2008) provide evidence from a visual world experiment that a contrastive L+H* accent facilitates the recognition of relevant alternatives in online processing relative to a non-contrastive H* accent. They conceptualize a contrastive accent as one involved in corrective exchanges like (5a), whereas a non-contrastive accent occurs in replies to questions (5b).[4] A sample item with used audio recordings to illustrate how contrast was employed is given in (6).[5]

(5) a. A: Did Carmen cook risotto? B: No, he cooked spaghetti. [audio]
b. A: What did Carmen cook? B: He cooked spaghetti. [audio]

(6) Click on the camel and the dog.
Move the dog to the right of the square.
Now, move the CAMEL/CANDLE to the left of the diamond.
[contrastive], [non-contrastive]

Additional evidence for the influence of contrastive accents on aspects of language comprehension comes from a cross-modal priming study from Husband and Ferreira (2016) and recognition studies by Fraundorf et al. (2010). Similar effects have also been found for Dutch and German by Braun and Tagliapietra (2010); Braun et al. (2018); Braun and Biezma (2019), in addition to effects on exhaustivity by Gotzner (2019). Although the majority of the findings of these studies primarily pertain to processing, they nonetheless point to the relevance of distinguishing pitch accents and their semantic and pragmatic contributions, and hence constitute relevant evidence against the idea that all pitch accents equally indicate Focus.

---

[4] Note that both instances would count as Focus in Alternative Semantics. The authors discuss that this difference hence would not have to be about a binary distinction between evoking alternatives or not but potentially in the restrictions on the contrast set (see also Repp, 2016).

[5] Thanks to Duane Watson for sharing the audio files.

6.2.2 The L*+H Pitch Accent

As the review above shows, previous research has mostly focused on effects of the L+H* accent, at least in terms of prosodic labels. The present study will instead investigate the L*+H accent, which differs from the H* and L+H* in the accented syllable being at a low pitch level rather than a high one and then rising in pitch afterward, often such that the pitch peak falls on the following syllable. An illustration of the difference between H* and L*+H from Ladd (2008) is given in (7), with the respective annotated spectrogram and pitch tracks in Figures 6.1 and 6.2.

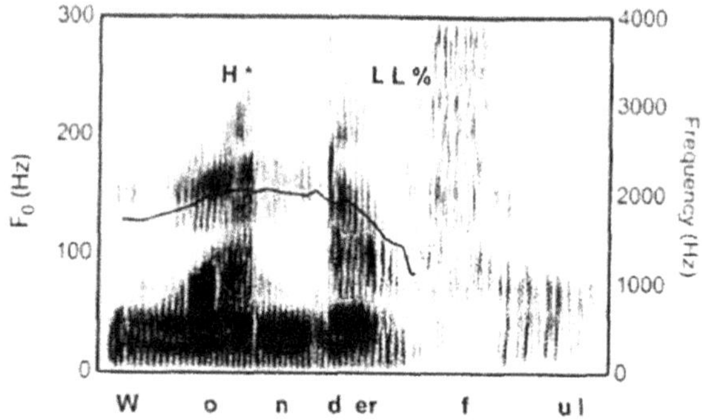

Fig. 6.1 Spectrogram and pitch track for H* in (7) from Ladd (2008: Figure 3.4a)

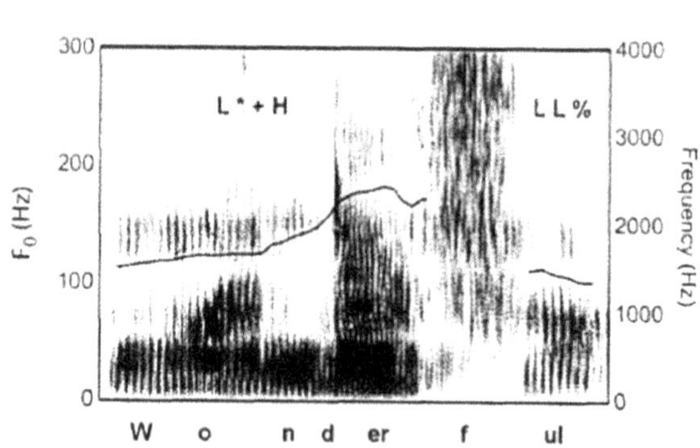

Fig. 6.2 Spectrogram and pitch track for L*+H in (7) from Ladd (2008: Figure 3.4b)

(7) Wonderful. [H*], [L*+H] (Ladd, 2008: 95)

Although the L*+H accent has been less studied in a minimal contrast to H* or L+H*, it is featured in the so-called rise-fall-rise contour (RFR, Ward & Hirschberg 1985), and its contribution hence has been studied indirectly as part of this contour. Prior research has characterized the RFR as conveying uncertainty (Ward and Hirschberg 1985) or incompleteness (Constant, 2012; Wagner, 2012). In contrast, recent work by Göbel and Wagner (2023b) has highlighted limitations of these accounts for dialogues like (8) where the RFR is used to provide a counterpoint to a previous (evaluative) statement, but is only felicitous when the counterpoint is positive in reply to a negative statement (8a) and not vice versa (8b). Göbel and Wagner , following Göbel (2019), hence argue that the RFR requires a higher alternative on a scale.

(8) a. A: The new iPhone is really terrible.
B: It has a lot of storage... [audio]
b. A: The new iPhone is really great.
B: #It has little storage... [audio]

By virtue of its occurrence in the RFR, Pierrehumbert and Hirschberg (1990) in their account of assigning meanings to individual subcomponents of contours propose that the L*+H evokes a scale. Building on this proposal, we adopt the more narrow hypothesis below:

(9) Evaluative Scale Hypothesis
The L*+H pitch accent in Mainstream American English evokes an evaluative scale.

The way in which this hypothesis will be tested here is in relation to an intuition about the interaction of pitch accents with the interpretation of the English Focus-particle *at least*. *At least* is in principle ambiguous between an epistemic interpretation (10a), which can be paraphrased as "this much and maybe more", and a concessive interpretation (10b), paraphrasable as "it could've been worse" (Biezma, 2013; Nakanishi & Rullmann, 2009).[6]

(10) a. Grover ate **at least** [the chicken]$_F$ (maybe even the tuna).
b. **At least** Grover ate [the chicken]$_F$ (he could've eaten nothing at all).

The intuition we aim to test in Experiment 1 is that concessive *at least* correlates with the use of the L*+H accent. Such a correlation would be in line with the hypothesis, and it crucially allows us to render the subtlety of any pitch accent difference more concrete. While the meaning difference between L*+H and other pitch accents is hard to pin down intuitively, the difference between epistemic and concessive *at least* seems quite clear. As a result, if the L*+H correlates with *at least* being used concessively, we can use the interpretation of *at least* as way to tap into the effect of the pitch accent. Experiment 1 aims to do so by employing an auditory rating task.

6.3 Experiments

6.3.1 Experiment 1: Accent Comparison with *at Least*

6.3.1.1 Materials & Design

The goal of this experiment was to assess the hypothesis that the L*+H accent evokes an evaluative scale by testing its effect on the interpretation of *at least*. To do so, we used dialogues as in (11) that varied in the assumed compatibility of a context sentence with the interpretation of *at least* in the target sentence: Context sentences were either *how many* questions taken to be more compatible with an epistemic interpretation of *at least* (11a), or assertions expressing some negative attitude toward

[6] Note that it is not obvious how concessive *at least* relates to other meanings labeled as concessive, such as connectives like *although*. However, in order to not cause confusion with respect to previous literature, I will adopt the epistemic-concessive distinction, but see Göbel and Wagner (2023a) for arguments in favor of "evaluative" *at least*.

the falsity of a higher alternative taken to be more compatible with a concessive interpretation (11b). To render *at least* principally ambiguous, the target sentence contained *at least* sentence-initially associating with the subject, to avoid the influence of syntactic cues for disambiguation as used in (10) above. As a second factor, the target sentence varied in intonation: The target word—here *some* —either carried an H* accent preceded by an accent on *at least*, or an L*+H accent with *at least* deaccented.[7] Target stimuli came from a female native speaker, who was recorded with a portable microphone in a session with the author of this paper to provide instructions, and context stimuli from a separate speaker. (This setup was the same for the remaining experiments.) Pitch tracks of the relevant parts of the target sentence for both conditions are shown in Figures 6.3 and 6.4. The remainder of the target sentence was deaccented and ended with a fall.

(11) Sample Item, Experiment 1
a. *Epistemic context*

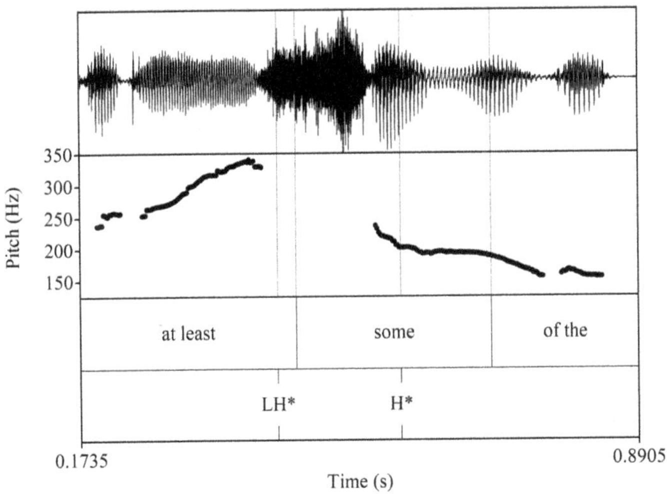

Fig. 6.3 Pitch track for (LH*+)H* condition

[7] The additional accent in the H* condition was used based on our impression from a previous natural production study. We will come back to this issue in the discussion.

A: How many of the children do you think ate their broccoli?
B: At least some of the children ate their broccoli. [(LH*+)H*], [(0/+)L*H]

b. *Concessive context*
A: I'm surprised that not all of the children ate their broccoli.
B: At least some of the children ate their broccoli. [(LH*+)H*], [(0/+)L*H]

As an additional exploratory between-item factor, dialogues varied in whether the target sentence contained *some*, as above, or a numeral between *one* and *four*. While epistemic contexts remained unchanged with numerals, the evaluative contexts were adjusted to contain *not more* instead of *not all*. The comparison between *some* and numerals was used to see how any potential effect would generalize across different types of scalar items (see Alexandropoulou, 2021 for relevant findings).

(12) Sample Item, Experiment 1: numerals

a. *Epistemic context*
A: How many of the customers do you think gave a tip?
B: At least three of the customers gave a tip.

b. *Concessive context*
A: I'm shocked that not more of the customers gave a tip.
B: At least three of the customers gave a tip.

The design was thus a 2 × 2 × 2 with within-item factors CONTEXT (epistemic vs concessive) and INTONATION (H* vs L*+H) and between-item factor SCALE-TYPE (*some* vs *numeral*). The factors were Latin-squared such that participants only saw one combination of context and intonation per item. There were 24 items in combination with 24 fillers.[8]

6.3.1.2 Procedure

The experiment started with a headphone screener test where participants listened to three sounds and had to identify the loudest one, which

[8] All stimuli as well as results files and analysis scripts for all experiments presented here can be accessed at the associated OSF repository at https://osf.io/3dtpx.

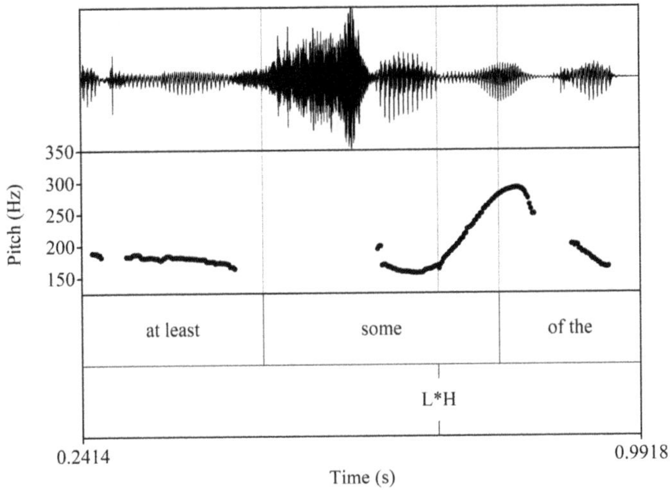

Fig. 6.4 Pitch track for (Ø+)L*H condition

was intended to be difficult if the sound came from a single source, in order to check if participants were wearing headphones. The headphone screener was followed by a consent form and a demographic survey. Participants were then told to rate items according to naturalness on a scale from 1 to 6. Dialogues were presented only auditorily without displaying any items in written form. There were three practice trials that varied in naturalness before the main part of the experiment began. At the end, participants had the option to provide feedback.

6.3.1.3 Participants

47 participants were recruited from Prolific.ac and compensated with $2.00 each. 7 participants were excluded due to failing the headphone check, leaving 40 for data analysis.

6.3.1.4 Predictions

On the hypothesis that the L*+H accent evokes an evaluative scale, its presence should bias toward a concessive interpretation of *at least*, whereas we assume the H* accent to be more neutral. As a result, we predict an interaction between CONTEXT and INTONATION such that the difference between H* and L*+H (i.e., the rating resulting from L*+H minus that for H*) should be smaller for concessive contexts than epistemic contexts. However, we remain agnostic about the exact shape this interaction may take given uncertainty about the independent baseline ratings for intonation and contexts.

6.3.1.5 Results

Data were analyzed in R using ordinal mixed-effects model with random intercepts for subjects and items and sum-coded factors. The mean ratings by condition are shown in Figure 6.5, with numerical values in Table 6.1. Looking first at *some*, we see higher ratings for H* than for L*+H in epistemic contexts, and no notable difference in concessive contexts. Additionally, concessive contexts were overall rated as more natural. For numerals, there is a similar pattern of H* above L*+H for epistemic contexts, which again decreases in concessive contexts. Moreover, epistemic contexts were overall higher rated than concessive ones, contrasting with *some*.

Model outputs reveal significant main effects of INTONATION ($z = -2.73$, $p < .01$), with higher ratings for H*, and SCALE-TYPE ($z = 2.60$, $p < .01$), with numerals better than *some*, while CONTEXT was not significant ($z = -0.67$, $p = 0.50$). Regarding interactions, there was a significant effect for CONTEXT and SCALE-TYPE ($z = -7.14$, $p < 0.001$), with concessive contexts rated higher than epistemic contexts for *some* but epistemic contexts rated higher than concessive contexts for numerals. Crucially, the interaction between INTONATION and CONTEXT was significant ($z = 1.97$, $p < 0.05$), with a larger difference between H* and L*+H in epistemic contexts than concessive ones. The interaction between INTONATION and SCALE-TYPE as well as the three-way interaction was not significant ($z = -0.22$, $p = 0.82$; $z = -0.71$, $p = 0.48$).

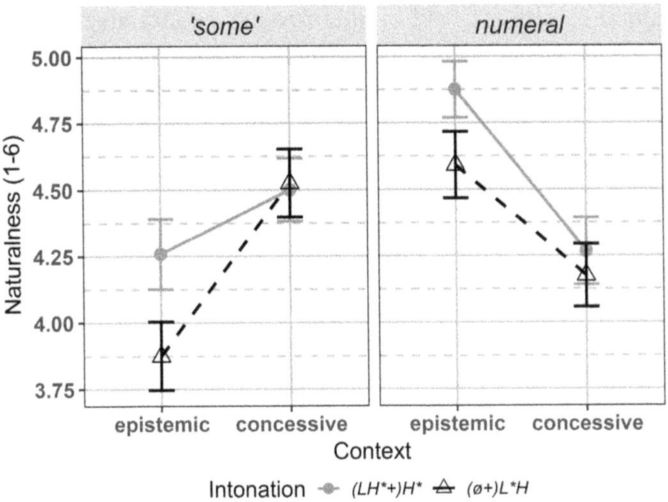

Fig. 6.5 Mean ratings by condition, Experiment 1

Table 6.1 Mean ratings (with standard error) by condition, Experiment 1

	'Some'		Numeral	
	Epistemic	Concessive	Epistemic	Concessive
H*	4.26 (0.13)	4.50 (0.12)	4.87 (0.11)	4.27 (0.13)
L*+H	3.87 (0.13)	4.52 (0.13)	4.59 (0.12)	4.17 (0.12)

6.3.1.6 Discussion

This experiment aimed to address the question whether the type of pitch accent has an influence on the interpretation of *at least*. The hypothesis was that an L*+H accent should be more compatible with a concessive interpretation of *at least* than an epistemic interpretation due to L*+H evoking an evaluative scale in line with the meaning of concessive *at least* and at odds with the meaning of epistemic *at least*. The results are in line with this prediction: the particular pattern we found was that the difference between L*+H and H* was larger in epistemic contexts, with L*+H being rated lower, than in concessive contexts, where there was no notable difference between pitch accents. This pattern could then be explained by either L*+H biasing toward a concessive interpretation, which is deemed less natural in epistemic contexts, or some additional effort associated with finding the contextually more appropriate interpretation when encountering L*+H in epistemic contexts.[9] This pattern was present for both *some* and numerals, although numerically more pronounced for *some*.

However, *some* and numerals differed in another way: while concessive contexts were rated better than epistemic ones for *some*, the reverse was true for numerals, with concessive contexts rated worse than epistemic ones. A possible explanation for this could be that the reply with *some* in epistemic contexts is deemed less informative than a reply with a numeral. In epistemic contexts, the *how many* question posed by speaker A may be taken as pragmatically presupposing the underlying existential statement, namely—with respect to (11a)—that at least one child ate their broccoli. Replying with *at least some* in this case would thus contribute little additional information. In contrast, using a numeral would at least narrow down the possible options slightly more, going beyond what would be entailed by an existential presupposition and satisfying basic informativity requirements of conversation. This difference could thus account for why *some* is rated lower in epistemic contexts than numerals and in turn why *some* and numerals differ with respect to which of the contexts is rated higher for the respective scale-type.

A potential confound of the experiment, on the other hand, is that the two intonation conditions varied not only in the pitch accent on the target word but also in the presence/absence of an accent on *at least*. The results may thus be solely driven by the prosody on *at least* or an interaction of it with the pitch accent on the target. Moreover, from a theoretical perspective, there is an open question whether the potential effect of L*+H is due to it serving as a cue for disambiguating *at least*, and hence mediated by the presence of an applicable ambiguity, or whether

[9] Notably, a more definitive interpretation of the results is not possible given the lack of an assessment of the baseline naturalness for the two intonation conditions outside the experimental design. That is, it might also be the case that L*+H is generally deemed less natural than H*, and that the interaction is driven by L*+H leading to more concessive interpretations in concessive contexts and hence higher ratings. However, a significant interaction would crucially constitute evidence for our hypothesis in either case.

the pitch accent itself makes an independent meaning contribution. The next experiment aims to address both of these issues.

6.3.2 Experiment 2: Accent Comparison Without *at Least*

6.3.2.1 Materials & Design

In order to test whether the L*+H pitch accent makes its own contribution, the experiment used the same design and materials as Experiment 1, but removed *at least* from the target sentences. The modification was done by manually cutting off the portion of the audio recordings corresponding to *at least*.[10] This change also removes the potential confound regarding the influence of the prosody on *at least*, given that there now is no *at least* anymore. A sample item is shown below for completeness:

(13) Sample Item, Experiment 2

a. *Epistemic context*
A: How many of the children do you think ate their broccoli?
B: Some of the children ate their broccoli. [H*], [L*H]

b. *Concessive context*
A: I'm surprised that not all of the children ate their broccoli.
B: Some of the children ate their broccoli. [H*], [L*H]

We used the same 24 item sets with the same 24 fillers from Experiment 1 in the same Latin-square design.

6.3.2.2 Procedure

The procedure was the same as Experiment 1.

10 Note that for the *some* items, all parts of the initial fricative identifiable in Praat were kept for consistency despite sometimes noticeable co-articulation with the preceding *at least*, which may have led to some recordings sounding slightly less natural.

6.3.2.3 Participants

37 participants were recruited from Prolific.ac and compensated with \$2.00 each. 1 participant was excluded due to failing the headphone check, leaving 36 for data analysis.

6.3.2.4 Predictions

If the L*+H accent makes a contribution that is independent of its effect on an applicable ambiguity, we should again find an interaction between CONTEXT and INTONATION, although the exact shape of the results pattern may differ given the removal of *at least*. If the L*+H accent does not have any independent effect, INTONATION should not interact with the other factors.

6.3.2.5 Results

The results, shown in Figure 6.6 and Table 6.2, were again analyzed with a sum-coded ordinal mixed-effects model with random intercept for participants and items. To again first descriptively characterize the results, for *some* we see numerically slightly higher ratings for H* compared to L*+H in epistemic contexts, and this difference being reversed and becoming larger for concessive contexts. This pattern is almost identical for numerals, except that epistemic contexts are overall much more natural than concessive ones.

In line with this characterization, the model revealed a significant effect of CONTEXT ($z = -8.05$, $p < 0.001$), with higher ratings for epistemic contexts than concessive ones, a significant effect of SCALE-TYPE ($z = 4.80$, $p < 0.001$), with numerals rated higher than *some*, as well as significant interactions of CONTEXT and INTONATION ($z = 2.56$, $p < 0.05$), and CONTEXT and SCALE-TYPE ($z = -7.78$, $p < 0.001$). All other effects were non-significant (INTONATION: $z = 0.60$, $p = 0.55$; INTONATION*SCALE-TYPE: $z = -0.47$, $p = 0.64$; CONTEXT*INTONATION*SCALE-TYPE: $z = 0.32$, $p = 0.75$). The analysis thus shows almost exactly the same significant factors as Experiment

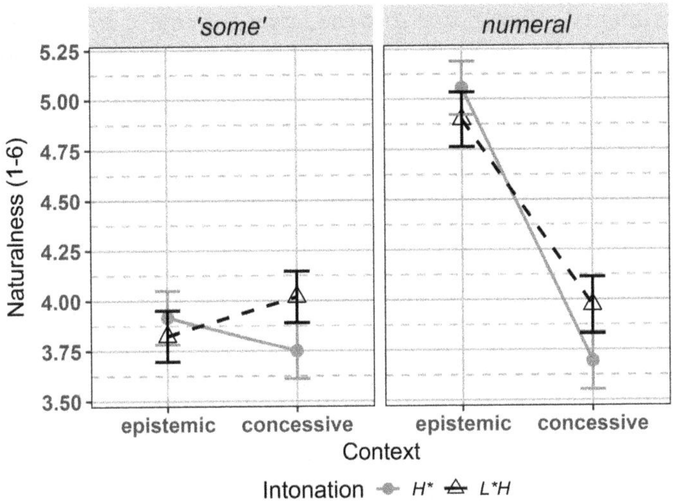

Fig. 6.6 Mean ratings by condition, Experiment 2

Table 6.2 Mean ratings (with standard error) by condition, Experiment 2

	'Some'		Numeral	
	Epistemic	Concessive	Epistemic	Concessive
H*	3.92 (0.13)	3.75 (0.14)	5.06 (0.13)	3.69 (0.14)
L*+H	3.82 (0.13)	4.02 (0.13)	4.90 (0.14)	3.97 (0.14)

1, the only difference being that Experiment 1 showed a main effect of INTONATION where Experiment 2 shows a main effect of CONTEXT.

6.3.2.6 Discussion

The data provide evidence for a genuine contribution of the L*+H pitch accent. More specifically, the L*+H's contribution seems to resemble that of concessive *at least* given how similar the pattern of results is to that of Experiment 1: independent of scale-type, L*+H received numerically higher ratings than H* in concessive contexts, and—albeit with a smaller difference—numerically lower ratings in epistemic contexts. In relation to Experiment 1, that means that the larger difference is now in concessive contexts rather than epistemic ones, but is nonetheless consistent with the hypothesis of L*+H being evaluative. The change in results patterns may be due to a small overall decrease in ratings for H* in both contexts in the absence of *at least*. For epistemic contexts, the issue of the reply being uninformative may be exacerbated without (an epistemically interpreted) *at least*, as the reply is now fully equivalent to the existential presupposition of the question. For concessive contexts, on the other hand, H* may be more likely to be taken as corrective/exhaustive—also due to it now being the most prominent accent—which seems somewhat incoherent as a reply. This characterization of H* is in line with research questioning whether the distinction between H* on the one hand and the L+H*, which is usually associated with contrast and its pragmatic effects, on the other is always categorical (Bartels & Kingston, 1999).

This issue, that the lack of informativity in epistemic contexts is worse for H* in this experiment, may also be reflected in the interaction of CONTEXT with SCALE-TYPE. In the absence of *at least*, the response with a bare numeral is now maximally informative, whereas *some* maximally uninformative, on the view that the question triggers an existential presupposition.

To sum up, the results provide evidence that L*+H does not merely serve as a cue to resolve an appropriate ambiguity, but that it has its own meaning contribution, which aligns with that of concessive *at least*. Moreover, the data resolved the potential confound of the influence of the prosody on *at least* given that target sentences here only differed in the pitch accent on the target word, since *at least* was no longer present as a point of variation.

However, the question remains how to characterize the meaning of L*+H more precisely. Superficially, it may be that L*+H is simply a way to communicate a meaning indistinguishable from concessive *at least*. Alternatively, as discussed by Göbel (2019), the accent seems to be compatible with a broader range of contexts. More specifically, Göbel argues that the contribution of L*+H is simply to evoke an evaluative ranking of alternatives, with the directionality of that ranking (i.e., from worse to better, or vice versa) being left underspecified. The following experiment aims to address this open question to further narrow down the possible contribution of L*+H.

6.3.3 Experiment 3

6.3.3.1 Materials & Design

To differentiate between the possible accounts of L*+H discussed above, this experiment makes use of the oddness of concessive *at least* in sentences that describe a negative state of affairs (Göbel & Wagner, 2023a; Kay, 1992). As shown in (14), while concessive *at least* is perfectly natural in (14a) when relating a positive albeit not perfect outcome, using *at least* in (14b) is odd because it conveys that people getting injured is somehow desirable. With respect to the goals of this experiment, we can thus examine whether the L*+H behaves similarly in the absence of *at least*.

(14) a. At least in that big train wreck several people were saved.
b. #At least in that big train wreck several people were injured.
(Kay, 1992: 22)

The experiment used a 2 × 2 × 2 × 2 Latin-square design, with a sample item shown in (15). CONTEXT was manipulated to generate the pattern in (14) but in a dialogue setting as in previous experiments. The *negative-positive* condition closely resembled the *concessive* condition of Experiments 1 and 2, only changing the attitude predicate to something more unambiguously negative (e.g., *unfortunate* instead of *shocked*). The *positive-negative* condition reversed the attitude of the statements conveyed by speakers A and B by changing the attitude predicate to something positive, e.g., *great*, and adding some negatively connotated predicate, e.g., *refuse*, or using an antonym or opposite where appropriate (e.g., *pass the test* instead of *fail the test*). As a second factor, the TARGET either contained *at least* or was *bare*, essentially combining the difference between Experiments 1 and 2. Thirdly, target sentences were varied in INTONATION as before, with the target word—here *some*—pronounced either with a falling H* pitch accent or the L*+H, including the pitch accent on *at least* from Experiment 1 when present. Lastly, as a between-item factor of SCALE-TYPE, the target word was either *some* or a numeral, with an even split as in previous experiments. However, since SCALE-TYPE did not substantially affect the results and the design is otherwise more complex, we will put it aside here (but see the OSF repository for more details).

(15) Sample Item, Experiment 3

a. *Negative-positive context*
A: It's unfortunate that not all of the children ate their broccoli.
B: (At least) Some of the children ate their broccoli. [(LH*+)H*], [(0/+)L*H]

b. *Positive-negative context*
A: It's great that not all of the children refused to eat their broccoli.
B: (At least) Some of the children refused to eat their broccoli. [(LH*+)H*], [(0/+)L*H]

The number of items was increased to 36 to accommodate the additional factor, but reusing previously used items as far as possible, including previously used recordings for the target sentences in the *negative-positive* condition. There were 36 filler items.

6.3.3.2 Procedure

The procedure was the same as in Experiments 1 and 2.

6.3.3.3 Participants

72 participants were recruited from Prolific and paid $3.00 each, with one additional participant contributing data without being listed. Data for 9 participants were excluded due to failing the headphone screener

test. An additional 12 participants were excluded to even out the participants for each list, since one of the eight lists had more than twice as many as any other due to a coding error, leaving 52 for data analysis.[11]

6.3.3.4 Predictions

To recap, the empirical question this experiment aims to address is whether the L*+H pitch accent makes a meaning contribution that is essentially equivalent to that of concessive *at least*, or whether its use accompanies a wider array of meanings. To distinguish between these two hypotheses, we are interested in whether using L*+H in the absence of *at least* leads to the same oddness that has been observed when concessive *at least* is used to express undesirable attitudes. Applied to the present design, the first thing to expect then is that for target sentences with *at least*, ratings for *negative-positive* contexts should be higher than for *positive-negative* contexts, as a type of sanity check. Although the influence of intonation on this pattern has not been previously tested, the effect should specifically be present with L*+H, assuming that this accent most clearly disambiguates toward a concessive interpretation. Secondly and more crucially, this effect of context should be smaller for bare targets if L*+H is not restricted to a concessive interpretation and indistinguishable otherwise. One central prediction thus concerns the interaction between CONTEXT and TARGET. Moreover, to ensure that the effect is indeed due to the meaning of L*+H, the H* accent should pattern differently, resulting in a three-way interaction between CONTEXT, TARGET and INTONATION. To assess these predictions in line with the reasoning laid out here, all factors will be dummy coded, with *at least*, *negative-positive*, and L*+H as reference levels, respectively.

6.3.3.5 Results

A summary of the mean ratings by condition is shown in Figure 6.7 and Table 6.3. The first thing to note is that there was a substantial decrease

[11] The main tendencies of the data were not affected by this last correction.

for *positive-negative* contexts relative to *negative-positive* ones when *at least* was present, as expected. This decrease seemed to be present for both L*+H and H*, with L*+H appearing overall slightly less acceptable. For *bare* targets, we observed a quite different pattern. With L*+H, *negative-positive* contexts appeared to receive slightly higher ratings, but to a much smaller margin than with *at least*. Moreover, with H* the pattern was flipped, showing higher ratings for *positive-negative* contexts than *negative-positive* ones.

Again using ordinal mixed-effects models to assess these observational patterns statistically and focusing on the effects of interest, we found a significant effect of CONTEXT ($z = -5.48$, $p < 0.001$), with *negative-positive* rated higher than *positive-negative*, a significant interaction of

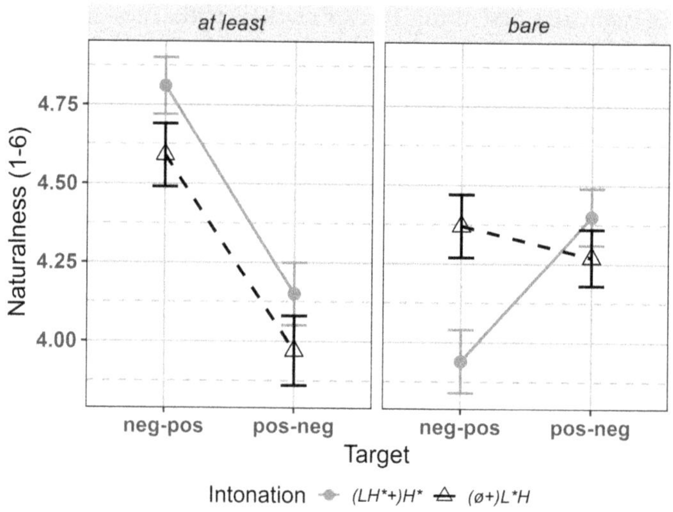

Fig. 6.7 Mean ratings by condition, Experiment 3

Table 6.3 Mean ratings (with standard error) by condition, Experiment 3

	'At least'		Bare	
	Neg-pos	Pos-neg	Neg-pos	Pos-neg
H*	4.81 (0.09)	4.15 (0.10)	3.94 (0.10)	4.40 (0.09)
L*+H	4.59 (0.10)	3.97 (0.13)	4.37 (0.10)	4.27 (0.09)

CONTEXT and TARGET ($z = 3.62$, $p < 0.001$), with the preference for negative-positive being larger—or restricted to —sentences with *at least*, and a significant three-way interaction between CONTEXT, TARGET, and INTONATION ($z = 2.51$, $p < 0.05$).[12]

6.3.3.6 Discussion

The experiment overall provided evidence against the notion that L*+H is simply a different way for conveying the meaning of concessive *at least*. While there was a decrease in ratings when *at least* was used to express something undesirable with L*+H, this decrease was significantly smaller when *at least* was not present. Moreover, the pattern shifted when the H* accent was used instead, specifically for bare target sentences. Hence, participants remained sensitive to the difference between the two pitch accents, particularly when there were no further restrictions imposed on the interpretation of the target sentence by the presence of a Focus-particle. These results are thus incompatible with a view that equates L*+H and concessive *at least* and speak in favor of a broader meaning of the pitch accent.

Despite the clear implications of the overall pattern for the main research question, a surprising aspect of the results were the ratings of the H* accent on bare target sentences. Negative-positive contexts received considerably lower ratings than positive-negative ones, reversing the pattern found for *at least*. The negative-positive contexts with bare targets thus constituted the clearest case of intonation having an impact. While this pattern does not affect the conclusions regarding the main research question, it is worth discussing possible explanations for it.

As a starting point, I want to suggest that the effect of the bare H* accent is one of correction in the cases here, much like corrective Focus, as already noted in the discussion of Experiment 2. In negative-positive contexts, there is thus an issue with what is supposed to be corrected. Given that the use of *not all* in A's sentence entails B's reply with

12 Of the remaining effects, all but the interaction between CONTEXT and INTONATION were significant ($z = -0.46$, $p = 0.64$; TARGET: $z = -2.54$, $p < 0.05$; INTONATION: $z = 2.03$, $p < 0.05$; TARGET*INTONATION: $z = -3.80$, $p < 0.001$).

some, the target sentence is rendered essentially redundant, which may be responsible for the low ratings. However, the same reasoning applies to positive-negative contexts, since the change in attitude does not affect the logical implications. What may be happening then is that the reply in positive-negative contexts is interpreted as a correction of the attitude expressed by speaker A: by highlighting the fact that there was still some negative outcome, speaker B may be able to express disagreement with speaker A's positive attitude, hence improving the overall coherence of the exchange.

We may ask why the same reasoning does not apply to negative-positive contexts, with highlighting something positive in reply to A's negative attitude. The issue here is that this communicative move is most compatible with concessive *at least* or L*+H. That is, the meaning of concessive *at least* appears to align perfectly with the need to provide a positive counterpoint to an initial negative attitude. Thus, the rating differences suggest that there is more to the acceptability of a dialogue than whether one expresses a disagreement or not. Rather, what may be at play here is how the attitude expressed by the reply aligns with what was previously said. In positive-negative contexts, a correction via H* may therefore fare better because it also corrects the attitude expressed by speaker A due to the correction expressing a somewhat negative attitude itself. In contrast, attempting a correction via H* in negative-positive contexts fails to correct the negative attitude of speaker A, diminishing overall discourse coherence. Put differently, the interpretive range of H* as corrective may be more restricted, with corrections only allowing association with a disagreement that, casually speaking, puts people down rather than lifting them up. While this proposal should only be seen as tentative and in need of future examination, the results may thus not only reveal something about the meaning contribution of L*+H but also point toward a more nuanced understanding of corrective Focus. The next section provides further discussion of the full experimental results in the context of the initial research questions and this volume.

6.4 General Discussion

The goal of the presented experiments was to examine the meaning of the L*+H pitch accent. The first experiment compared L*+H with H* with respect to the two interpretations of *at least* and corresponding contexts. The L*+H rendered contexts geared toward an epistemic interpretation less acceptable compared to H*, providing initial evidence for L*+H being associated with an evaluative component that is at odds with the intended epistemic meaning. Experiment 2 used the same manipulation but removed *at least* from target sentences to assess if L*+H makes its own independent contribution or is merely mediated by an ambiguity that needs to be resolved. Concessive contexts showed a preference for L*+H over H*, again in line with the idea of L*+H being evaluative and moreover in support of its contribution being genuinely independent. The final experiment aimed to separate the apparent overlap between L*+H and concessive *at least* to see if the two meanings can be considered equivalent or if the pitch accent can take on a broader range of meanings, using the incompatibility of concessive *at least* with undesirable states of affairs as test environment. While target sentences with *at least* showed the expected pattern regardless of intonation, the respective decrease was much less pronounced without *at least* and crucially specific to target sentences with L*+H. The combined results thus provide evidence for an independent evaluative contribution of L*+H that goes beyond that of concessive *at least*.

We may now ask how these results relate to the initial question of this paper regarding the relationship between alternatives and grammar. As a starting point, we can think of a binary split between alternatives being evoked and alternatives being operated on, along the lines of our framing of Rooth's Alternative Semantics. In a language like English, the role of evoking alternatives belongs to pitch accents like H* or L+H*, and the role of operating over alternatives belongs to Focus-particles like *only* and *even*. This split is represented formally by Focus-particles functioning as operators that take the alternative set generated by Focus as their argument. From this perspective, we might think of L*+H as an instance of the former class by virtue of inducing an evaluative meaning on the evoked alternatives. However, this categorization raises immediate issues.

For instance, L*+H would have to both evoke alternatives and operate on them, given that it replaces the H* accent. Therefore, I want to take a step back first and look more closely at the range of meanings expressed by Focus-particles in English.

The main cases to consider are *only*, *even*, *also*(/*too*), and *at least*. While the details of more nuanced analyses for these lexical items may vary, let's assume the simplified meanings below:

(16) Exhaustive *only*

a. **Only** [Sydney]$_F$ makes a tremendous risotto.

b. $\lambda C.\lambda p.\ \forall q\ [q \in C\ \&\ q \neq p \rightarrow q = 0]$

c. ≈ For all propositions in the alternative set that are not the prejacent, they are false.

(17) Evaluative/Scalar *only*

a. Carmy's restaurant **only** has [two stars]$_F$.

b. $\lambda C.\lambda p$: $\forall q\ [q \in C\ \&\ q \neq p \rightarrow p <_{eval}\ q]$. p

c. ≈ For all propositions in the alternative set that are not the prejacent, they are better (= ranked higher evaluatively).

(18) Scalar *even*

a. **Even** [Richie]$_F$ is helping in the kitchen.

b. $\lambda C.\lambda p$: $\forall q\ [q \in C\ \&\ q \neq p \rightarrow p <_{likely}\ q]$. p

c. ≈ For all propositions in the alternative set that are not the prejacent, they are more likely (= ranked higher in terms of likelihood).

(19) Additive *also*(/*too*)

a. [Marcus]$_F$ is **ALSO** creating new recipes.

b. $\lambda C.\lambda p$: $\exists q\ [q \in C\ \&\ q \neq p \rightarrow p = 1]$. p

c. ≈ There is a proposition in the alternative set that is not the prejacent, which is true.

(20) Epistemic at least
  a. Tina made **at least** [five sandwiches]$_F$.
  b. $\lambda C.\lambda p.\ \forall q\ [q \in C\ \&\ q < p \rightarrow q = 0]$
  c. ≈ For all propositions in the alternative set that are lesser than the prejacent, they are false.

(21) Concessive *at least*
  a. **At least** Tina made [five sandwiches]$_F$.
  b. $\lambda C.\lambda p$: $\exists q\ [q \in C\ \&\ q < p \rightarrow q <_{eval} p]$. p
  c. ≈ For all propositions in the alternative set that are lesser than the prejacent, they are worse (= ranked lower evaluatively).

Looking across these different meanings, there are several points of variation worth mentioning. First, Focus-particles vary in whether they contribute at-issue content (exhaustive *only*, epistemic *at least*) or not at-issue content (scalar *only*, *even*, *also*, concessive *at least*).[13] Second, some meanings are concerned with truth values more directly insofar as they imply the truth or falsity of some other proposition(s) (exhaustive *only*, *also*, epistemic *at least*), while others involve rankings of some kind (scalar *only*, *even*, concessive *at least*). Within the latter group, there

[13] The diagnostic for distinguishing at-issue from not at-issue content assumed here is the direct denial test (Potts, 2005; Tonhauser et al., 2013), illustrated in (i) for the two interpretations of *only*. While it is perfectly natural to deny the exhaustive contribution of *only* in (ia), attempting the same for the evaluative "not much" contribution of *only* in (ib) results in infelicity. (For space reasons, I will leave the application of the test to the other Focus-particles to the interested reader.)

(i) a. A: **Only** Sydney makes a tremendous risotto.
  B: That's not true, Terry makes a tremendous risotto as well!
 b. A: Carmy's restaurant only has two stars.
  B: #That's not true, having two stars is really good!

is then variation in what the ranking involves, either likelihood or an evaluation.[14]

How could we characterize the meaning of L*+H relative to this repertoire? Crucially, while Experiments 1 and 2 hinted at a strong similarity to concessive *at least*, which would suggest that L*+H communicates relevant alternatives to be worse and thereby leading to its optimistic connotation, the results of Experiment 3 would be incompatible with such a characterization. Looking at a particular example in (22), the intuitive effect seems to be almost the opposite, with B acting as a bit of a downer who intends to dampen A's expectation. To cover both of these cases, the evaluation L*+H contributes hence has to be open to context. That is, there cannot be a fixed ranking as in the case of (21). The corresponding proposal by Göbel (2019) is given in (23).

(22) A: It's great that not all of the children refused to eat their broccoli.
B: Some of the children refused to eat their broccoli.

(23) $[\![L^*{+}H]\!] = \forall p \forall q[p,\ q \in C\ \&\ p \neq q \rightarrow p <_{eval} q \vee p >_{eval} q]$
(= *for all distinct propositions p, q in C, p is either ranked below or above q)*

On this proposal, the contribution of L*+H would be quite unique insofar as no other Focus-particle offers this amount of flexibility. Moreover, in order to capture that alternatives have to be evoked as well, Göbel (2019) proposes that L*+H includes the meaning of the Focus-operator ~, with the evaluative component in (23) as added meaning. An interesting question such an approach would raise for the processing of Focus and alternatives is at what stage the evaluative component enters the computation. Gotzner and Spalek (2019) argue based on a review of the previous literature in this area that Focus activates a broader range of alternatives initially before restricting the set to what is immediately relevant (but see Muxica & Harris (this volume) for a counter-argument).

[14] It is important to note that there are formal accounts that aim to unify the meaning of cases like *only* by treating its truth value-oriented interpretation in terms of a ranking of informativity (e.g., Beaver & Clark, 2008). On such approaches, we would thus deal with one less point of variation.

Additionally, Focus-particles like *only* and *even* lead to competition among alternatives in the set, inhibiting processing at earlier stages. Conceptually, we may thus ask whether the evaluative component of L*+H would behave like a Focus-particle during the incremental activation of alternatives, or whether inducing the ranking constitutes a distinct step. If the latter, we might expect the relationship between alternatives regarding their relative ranking to become important beyond their semantic similarity or being mentioned in the discourse. For instance, a target like *gold* might be primed differentially from a target like *iron* in the context of an L*+H accent on a word like *silver* after semantic relatedness is taken into account due to the associated ranking. While the details of such a hypothesis would require more work, I believe the results presented here have a clear connection to research on the cognitive aspects of alternatives and may lead to interesting insights in this area.

6.5 Conclusion

Alternatives play an important role in contemporary linguistic theorizing. This paper looked at Focus and some parts of the grammar that relate to it. While intonation has been central in the way Focus evokes alternatives, it has received less attention in the ways it may itself operate over alternatives. Three auditory rating experiments examined the meaning of the less studied L*+H pitch accent, providing evidence for its characterization as ranking alternatives evaluatively. These results thus add to our understanding of the ways in which the grammar interacts with alternatives and raise interesting questions about its integration into research on their cognitive representations.

References

Alexandropoulou, S. (2021). Scalar diversity and ignorance inferences: An experimental study on *at least* as a modifier of numerals vs. adjectives. In *Proceedings of SALT XXXI* (pp. 506–529). Cornell University.

Bartels, C., & Kingston, J. (1999). Salient pitch cues in the perception of contrastive focus. In M. W. Dickey & S. Tunstall (Eds.), *University of Massachusetts occasional papers 19: Linguistics in the laboratory* (pp. 1–26). GLSA.

Beaver, D., & Clark, B. (2008). *Sense and sensitivity: How focus determines meaning*. Blackwell.

Beckman, M., Hirschberg, J., & Shattuck-Hufnagel, S. (2005). The original ToBI system and the evolution of the ToBI framework. In S.-A. Jun (Ed.), *Prosodic typology: The phonology of intonation and phrasing* (pp. 9–54). Oxford University Press.

Biezma, M. (2013). Only one 'at least': Refining the role of discourse in building alternatives. *In Proceedings of Penn Linguistics Colloquium, 36*, 11–19.

Bolinger, D. (1965). *Forms of English: Accent, morpheme, order*. Harvard University Press.

Braun, B., Asano, Y., & Dehé, N. (2018). When (not) to look for contrastive alternatives: The role of pitch accent type and additive particles. *Language and Speech, 62*, 751–778.

Braun, B., & Biezma, M. (2019). Prenuclear L*+H activates alternatives for the accented word. *Frontiers in Psychology, 10*, 1–22.

Braun, B., & Tagliapietra, L. (2010). The role of contrastive intonation contours in the retrieval of contextual alternatives. *Language and Cognitive Processes, 25*, 1024–1043.

Büring, D. (1997). *The meaning of topic and focus: The 59th street bridge accent*. Routledge.

Büring, D. (2003). On D-trees, beans, and B-accents. *Linguistics and Philosophy, 26*, 511–545.

Constant, N. (2012). English rise-fall-rise: A study in the semantics and pragmatics of intonation. *Linguistics and Philosophy, 35*, 407–442.

Constant, N. (2014). *Contrastive topic: Meanings and realizations* (Ph. D. thesis). University of Massachusetts, Amherst.

Fraundorf, S. H., Watson, D. G., & Benjamin, A. S. (2010). Recognition memory reveals just how contrastive contrastive accenting really is. *Journal of Memory and Language, 63*, 367–386.

Gotzner, N. (2019). The role of focus intonation in implicature computation: A comparison with 'only' and 'also'. *Natural Language Semantics, 27*, 189–226.

Gotzner, N., & Spalek, K. (2019). The life and times of focus alternatives: Tracing the activation of alternatives to a focused constituent in language comprehension. *Language and Linguistics Compass, 13*, 1–26.

Göbel, A. (2019). Additives pitching in: L*+H signals ordered focus alternatives. In *Proceedings of SALT 29* (pp. 279–299).

Göbel, A., & Wagner, M. (2023a). How the position of 'at least' affects its interpretation: experimental data. *Glossa: A Journal of General Linguistics 8*.

Göbel, A., & Wagner, M. (2023b). On a concessive reading of the rise-fall-rise contour: Contextual and semantic factors. *In Proceedings of ELM, 2*, 83–94.

Husband, E. M., & Ferreira, F. (2016). The role of selection in the comprehension of focus alternatives. *Language, Cognition and Neuroscience, 31*, 217–235.

Ito, K., & Speer, S. R. (2008). Anticipatory effects of intonation: Eye movements during instructed visual search. *Journal of Memory and Language, 58*, 541–573.

Jackendoff, R. (1972). *Semantic interpretation in generative grammar*. MIT Press.

Kay, P. (1992). At least. In A. Lehrer & E. F. Kittay (Eds.), *Frames, fields, and contrasts: New essays in semantic and lexical organization* (pp. 309–332). L. Erlbaum Associates.

Ladd, R. D. (2008). *Intonational phonology*. Cambridge University Press.

Lee, C. (1999). Contrastive topic: A locus of the interface. In K. Turner (Ed.), *The semantics/pragmatics interface from different points of view* (pp. 317–341). Elsevier.

Martens, G. (2022). *What about those B-accents and hat patterns? Form and meaning of contrastive topics in English, Dutch, and German* (Ph. D. thesis). McGill University.

Nakanishi, K., & Rullmann, H. (2009). *Epistemic and concessive interpretation of* at least. Talk presented at Canadian Linguistics Association.

Pierrehumbert, J. B., & Hirschberg, J. (1990). The meaning of intonational contours in the interpretation of discourse. In P. R. Cohen, J. Morgan, & M. E. Pollack (Eds.), *Intensions in communication* (pp. 271–311). MIT Press.

Potts, C. (2005). *The logic of conventional implicatures*. Oxford University Press.

Repp, S. (2016). Contrast: Dissecting an elusive information-structural notion and its role in grammar. In C. Féry & S. Ishihara (Eds.), *The Oxford handbook of information structure* (pp. 270–289). Oxford University Press.
Sedivy, J., Tanenhaus, M., Chambers, C., & Carlson, G. (1999). Achieving incremental semantic interpretation through contextual representation. *Cognition, 71*, 109–147.
Tonhauser, J., Beaver, D., Roberts, C., & Simons, M. (2013). Toward a taxonomy of projective content. *Language, 89*, 66–109.
Wagner, M. (2012). Contrastive topics decomposed. *Semantics and Pragmatics, 5*, 1–54.
Ward, G., & Hirschberg, J. (1985). Implicating uncertainty: The pragmatics of fall-rise intonation. *Language, 61*, 747–776.
Watson, D. G., Tanenhaus, M. K., & Gunlogson, C. A. (2008). Interpreting pitch accents in online comprehension: H* vs. L+H*. *Cognitive Science, 32*, 1232–1244.
Zondervan, A. J. (2010). *Scalar implicatures or focus: An experimental approach* (Ph. D. thesis). University of Amsterdam.

7

Answerability Constraints on Alternative-Introducing Salient Sentences: Support from the Evaluativity Effects of *Only* and from Scalar Implicatures

Yael Greenberg

7.1 Introduction

We will propose that in order to be used as a basis for an alternative to a proposition *p*, a salient sentence must obey an answerability-based constraint.

Of course, neither the effects of salient sentences on the construction of alternatives, nor that of answerability constraints, are new topics in the literature on alternatives. Regarding the former, there is a body of experimental research on the activation of alternatives which found that alternatives constructed based on previously uttered sentences have a prioritized status relative to those based on, e.g., the lexicon (see, e.g., Fraundorf et al. (2013), Kim et al. (2015), Gotzner (2015) and Gotzner et al. (2016)). From the more theoretical perspective Fox and Katzir (2011), Katzir (2014) and subsequent work argue that salient material can be used to construct alternatives which are usually not allowable in

Y. Greenberg (✉)
Bar Ilan University, Ramat Gan, Israel
e-mail: Yael.Grinberg@biu.ac.il

N. Gotzner et al. (eds.), *Alternatives in Grammar and Cognition*, Palgrave Studies in Pragmatics, Language and Cognition, https://doi.org/10.1007/978-3-031-76676-3_7

the set of alternatives, namely those with material which is more complex than the substituted focused element. This is illustrated in Katzir's (2014) complexity-based constraint on formal alternatives in (1):

(1) X′ is at most complex as X if X′ can be derived from X by successive steps in which a sub-constituent *z* of X is replaced with an element of the substation source for s in C, SS(z,C)
Where the substation source for s in C, SS(z,C), is the union of
a. The lexicon
b. The sub-constituents of z
c. **The set of salient constituents in C (that is, constituents of the structures of utterances made in recent discourse).** (My emphasis)

As to answerability-based constraints, this topic too has been already proposed and discussed with regard to sets of alternatives, but usually with respect to the alternatives themselves, and not with respect to the salient sentences that introduce them into the set. In particular, various theories suggested that the focus alternatives to a proposition *p* in C—the set of contextually relevant alternatives (Rooth, 1992) can be only those which are relevant with respect to the Question Under Discussion, i.e., those that constitute a (partial) answer to the question that *p* answers (see, e.g., Spector, 2007; Trinh, 2019). Thus, for, example, given the Hamblin-like approach to questions as denoting sets of propositions, and the view that focus should be congruent to the QUD (e.g. Beaver & Clark, 2008; Roberts, 1996; Rooth, 1992), all focus alternatives to *John danced with [Mary]$_F$*, namely *John danced with Susan, John danced with Ann,* etc. should answer the same question that the original sentence answers—*Who did John dance with*?

In this chapter, though, we will not concentrate on answerability constraints on alternatives, but on salient sentence which introduce those alternatives into the set. We will take as a starting point a proposal in Greenberg, 2022 which deals with the way different salient sentences affect the mirror-imaged (in)felicity of sentences with *only* and *even*. Based on this examination that paper argues that, when properly constrained, salient sentences have a prioritized status relative to alternatives based on the lexicon, in that the former, but not the latter, cannot be ignored when constructing alternatives into the set of alternatives to the prejacents of *only* and *even*. Thus, alternatives based on salient sentences must enter the set of alternatives (even when leading to a presupposition failure), whereas those based on the lexicon which can, but do not necessarily enter the set.

What will be relevant for us here is Greenberg's (2022) claim that the proper constraint on these salient sentences concerns answerability, and in particular, the requirement that the salient sentence is used to answer same question that the prejacent of *even* or of *only* answers.

The goal of this chapter is to extend the examination of answerability-based constraints on alternatives-introducing salient sentences. We will propose that such a constraint is operative not only with those salient sentences which MUST be used to construct alternatives, but also with those which ARE ABLE to do that. To support this proposal we will examine two cases where the alternatives to the prejacent cannot be based on any other source but the salient sentence (albeit for two different reasons). These two cases concern the effect of salient sentences on (a) the (dis)appearance of evaluativity effects with *only*, namely its (in)felicity with 'large' associates and on (b) The presence vs. absence of scalar implicatures, where the focused element is substituted by 'more complex' material.

The chapter is structured as follows. In Sect. 7.2 we present two sets of novel, and so-far unaccounted for data, regarding salient sentences which do not have their expected effects (a) in canceling the evaluativity effects of *only* and (b) leading to scalar implicatures which are otherwise unattested. Section 7.3 reviews Greenberg's (2022) observations regarding the mirror-imaged infelicity of *only* and *even* when appearing after salient sentences with material which is weaker / stronger of their associate, respectively. The important part for us will be the proposal regarding an answerability-based constraint on salient sentences, which, when obeyed, leads to a necessary membership of alternatives based on these sentences into the set of alternatives. Section 7.4 turns to the evaluativity effects of *only*, illustrated by its infelicity with 'too large' associates (e.g., *#John only has [12]$_F$ kids*), and which was observed to disappear after salient sentences with even 'larger' materials. In this section we will examine more closely the novel observation from Sect. 7.2, showing that not any such salient sentence can have this effect. In Sect. 7.5 we will reject an explanation of the new data in terms of a plausibility/entertainability, and in Sect. 7.6 propose that the distinction between salient sentences which can vs. cannot cancel the evaluativity effects of *only* is accounted for if we assume an answerability-based constraint, requiring that a salient sentence can only introduce alternatives into the set if it is used to answer the same question that the *p*-sentence answers. Section 7.7 proposes that the answerability-based constraint can also help explain the data, mentioned in Sect. 7.2, showing that some, but crucially not all salient sentences can lead to scalar implicatures with 'complex' material.

Before we start, here is some terminology we will try to keep unified throughout the chapter: we will use the term 'salient sentences' to refer to those sentences which are mentioned / uttered before the sentences with the focused element. Following Rooth, 1992 and much subsequent work, we will refer to the set of alternatives that the operator (*only* / *even* / *exh*) ends up operating over as C,[1] or simply as 'the set of alternatives'. Finally, we will refer to the prejacents of the operators (*only*, *even*, etc.), denoting the proposition p, as S_p, and to sentences which denote propositions q which are (potential) alternatives to p, as S_q.

7.2 Two Puzzles About Salient Sentences

7.2.1 Salient Sentences Which Do vs. Do Not Cancel the Evaluativity Effects of *Only*

Only has been long observed to have **mirative / evaluative** effects (cf. Alxatib, 2013; Beaver & Clark, 2008; Klinedinst, 2004, 2005; Roberts, 2011; Zeevat, 2009, 2013 and others). These effects are both interpretational and distributional. In terms of interpretation, a sentence with *only* leads to the inference that its associate is 'small', i.e., smaller than expected (cf. Zeevat, 2008, 2013), or smaller than the contextual standard on the relevant scale (cf. Alxatib, 2013). Thus, for example, the presence of *only* in (2) indicates that having 2 children is somehow less

[1] Notice that this is different from the terminology in, e.g., Katzir (2014) and subsequent work, where *C* refers only to the set of propositions in the context, which intersects with the set of formal alternatives, *F(S)*, to create the set of actual alternatives *A*.

than expected, or than the contextual norm regarding the number of children:

(2) John has (only) $[2]_F$ kids

Distributionally, *only* was often observed to be degraded when its associate is 'large':

(3) John has (#only) $[12]_F$ kids (odd in typical Western contexts (cf. John has (only) $[2]_F$ kids)

While some theories (e.g., Beaver & Clark, 2008; Zeevat, 2013) take the evolutive / mirative inference to be hardwired into the semantics of *only*, other (e.g., Alxatib, 2020, Greenberg, 2022; Homer, 2019; Roberts, 2011) argued that it is derived, based on the observation that these effects are cancelable. An observation we will focus on below, made in Greenberg (2022), is that the cases where these effects typically arise is in 'out of the blue' utterances, or as answers to questions, but that they tend to disappear when the sentence with *only* appears after a salient sentence with material larger than the associate of *only*. To illustrate, compare the oddness of *only* in (3) above to its much better status in (4)-(5):

(4) A: John has 13 kids
B: Wow! That's a lot!!! And what about Bill?
A: He has only $[12]_F$ - This is also a lot, but less than what John has

(5) John always wanted to have 13 kids. I have no idea why. But he only has $[12]_F$

A novel observation we make in this chapter, however, is that not any such salient sentence can have this effect. Some examples illustrating this observation are in (6)-(8):

(6) I have (#only) $[80]_F$ dresses in my wardrobe (cf. I have (only) $[2]_F$ dresses in my wardrobe)

(7) a. My sister has 100 dresses in her wardrobe. I myself have (only) $[80]_F$
b. I want to have 100 dresses in my wardrobe. (But) I (only) have $[80]_F$

(8) a. Most of my family really loves fashion. My grandmother, for example, designed 100 dresses. I myself have (#only) $[80]_F$ dresses in my wardrobe (cf. I myself have only $[2]_F$ dresses)
b. My sister always dreamt that she would have 100 dresses in her wardrobe. I myself have (??only) $[80]_F$ dresses in my wardrobe (cf. I myself have only $[2]_F$ dresses in my wardrobe)

The pattern we see in (6) and in (7) is the same as mentioned above: The 'out of the blue' (6) displays the evaluativity effects of *only*, namely its infelicity with a 'large' associate ('80'). In (7a)-(7b), on the other hand, the presence of the salient sentences which mention '100 dresses', makes the association of *only* with *80* much better.

The novel data is in (8a,b): Here the salient sentences, which again mention '100 dresses', do not have the effect seen in (7a,b): *only* keeps its oddness with a 'large' material (80) in these sentences, as it does in the 'out of the blue' (6).

The first puzzle we are facing, then, can be phrased as in (9):

(9) **A puzzle regarding the effect of salient sentences on evaluativity effects of *only*:**
Why is it that the evaluativity effects of *only* (namely its infelicity with 'large' associates) disappears in the presence of some salient sentences with an even larger material, but not with all such salient sentences?
What is the factor which teases these two types of salient sentences apart?

7.2.2 Salient Sentences Which Do vs. Do Not Lead to Scalar Implicatures with a 'More Complex' Substitute

An apparently unrelated puzzle concerns a much more well-studied effect of salient sentences, namely their ability to lead to scalar implicatures which cannot arise in 'out of the blue' utterances. This effect is illustrated in (10)-(11):

(10) Bill was required to answer some of the questions
Implicatures:
a. He was not required to answer all of the questions
b. ~~He was not required to answer some but not all of the questions~~

(11) John was required to answer some but not all of the questions
Bill was required to answer some of the questions
Implicatures:
a. He was not required to answer all of the questions
b. He was not required to answer some but not all of the questions

In both (10) and (11) the (a) implicatures, where *some* is substituted by *all* arise. But, whereas the (b) implicature, where *some* is substituted by the more complex *some but not all* cannot arise in (10), it does arise in (11), where this more complex quantifier is made salient in the first sentence. This is captured by Katzir's (2014) substitution source in (1) above.

But again, we now observe that not any salient sentence has this effect. Consider first (12)[2]:

(12) Some but not all of the kids arrive to class on time
The teacher required that they answer some of the questions
Implicatures:
a. The teacher did not require them to answer all of the questions
b. ~~The teacher did not require them to answer some but not all of the questions.~~

Unlike what we saw in (11), in this case the implicature in (b) does NOT arise, despite the fact that *some but all* is made salient in the first sentence.

A similar pattern is seen in (13), where the DP *some but not all of the questions* is made salient in the first sentence. Here too, the (b) implicature does not arise:

[2] Thanks to Roni Katzir (p.c.) for this example.

(13) (Context: I spent 3 weeks at a math camp last year. We got 100 questions to solve)
On the first day the instructors gave us some but not all of the questions. (The rest were given to us on the second day)
The instructors required that we submit the answers to some of the questions already by the end of the first week
Implicatures:
a. They did not require that we submit the answers to all of the questions by the end of the first week
b. ~~They did not require that we submit the answers to some but not all of the questions by the end of the first week.~~

To the best of our knowledge this kind of data has not been examined so far in current theories of scalar implicatures, and is not predicted by them. The puzzle we are facing, then, can be phrased as in (14):

(14) **A puzzle regarding the effect of salient sentences on scalar implicatures with 'complex' material:**
Why is it that scalar implicatures which are based on substitution of focused material with more complex material can arise in the presence of some salient sentences with this complex material, but not with all such salient sentences?
What is the factor which teases these two types of salient sentences apart?

7.2.3 The Plan

On the surface, the two types of puzzling data in Sect. 2.1—concerning evaluativity effects of *only*, and in 2.2—concerning scalar implicatures, do not seem related. We will argue, however, that there is an important similarity between them: The 'well-behaved' cases with both types of data, namely (7) in Sect. 2.1 and (11) in Sect. 2.2, are those where the salient sentences can be the only possible basis for alternatives in C (albeit for two independent reasons). In particular, we argue below that it is only the ability of the salient sentence in (7) to introduce an alternative with an 'extremely large' material which cancels the evaluativity effects of *only*, i.e., which allows it to associate with a large associate. Similarly, it is only the ability of the salient sentence in (11) to introduce an alternative with 'complex' material which licenses the scalar implicature in (11b), where *some* is substituted by the more complex *some but not all.* Besides the salient sentences, the alternatives to *p* in both types of data cannot be based on any other source (e.g., the lexicon).

Thus, the observation that there are some salient sentences which are 'not well-behaved', i.e., cannot introduce alternatives into the set, and thus, like (8), cannot cancel the evaluativity effects of *only,* and, like (12), cannot lead to scalar implicatures with 'complex' material, is significant. In particular, comparing those salient sentences which can be used to construct alternatives vs. those which cannot do so, is an opportunity to investigate how alternatives-introducing salient sentences are constrained. We will argue that there is actually one and the same constraint—based on answerability—which is at work with both kinds of phenomena.

To do that we will first review, in Sect. 7.3, an answerability-based constraint proposed in Greenberg (2022) on salient sentences which *must* introduce alternatives into C, and which is based on an observed mirror-imaged infelicity pattern with *even* and *only*. In Sects. 7.4–7.6 we will turn to the way salient sentences can vs. cannot cancel the evaluativity effect of *only*, and in Sect. 7.7 to the way salient sentences can vs. cannot lead to scalar implicatures which are otherwise non-attested. Based on these examinations we will conclude, in Sect. 7.8 that the answerability-based constraint dictates not only which salient sentences must introduce alternatives into C, but also which are able to do so.

7.3 An Answerability-Based Constraint on Salient Sentences Which Must Introduce Alternatives into C: Support from the Mirror-Imaged Infelicity Patterns with *Only* and *Even*

1. <u>The Mirror-Imaged Infelicity Pattern of *Only* and *Even* and Their Proposed Mirror-Imaged Superlative Scalar Presuppositions</u>

As observed in Greenberg (2022), *only* and *even* manifest a mirror-imaged infelicity pattern in cases like (15)-(16) (see Orenstein & Greenberg, 2013, Orenstein, 2016) for the original observation regarding *only*):

(15) A: How many chapters have your faculty members written during the last three years?
B Let's see: Ann wrote 10 papers, Sam wrote 8, Henry wrote 5, Tom wrote 6, Ted wrote 7, Ian wrote 3, and Bill (#only) wrote $[4]_F$

(16) A: How many papers have your faculty members written during the last three years?
B: Let's see: Ann wrote 4 papers, Sam wrote 3, Henry wrote 5, Tom wrote 7, Ted wrote 6, Ian wrote 10, and Bill (#even) wrote $[8]_F$

Given the salient sentences, the C sets for p in these cases seem to be as in (15')-(16'), where the p alternative denoted by the prejacent (S_p) is underlined:

(15') {<u>Bill wrote 4 papers</u>, Bill wrote 3 papers, Bill wrote 6 papers, Bill wrote 7 papers, Bill wrote 5 papers, Bill wrote 8 papers, Bill wrote 10 papers, …}

(16') {<u>Bill wrote 8 papers</u>, Bill wrote 10 papers, Bill wrote 6 papers, Bill wrote 7
papers, Bill wrote 5 papers, Bill wrote 3 papers, Bill wrote 4 papers, …}

Importantly, the infelicity of *even* in (16) can be straightforwardly explained by assuming the widely held view (Horn, 1969; Karttunen & Peters, 1979; Rooth, 1985, 1992 and much subsequent work) that this particle triggers a 'superlative' scalar presupposition along the lines of (17), requiring p to be the strongest alternative in C:

(17) $||\textbf{even C S}||^{g,c} = ||S||_O(w) = 1$. Only defined iff $\forall q \in C\ [q \neq ||S||_O \rightarrow ||S||_O >$

This 'superlative' presupposition fails in the C set in (16') because p is not the strongest alternative in C - Bill *wrote 10 papers* is stronger than it. Hence *even* is correctly predicted to be infelicitous in (16).

In contrast, the mirror-imaged infelicity of *only* in (15) is not predicted, at least not in a straightforward manner, by the common lexical entries of this particle proposed in the literature. We take the scalar entry in (18) as an example (see Alxatib, 2013; Beaver & Clark, 2008; Coppock & Beaver, 2014; Horn, 1969; Klinedinst, 2005; Liu, 2017; Roberts, 2011 for variants):

(18) $||$**only C S**$||^{g,c}$ = for all q in C such that $q > ||S||_O \rightarrow q = 0$
Only defined iff $||S||_O$ (w) = 1

Given this entry *only* presupposes that *p* is true, and asserts that those alternatives in C which are stronger than *p* on a scale are false. Crucially, however, *only* does not ban in any way the mere existence of alternatives which are weaker than *p* in C. What, then, can explain the infelicity of *only* in (15)?

Two existing constraints on *only* which come to mind when trying to explain its infelicity in (15) are examined and rejected in Greenberg (2022). First, trying to derive this infelicity by requiring that there is at least one / a salient alternative in C which is stronger than *p* (so the operation of *only* is not vacuous) is problematic. This is because such salient stronger alternatives do exist in the C set in (15'), namely *Bill wrote 6 papers, Bill wrote 7 papers,* etc. In addition, the associate of *only* in (15) can be easily considered 'small' relative to the alternatives (since most alternatives indicate a larger number of papers). Thus, the infelicity of *only* in (15) cannot be attributed to failure of a mirative / evaluative presupposition, requiring that *p* indicates a degree lower than expected / lower than the norm (see Sect. 7.4 for a more detailed discussion of this requirement).

The conclusion in Greenberg (2022), then, is that the lexical entry for *only* in (18) is not enough explain its infelicity in sentences like (15).

Instead, to explain this infelicity of *only*, and the fact that it mirror-images the infelicity of *even* in (16), the semantics of *only* is revised in Greenberg (2022) so it includes a superlative scalar presupposition which mirror-images that of *even*.[3] This is summarized in (19):

---

[3] See Xiang (2020) for an attempt to explain the mirror-imaged infelicity of *only* and *even* without using a superlative presupposition, and challenges for this attempt discussed in Greenberg (2022).

(19) **A superlative scalar antonymy presupposition for *only* and for *even*[4]:**

a. *Only C* S_p presupposes that all alternatives in C are stronger than $||S_p||_O$, i.e., that *p* is the weakest alternative in C

b. *Even C* S_p presupposes that all alternatives in C are weaker than $||S_p||_O$, i.e., that *p* is the strongest alternative in C

2. The Privileged Status of Salient Sentences in Constructing Alternatives into C.

As pointed out in Greenberg (2022), using the superlative scalar presuppositions in (19) to explain the mirror-imaged infelicity pattern with *only* and *even* in (15)-(16) can be successful only if we follow the assumption in (20):

(20) The necessary membership of alternatives in C given prior discourse (First version): Contextually relevant focus alternatives to $||S_p||_O$ (i.e., to *p*) must be in C if they are constructed based on salient sentences (e.g., those which are previously uttered)

Where, following Rooh (1985, 1992) and much subsequent work, an alternative *p* to $||S_p||_O$ is constructed based on a discourse salient sentence by substituting the focused material in $||S_p||_O$ by parallel material in this sentence.

Thus, for example, *only* and *even* are infelicitous in C because, given (20), the salient sentences *Ian wrote 3 papers* in (15), and *Ian wrote 10 papers* in (16) must introduce into C an alternative which is weaker than *p* (in (15)), and stronger than it (in (16)) respectively, thus leading to the violation of the superlative presuppositions of *only* and *even*. If such salient sentences could be ignored, so the alternatives based on them did not have to be in C, no presupposition failure would occur and *only* and *even* would be wrongly predicted to be felicitous in these sentences.

[4] Notice that similar versions of (19) were independently proposed in the literature (in e.g. Guerzoni (2003), König (1991), Crnič (2012), Charnavel (2017) and Liu (2017)), but were not used to explain the mirror-imaged infelicity pattern of *only* and *even*.

The assumption in (20) can also explain cases like (21–22) from Kay (1990) where *even* is felicitous although its associate is not 'at the end of the scale':

(21) Not only did Mary win her first-round match, she even made it to the [semi-finals]$_F$

(22) The administration was so bewildered that they even had [lieutenant colonels]$_F$ making policy decisions

Kay points out that *even* is felicitous in these examples although *p* does not seem to be the strongest alternative. For example, in (21) 'making it to the semi-finals' is not the end of the scale point ('making it to the finals' is more extreme) and in (22) "having majors, captains or sergeants making major police decisions would provide the basis for even more extreme assertions" (1990: 90). Kay thus rejects a superlative scalar presupposition for *even* and instead adopts an existential presupposition, according to which *even p* requires that *p* is stronger than some (salient) alternatives.

As mentioned above, though, an existential presupposition would not be enough to explain the infelicity of *even* in (16). In contrast, given the assumption in (20) about salient sentences the felicity of *even* in (21)-(22) is fully compatible with a superlative scalar presupposition in (19): The 'more extreme' alternatives are not necessarily members of C in such cases, since they are not based on salient, i.e., previously uttered sentences, but need to be accommodated. Hence, *p* can still be taken to be the strongest alternative in C.

The same rationale can be now applied to explain felicity contrasts as in (23) with *even* and in (24) with *only*:

(23) a. Last year Bill won the bronze medal. This year he even won [silver]$_F$

b. Two years ago Bill won the bronze medal. Last year he won gold and this year he (#even) won [silver]$_F$

(24) a. Last year Bill won the gold medal. This year he only won [silver]$_F$

b. Two years ago Bill won the gold medal. Last year he won bronze and this year he (#only) won [silver]$_F$

The superlative presupposition of *even* and of *only* phrased in (19) fails only in the (b) cases, where alternatives stronger than and weaker than *p*, respectively, are necessarily members of C due to being constructed based on previously uttered sentences. In contrast, when the alternatives are constructed based on the lexicon (e.g., the stronger alternative *Bill won silver* in (23), and the weaker *Bill won bronze* in (24)), they can be left out of C so the superlative scalar presupposition can be met.

A more general conclusion, then, is that given (20) alternatives based on discourse salient sentences have a privileged status over those based on the lexicon: Only the former, but not the latter, are necessarily members of C.

3. Alternative-Introducing Salient Sentences with *Only* and *Even* Are Subject to an Answerability-Based Constraint

Despite the ability of the assumption in (20) to help explain the mirror-imaged infelicity of *only* and *even*, it needs to be revised. In particular, as pointed out in Greenberg (2022), this assumption makes wrong predictions regarding some felicity contrasts with *only* and *even*. To illustrate, consider (25) and (26) (variants on the original examples in Greenberg, 2022):

(25) a. Two years ago John reviewed 5 papers and wrote 3. Last year he reviewed (only) $[4]_F$ papers
b. Two years ago John reviewed 5 papers and wrote 3. Last year he wrote (#only) $[4]_F$ papers

(26) a. Two years ago John reviewed 5 papers and wrote 3. Last year he (#even) reviewed $[4]_F$ papers
b. Two years ago John reviewed 5 papers, and wrote 3. Last year he (even) wrote $[4]_F$ papers[5]

Consider, for example, the felicity contrast with *only* in (25). Given the constraint in (20) above concerning the necessary membership in C of alternatives based on salient sentences, the C sets of (25a) and (25b) are as in (25'a) and (25'b), respectively:

[5] For some reason *even* sounds more natural before the verb than between the verb and the numeral associate, whereas *only* sounds natural in both positions. We are not sure what the reason for this contrast is, but we assume it does not make a difference w.r.t. the main claims here.

(25′) a. {Last year John reviewed 4 papers, Last year John reviewed 3 papers, Last year John reviewed 5 papers, ...}
b. {Last year John wrote 4 papers, Last year John wrote 3 papers, Last year John wrote 5 papers, ...}

Crucially, in both cases p is not the weakest element in C. Thus, assuming a superlative scalar presupposition for *only* as in (19), (20) wrongly predicts that *only* is infelicitous in *both* cases.[6]

A revised version of (20), then, which constrains those salient sentences which necessarily introduce alternatives into C, is proposed in Greenberg (2022). This version can be phrased as in (27):

(27) **The necessary membership of alternatives in C given prior discourse (Revised version):** A focus alternative q to p necessarily enters the set of alternatives to p, C iff the following two conditions hold:
(a) q is constructed based on a salient sentence S_q (uttered before S_p) and
(b) this salient sentence S_q answers the same question in the context that S_p answers

Indeed, (27) now correctly accounts for the felicity contrast with *only* in (25a)-(25b). The natural intonational pattern of the prejacent in (25a) is a Contrasive Topc-FOCUS one (*Last year$_{CT}$ John reviewed [5]$_F$ papers*). Hence, following Roberts' (1996) notion of 'strategy of inquiry' for QUDs, Büring's (2003) ideas about Topic-Focus intonation patterns and subsequent work, we assume that such a structure indicates the presence of a salient super-QUD as in (28), with the following two sub-questions:

(28) How many papers did John review every year?
Sub-questions:
How many papers did John review two years ago?
How many papers did John review last year?

[6] Importantly, (20) makes the wrong predictions here even if one rejects the superlative presupposition in (19) and adopts instead an existential one (requiring that p is weaker than at least one (salient) alternative). In this case (20) wrongly predicts that *only* is felicitous in *both* (24a) and (25b). What that means is that the assumption in (20) needs to be revised no matter which scalar presupposition one adopts for *only*. The same holds for the cases with *even* in (26).

Thus, the salient sentence S_q in (25a) (*Two years ago John reviewed 5 papers*) can be safely taken to answer the same question that S_p (*Last year John reviewed 4 papers*) answers, since it answers a sub-question of the same super-question. S_q, then, obeys the constraint in (27) and hence must introduce an alternative to *p* into C.

In contrast, the salient sentence *Two years ago John wrote 3 papers* does not answer this question, and hence does not need to introduce an alternative to *p* into C. The real C set for (25a), then, is not (25'a) above, but rather (25"a) below:

(25") a. {Last year John reviewed 4 papers, Last year John reviewed 5 papers}

Importantly, in this set *p* is the weakest element, so the superlative scalar presupposition of *only* is met, correctly predicting its felicity.

In contrast, given the CT-FOCUS pattern on S_p, the salient question that is answered by (25b) is (29):

(29) How many papers did John write every year?
Sub-questions:
a. How many papers did John write two years ago?
b. How many papers did John write last year?....

In this case, the salient sentence *John wrote 3 papers last year* answers the question in the context (as opposed to *John reviewed 5 papers last year*, which does not), so the alternative to *p* which is based on it must enter C. Hence the C set is as in (25b"), where *p* is not the weakest element. This correctly predicts that *only* is infelicitous due to the failure of the superlative scalar presupposition, requiring *p* to be the weakest alternative in C:

(25") b. {Last year John wrote 4 papers, Last year John wrote 3 papers, ...}

Finally, as pointed out in Greenberg (2022), there are also cases where the super-question that both S_p and S_q answer (in order for S_q to necessarily introduce an alternative into C) is not necessarily of a CT-FOCUS structure. To illustrate compare (30) and (31):

(30) A: To get into this playground one needs to be at least 10 years old. Can John and Bill get in?
B: Yes. Both are old enough to get in. $[\text{John}]_{CT}$ is 13 and $[\text{Bill}]_F$ is (#only) $[11]_F$

(31) A: To get into this playground, one needs to be at least 10 years old. Can John and Bill get in? They are of the same age, right?
B: Yes, both are old enough to get in, but they are not of the same age: $[\text{John}]_{CT}$ is 13 and $[\text{Bill}]_F$ is (only) $[11]_F$

Only is infelicitous in (30) because the question that B tries to answer is *Can John and Bill get into the playground*? In this case, the comparison to the age limit (*10 years old*) cannot be ignored and is relevant for answering the question. Hence when forming alternatives to *p* (*Bill is 11 years old*) in this case, an alternative based on the salient sentence in the background (*To get into this playground one needs to be at least 10 years old*) must enter C, as can be seen in (30'):

(30') C: {John is 11 years old, John is 13 years old, John is 10 years old}

The structure of the super-question and the sub-questions in this case can be seen in (30"):

(30") Salient question: Can John and Bill get into the playground?
Sub-questions:
a. Can John get in? (What is the contextually relevant standard age for getting into the playground?, What is John's age?)
b. Can Bill get in? (What is the contextually relevant standard age for getting into the playground?, What is Bill's age?)

Thus, *p* is not the weakest alternative in C and *only* is correctly predicted to be infelicitous in (30).

In contrast, the alternative to *p* based on the salient sentence in (31) need not enter C, so C looks as in (31'):

(31') C: {John is 11 years old, John is 13 years old}

The reason is that the question that B tries to answer in (31) does not concern the age limit anymore, but is rather the one in (31"). Thus, the salient sentence *To get into this playground, one needs to be a least 10 years old* is not used to answer the question that S_p answers, and hence the alternative based on it can be left out of C.

(31″) Salient question: Are John and Bill of the same age?
Sub-questions:
a. What is John's age?
b. What is Bill's age?

Thus *only* is correctly predicted to be felicitous in (31) because p is the weakest alternative in C, so the superlative scalar presupposition can be met.

The answerability-based constraint in (27), then, seems to make correct predictions regarding the (in)felicity of *only* in the presence of salient sentences with material weaker than the associate. The same conclusion applies to the (in)felicity of *even* in the presence of salient sentences with material stronger than the associate (as in (26)).

We have reviewed, then, claims in Greenberg (2022) regarding an answerability-based constraint (namely (27)), which concerns salient sentences which must introduce alternatives into C. In the next sections we turn to cases indicating that the same answerability-based constraint can also constrain which salient sentences CAN introduce alternatives into C. We start with existing, as well as novel observations concerning the effects of salient sentences on the (dis)appearance of evaluativity effects of *only*.

7.4 The (Dis)appearance of Evaluativity Effects with *Only* Given Salient Sentences: Existing and novel observations

7.4.1 Background: The Cancelable Evaluativity Effects of *Only* and Their Derivation

Remember the data is Sect. 7.2.1 above, showing that *only* has a 'smallness' inference, so it is often infelicitous with 'large' associates. This is illustrated again in (32), when uttered in a 'Western Culture' context:

(32) a. John has only $[3]_F$ kids (inference: having 3 kids is 'a little')
b. John has (#only) $[13]_F$ kids

Observations like these were the basis for the claims that *only* conveys that *p* falls short of what is expected (Zeevat, 2009, 2013), is lower than most/sufficiently many alternatives (Klinedinst, 2004, 2005), or is lower than the expected answer to the Current Question (Beaver & Clark, 2008). Such claims have been often used to characterize *only* as **mirative** (following the terminology of DeLancy, 1997).

A broader characterization of *only*, proposed in Alxatib (2013, 2020) takes it to be **evaluative**, in the sense used in some of the literature on gradable adjectives, as in Solt (2011), Rett (2015). Given this characterization *only* presupposes that its prejacent indicates a quantity or degree that is below what ought to be the case, or below the contextual norm or standard on a relevant scale (and not only below what is 'expected'). We will mainly use the latter characterization, and talk about the 'smallness' inference of *only*, and its infelicity with 'large' associates as illustrating its **evaluativity** effects.

There have been also claims in the literature that the mirative / evaluative effects of *only* mirror-image that of *even*. This kind of hypothesis is supported by data as in (33):

(33) (How do you think John will do in the quiz?)
a. He won't do so well. I think he can only/#even solve $[6]_F$ problems
b. He will do great. I think he can even/#only solve $[6]_F$ problems

However, such an 'evaluative-antonymy' hypothesis for *only* and *even* is rejected in Greenberg (2022). Instead, it is argued that while an evaluative inference ('largeness') is indeed hardwired into the scalar presupposition of *even* (along the superlative inference discussed above) the mirror-imaged evaluative effects of *only*, namely its 'smallness' inferences and its infelicity with 'large' associates, are cancelable.

A major motivation for this claim is the observation that there is an 'evaluative asymmetry' between *only* and *even*, illustrated in (34)-(35):

(34) (The average price for a dress is $50)
  a. The blue dress is expensive. It costs $100. The red dress is cheaper—it is only [$75]$_F$. (So it is also expensive, but costs less than the red one.)
  b. The blue dress is cheap. It costs $20. The red dress is more expensive—it is (#even) [$30]$_F$. (So, it is also cheap but costs more than the red one)

(35) a. John is tall. He is 1.92 m. Bill is shorter—he is only [1.88 m]$_F$ (but he is still tall)
  b. John is short. He is 1.52 m. Bill is taller. He is (#even) [1.58 m]$_F$ (but he is still short)

As can be seen in these cases, for *only* (in the (a) sentences) to be felicitous, it is enough that *p* indicates a degree that is lower than a degree mentioned in a salient sentence, crucially—even if this degree itself counts as high relative to the contextual norm. In contrast, with *even* (in the (b) sentences) just taking *p* to indicate a degree higher than a previously uttered degree is NOT enough. For it to be felicitous the degree expressed must be also higher than the norm.

The picture which emerges from these observations, then, is that while the evaluativity, i.e., the sensitivity to standards, of *even* is non-cancelable and hardwired into its semantics,[7] that of *only* is cancelable.

But if this is so, what is it which gives rise to the so-common evaluativity effects of *only,* i.e., to 'smallness' inference and to its infelicity with 'large' associates?

As an answer to this question it is proposed in Greenberg (2022) that the evaluative effects of *only* can be derived from the interaction between two ingredients. The first is its superlative presupposition, phrased in (19) above, requiring that *p* is the weakest alternative in C. The second follows ideas in Krifka (2000) about the cancelable mirativity of *still* (as in *Lydia is still 3 years old,* indicating a 'small' age, i.e., younger than expected), and *already* (as in *Lydia is already 3 years old*, indicating a 'large' age, i.e., older than expected). Krifka (2000) takes *still* and *already* to indicate that their 'prejacents' mark the lowest and highest alternatives along a temporal scale, respectively. He adds to that a general pragmatic

[7] See Greenberg 2015, 2018 for a degree-based semantics of *even* which embodies this claim.

constraint on constructing sets of alternatives, namely that "the alternative propositions must be considered reasonable, or entertainable, at the current point in discourse" (p. 405). The combined derived effect of these two ingredients, proposes Krifka, is the mirative effects of *still* and *already*:

> (*still* and *already*) express a deviation from expected values in a particular direction ... 'already' gives rise to the understanding that Lydia's age is greater than may have been expected, and *still* that it is smaller than may have been expected. These meaning components are conversational implicatures that arise from the fact that only such alternatives are constructed that can plausibly be entertained. (Krifka, 2000 p. 405)

As proposed in Greenberg (2022), these ideas can be applied to deriving the evaluative effects of *only*. Consider, again (32a):

(32a) John has only $[3]_F$ kids (Inference: 3 kids is 'small')

Given the superlative scalar presupposition of *only*, *p* has to be the weakest alternative in C:

(32a') C: {*John has 2 kids John has 3 kids, John has 4 kids, John has 5 kids…*}

Assuming that all alternatives to *p* in C must be, using Krifka's (2000) terminology, 'plausibly entertainable', the resulting inference is that having 3 kids is lower than the plausibly entertainable number of kids in the context, and hence 'small'.

A similar reasoning can explain why *only* is odd when its associate is 'large', as in (32b):

(32b) John (??only) has $[12]_F$ kids (odd in a 'Western' context, where the standard number of kids is much lower)

The reason for the infelicity of *only* in this case is that if we try to construct a C set where *p* is the weakest element (to follow the superlative scalar presupposition), the result will be (32b'):

(32b′) C: {{John has 12 kids John has 13 kids, John has 14 kids, John has 15 kids…}

But constructing such a set, the pragmatic constraint on having only 'plausibly entertainable' alternatives in C is violated in the 'Western culture' context. In fact, in this context no alternative stronger than *p* is plausibly entertainable. Thus, the real C set for (32b) is (32b"), where no alternative stronger than *p* is a member:

(32b″) C: {John has 12 kids}

This leads to the infelicity of *only*, due to its vacuous at-issue operation. In particular, rejecting all stronger alternatives in C will not be possible since no stronger alternatives can exist in C.

7.4.2 The Puzzle: Salient Sentences Which Can vs. Cannot Cancel the Evaluativity Effects of *Only*

As pointed out in Sect. 7.2.1 above and repeated here, an observation made in Greenberg, 2022 is that the contexts in which the evaluativity effects of *only* typically arise are those where the sentences with *only* appear 'out of the blue' or as an answer to a question. In contrast, these evaluativity effects typically disappear when the sentences with *only* appear after discourse salient sentences with material larger than the associate of *only* in *p*. This is illustrated in (36) (see also (34a)-(35a) above for the same observation1):

(36) a. A: How many kids does John have?
B: He has (#only) $[12]_F$ kids
b. A: Bill has 13 kids
B: Wow, that's a lot! And what about John?
A: He has only $[12]_F$ kids

(37) a. (How tall is Bill?)—He is (#only) 2.05 m tall
b. John is 2.10 m tall. Bill is shorter—he is only $[2.05\ m]_F$

The salient sentences in the (b) cases, then, lead to the disappearance of the evaluativity effects of *only*, so it is felicitous with a 'large' material.

Crucially, however, as also pointed out in Sect. 7.2.1, not *any* salient material can do this job. This is seen again in (38)-(40):

(38) I have (#only) $[80]_F$ dresses in my wardrobe (cf. I have (only) 2_F dresses in my wardrobe)

(39) a. My sister has 100 dresses in her wardrobe. I myself have (only) $[80]_F$

b. I want to have 100 dresses in her wardrobe. I (only) have $[80]_F$

(40) a. Most of my family really loves fashion. My grandmother, for example, designed 100 dresses. I myself have (??only) $[80]_F$ dresses in my wardrobe (cf. I myself have only $[2]_F$ dresses)

b. My sister always dreamt that she will 100 dresses in her wardrobe. I myself have (??only) $[80]_F$ dresses (cf. I myself have only $[2]_F$ dresses)

The pattern we see in (38) and in (39) should be by now familiar: The 'out of the blue' (38) displays the infelicity of *only* with a large associate. In (39a,b), on the other hand, the presence of the salient sentences which mention '100 dresses' makes the association of *only* with *80* much better.

But crucially, the salient sentences in (40a,b), which again mention '100 dresses', do not have this effect: *only* keeps its oddness with the 'large' associate in these sentences, i.e., its evaluativity effects are not canceled despite the presence of the salient sentences.

Importantly, this odnness of *only* here seems indeed to be due to its evaluativity effect , i.e., by its oddness with a 'large' associate, and not because of some other reason. That this is so, is evidenced by the fact that *only* is perfectly felicitous in the versions the 'small' associate *2* in these examples.

A similar pattern can be seen with other examples, as in (41)-(43):

(41) My grandmother is (#only) $[95]_F$ years old (cf. She is only $[65]_F$ years old)

(42) a. A: My grandfather is 102 years old

B: Wow! That's amazing! And what about your grandmother?

A: She is (only) $[95]_F$ years old. That is – she is very old, but still younger than my grandfather

b. My grandmother really wishes she could be 100 years old now, (but) she is (only) $[95]_F$

(43) If I get to be 100 years old I will be very grateful. My grandmother, is (??only) $[95]_F$ now, and she feels the same (cf. My grandmother is only $[65]_F$ years old now and she feels the same)

Here too we can see that while the infelicity of a sentence with *only* with a large associate can be sometimes avoided when appearing after a sentence with an even larger material, as in (42a.b), in other cases, as in (43), the presence of such a salient sentence does not have this effect, and cannot 'save' *only*.

We repeat, then, the puzzle that this data poses for us, as phrased in Sect. 7.2.1 above:

(44) **Why is it that the evaluativity effects of *only* (namely its infelicity with 'large' associates) disappears in the presence of some salient sentences with an even larger material, but not with all such salient sentences?**
What is the factor which teases these two types of sentences apart?

The puzzle becomes more general if we follow the ideas reviewed above regarding the derivation of the default evaluativity effects of *only*: Given these ideas, these effects are due to the fact that alternatives indicating degrees which are 'too large' in the context are not plausibly entertainable (following Krifka's, 2000 terminology), and hence are not allowable in C. Thus, the (in)ability of salient sentences to cancel the evaluativity effects of *only* (i.e., to allow *only* to felicity associate with 'large' material) reflects the (in)ability of such salient sentences to construct alternatives into C, respectively.

Thus, the puzzle in (44) can be more generally reframed as in (45):

(45) What is the factor which teases apart those salient sentences which are able to introduce alternatives into C, from those salient sentences which cannot do so?

In the next section we will look at one potential answer to this puzzle, in terms of plausibility / entertainability, following ideas in Greenberg (2022). We will argue, however, that this answer does not seem to be enough for explaining the full range of data concerning the (in)felicity pattern with *only*. In Sect. 7.6 we will turn to a second answer to the puzzle, in terms of an answerability-based constraint. We will then propose, in Sect. 7.7, that such a constraint can also explain the presence vs. absence of Scalar Implicatures with 'complex' material.

7.5 A 'Plausibility' / 'Entertainability'-Based Explanation of the Data Is Not Enough

1. 7.5.1 An hypothesized 'Plausibility' / 'Entertainability'-Based Explanation of the Effect of Salient Sentences on the Membership of Alternatives in C.

The observation that the default infelicity of *only* with 'large' associates disappears in the presence of salient sentences with an even larger material (see again (36)) is explained in Greenberg (2022) by following Krifka's (2000) claims reviewed above, concerning the plausibility/entertainability constraints on alternatives. In particular, it is proposed in this paper that the evaluativity-canceling effect of salient sentences is due to the fact that "alternatives constructed based on such sentences can be considered plausible/entertainable at the current point in discourse simply because they have been just entertained". Thus, alternatives based on salient sentences can enter C even if they contain 'too large' material. This is in contrast to the 'out of the blue' utterances, where the basis for constructing alternatives is common ground expectations or standards so alternatives with 'too large' material are considered not plausibly entertainable, and hence not allowable into C.

Let us try to make this explanation a bit more precise by considering again the data in (36) above, repeated here:

(36) a. A: How many kids does John have?
B: He has (#only) $[12]_F$ kids
b. A: Bill has 13 kids
B: Wow, that's a lot! And what about John?
A: He has only $[12]_F$ kids

We can propose, for example, that by comparing John to Bill in (36b) the speaker alludes to the possibility that they belong to the same comparison class regarding number of kids, which sets a higher standard for number of kids than the one prevailing in the 'Western' context in which the sentence is uttered. This, in turn, can make the alternative *John has 13 kids* 'plausibly entertainable', in Krifka's, (2000) terminology.

Given this direction, the problem with the 'out of the blue' case in (36a), is that the alternative proposition *John has 13 kids* is true in possible worlds which are too remote from ours ('outlandish worlds' in Beltrama & Hanink's 2019 terminology). But once the salient sentence *Bill has 13 kids* is uttered and the proposition it denotes is proposed to be added to the Common Ground (in Farkas & Bruce's, 2010 terminology, it is on the TABLE), a higher standard for number of kids is proposed to hold, so the alternative proposition *John has 13 kids* can be taken to be true in worlds closer to ours. This is what makes this alternative proposition 'plausibly entertainable' and hence allowable to enter C. The result, in turn, is the felicity of *only* in (36b).

This kind of idea can be applied also to (38)-(39) above: *Only* is odd in (38) because the distributional standard regarding the number of dresses in one's wardrobe (determined by an average or a median number of dresses one has, cf. Solt (2011)) is originally a number of dresses which is much lower than 80. Hence, alternatives to *p* (*I have 80 dresses in my wardrobe*) with an even higher number (e.g., *I have 90 dresses in my wardrobe*) will be true in worlds which are too remote from ours. This is what makes such alternatives not plausibly entertainable and hence not allowable in C. This, in turn, leads to the vacuous operation of *only* in (38) and its infelicity, as proposed above.

In (39a), on the other hand, the presence of the sentence *My sister has 100 dresses in her wardrobe* in the context allows worlds in which the standard of dresses is high to be considered closer to an ideal world which is normal relative to our world. Hence alternatives like *I have 90 dresses in my wardrobe, I have 100 dresses in my wardrobe,* etc. can be considered now 'plausibly entertainable and allowable' in C. Such higher alternatives can be thus negated by the at-issue component of *only*, leading to its felicity.

As to (39b), here an alternative like *I have 90 dresses in my wardrobe* is not taken to be true in worlds that are 'most normal' relative to our worlds. However, we can propose that given the salient sentence *I want to have 100 dresses in her wardrobe* such alternative can be taken to be true in worlds where the speaker's wishes in w_0 become true. This is what makes such alternatives 'plausibly entertainable' and hence allowable into C.

More generally, given this proposal, a salient sentence can turn an alternative from 'non-entertainable' to 'entertainable' (and hence to allow it to be a member of C) by making this alternative true in worlds which are reasonably accessible from our world (e.g., true in 'normal' worlds, true in buletically accessible worlds, etc.).

7.5.1 A Plausibility-Entertainability Based Explanation Cannot Explain the Whole Data

Despite the intuitive appeal of the plausibility-entertainability constraint on salient sentences, examining a wider range of data it seems that this direction is not enough to account for it, at least not as a sole explanation. To illustrate the problem consider again (40a)-(40b), repeated here, where *only* is odd with a large associate:

(40) a. Most of my family really loves fashion. My grandmother, for example, designed 100 dresses. I myself have (??only) $[80]_F$ dresses in my wardrobe (cf. I myself have only [2]F dresses)

b. My sister always dreamt that she will 100 dresses in her wardrobe. I myself have (??only) $[80]_F$ dresses (cf. I myself have only $[2]_F$ dresses)

Starting with (40a), given that the claim that most of my family loves fashion, and that my grandmother designed 100 dresses, I can rather easily be considered a member of a comparison class which sets a standard higher than usual regarding the number of dresses one has in one's wardrobe. This can make an alternative like *I have 100 dresses in my wardrobe* true in a set of accessible worlds which given this context can be considered not too remote from our world, and hence plausibly entertainable and allowable into C.

As to (40b), if *My sister always dreamt of having 100 dresses in her wardrobe* is true in the actual world, then one could reasonably take me, her sister, to have similar wishes as well, i.e., to be a member of the comparison class regarding the number of dresses one has in her wish-worlds. In such a case, then, an alternative like *I have 90 dresses in my wardrobe* will be predicted to be true in my own wish-worlds as well, similarly to what we proposed above for (39b). This, again, will make this alternative 'plausibly entertainable' and hence an allowable member of C. It will then wrongly predict that *only* will be as felicitous in (40b), just as in (39b).

A similar problem to the proposal above is (43) above, repeated here:

(43) If I get to be 100 years old I will be very grateful. My grandmother, is (??only) $[95]_F$ now, and she feels the same (cf. My grandmother is only $[65]_F$ years old now and she feels the same)

Given the salient sentence *If I get to be 100 years old I will be very grateful* the possibility of being 100 years old can be taken to be true in the speaker's wish-worlds. It can then be taken to be plausibly true in the speaker's grandmother wish-worlds as well (who is reported to feel the same). Given the proposal above, then, the alternative *My grandmother is 100 years old* can be considered true in not too remote worlds and hence 'plausibly entertainable', and allowed in C. This, however, will wrongly predict *only* to be felicitous in (43).

We conclude, then, that at least in its present version, an entertainability-based explanation for the effect of salient sentences on allowing alternatives into C does not seem to be enough for explaining the full range of data above regarding the (in)felicity of *only* with large associate. In particular, this proposed explanation cannot tease apart those salient sentences which can introduce otherwise non-allowable alternatives into C from those which cannot.

Instead of this proposal, then, we want to examine now a different direction for teasing apart the two types of salient sentences, based on answerability.

7.6 A Proposal: An Answerability-Based Constraint on Alternatives-Introducing Salient Sentences

Remember that in Sect. 3 above we reviewed Greenberg's (2022) examination of the mirror-imaged infelicity of *only* and *even*, and the proposal that only those salient sentences which obey an answerability-based constraint must construct alternatives into C.

When we turn now to the effect of salient sentences on the (dis)appearance of evaluativity effects with *only*, we will follow this direction, but make a stronger claim, namely that only those salient sentences which obey the answerability-based constraint CAN construct alternatives into C.

In particular, we propose that in order for a salient sentence to be able to construct an alternative to *p* into C (and hence to cancel the evaluativity effects of *only*) it is not sufficient that this sentence will contain a constituent that can substitute the focused element in *p*, and not even that this sentence will make the alternative based on it 'plausibly entertainable'. Rather, the salient sentence should be one which answers the same question in the context that the *p*-sentence answers. This is summarized in (46):

(46) A focus alternative *q* to *p*, which is constructed based on a salient sentence S_q, can enter the set of alternatives to *p*, C, only if S_q answers the same question in the context that S_p answers

As in the discussion of the mirror-imaged infelicity patterns with *only* and *even* in Sect. 3, we will take two sentences to answer the same question Q if each answers a sub-question of Q. A simple case illustrating this proposal is (39a) above. We assume again a natural Contrasive Topic-FOCUS pattern in this sequence of sentences, as seen in (47):

(47) [My sister]$_{CT}$ has [100]$_F$ dresses in her wardrobe. [I myself]$_{CT}$ have only [80]$_F$ dresses in my wardrobe

Following again Büring (2003) and subsequent work, then, it is easy to see that S_q and S_p each answer a sub-question of the same super-question, as seen in (48):

(48) How many dresses do you and your sister have in your wardrobes?
Sub-questions:
How many dresses does your sister have in her wardrobe?
How many dresses do you have in your wardrobe?

As we also saw, though, the super-question that the sequence of sentences S_q and S_p answer is not always of a CT-FOCUS pattern. We think that the same can happen here. An example is (49):

(49) I want to have 100 dresses in my wardrobe, (but) I only have $[80]_F$

One super-question that we can be reasonably asked in the context is (50), where the sub-questions are indicated below:

(50) What makes you disappointed (w.r.t the number of your dresses)?
Sub-questions:
How many dresses do you want to have?
How many dresses do you have?

Another possible super-question is the polar question in (51). In this case the answers to the two sub-questions given in (49) by S_q and S_p help entail a negative answer to this polar question:

(51) Do you have the same number of dresses you want to have?
Sub-questions:
How many dresses do you want to have?
How many dresses do you have?

In contrast, consider again (40a), repeated here as (52), where *only* is infelicitous with a 'large' associate, i.e., where the salient sentence is not able to introduce an alternative into C and hence to cancel the evaluativity effects of *only*:

(52) Most of my family really loves fashion. My grandmother, for example, designed 100 dresses. I myself have (#only) $[80]_F$ dresses in my wardrobe (cf. I myself have only $[2]_F$ dresses in my wardrobe)

The problem here seems to be that it is hard to think of a super-question in the context that both S_q and S_p answer. For example the super-question in (53) seems odd:

(53) #Do you have the same number of dresses in your wardrobe as the number of dresses that your grandmother designed?
Sub-questions:
How many dresses did your grandmother design?
How many dresses do you have in your wardrobe?

Although technically S_p and S_q can help answer the super-question in (53), it is hard to think of a context where this kind of question will be asked. Similarly, consider again (40b) above, repeated here as (54):

(54) My sister wants to have 100 dresses in her wardrobe. I myself have (??only) $[80]_F$ dresses in my wardrobe (cf. I myself have only $[2]_F$ dresses in my wardrobe)

What question can both S_q *(My sister wants to have 100 dresses)* and S_p *(I have* 80_F *dresses)* answer? Two possible such questions are seen in (55) and (56). Again, however, finding a context where such questions will be asked seems hard, and they sound odd:

(55) #What is the number of dresses that your sister wants and that you have?
(56) #Do you have the same number of dresses that your sister wants to have?

If this direction is on the right track, the prediction is that if we can construct contexts where such questions will be reasonably asked, *only* will be better in the corresponding sequence.

This prediction seems to be borne out. Suppose, for example, that I was always jealous of my sister, and felt inferior relative to her. As a result, I decided that whatever my sister wants to have, I will immediately try to achieve in reality, so as to make her jealous of me instead. In such a context a question like (56) sounds reasonable to ask, and importantly, *only* becomes much better in (54) above, indicating that my goal (having the same number of dresses that my sister wants) has NOT been achieved.

Notice again that in both (52) and (54) *only* is perfectly felicitous with the 'small' associate *2*. This is significant as it indicates two points: First, there is no independent problem with using *only* in these structures. Second, and more importantly, the felicity of *only* with the 'small' associate is not because using it makes the 'odd' super-questions like (53), (54) or (55) easier to accommodate. Rather, this is because constructing alternatives to *I have 2 dresses in my wardrobe* can be done with no need to accommodate such super-questions to start with: Unlike the alternatives to *I have 80 dresses in my wardrobe*, with a 'small' associate the alternatives (e.g. *I have 3 dresses in my wardrobe I have 4 dresses in my wardrobe*, etc.) are plausibly entertainable, and are hence easily allowed into C based on the lexicon, with no need to rely on previously uttered salient sentences which obey the answerability constraint.

To summarize, so far we observed that while some salient sentences can cancel the evaluativity effects of *only* (leading the felicity of *only* with 'large' associates), not all of them can do so. Given our discussion of evaluativity effects in Sect. 7.4, we take this to mean that the former type of sentences, but not the latter, can introduce alternatives based on them into C. We argued that the difference between these two types of salient sentences cannot be characterized in terms of the entertainability of the alternatives based on them. Instead, we proposed that 'too large' alternatives can enter C only if they are constructed based on salient sentences which obey the answerability-based constraint in (46).

Given this constraint it is not enough that such salient sentences have a constituent which can substitute the focused element in *p*. Nor it is enough that the alternatives based on these sentences answer the same super-question that *p* answers. Rather, these salient sentences themselves need to answer the same super-question that the *p*-sentence answers. In cases where such a super-question does not seem reasonable to be asked in the context, it will be hard to accommodate it, and hence will be hard to take the salient sentence to obey the constraint and to construct an alternative into C.

Notice, then, that the distinction between those salient sentences which can vs. those which cannot introduce alternatives into C indirectly reduces to the distinction between those super-questions which can vs. those which cannot be reasonably asked in a context. A direction which might be useful for making this latter distinction more precise and testable is to follow ideas, e.g., Van Rooy's (2003), and related work, and try to rank questions by their helpfulness in the context, and more technically by their expected utility given the goals and information states of the interlocutors in a context. Such a task, though, is beyond the scope of the present chapter. We leave this and other possible directions for making the answerability-based constraint more precise to future research, and at this point continue to use its informal characterization above.

With this in mind, the next question that the proposal developed here raises is whether there is any additional empirical motivation for it. That is, is there any other alternative-sensitive phenomena, besides the (dis)appearance of evaluativity-based effects of *only*, where a salient sentence cannot introduce alternatives into C unless it obeys an answerability-based constraint of the sort developed here? Obviously, if no such phenomenon can be found, the proposal above should be seriously reconsidered.

Luckily, though, it seems that such an additional phenomenon can be found, namely the effect of salient sentences on the presence vs. absence of scalar implicatures with 'complex' material. We have already made some initial observations regarding this phenomenon in Sect. 7.2.2 above. We now turn to examining it in more detail.

7.7 The Relevance of the Answerability-Based Constraints to Scalar Implicatures

7.7.1 A Brief Background: Symmetry, Complexity and the Role of Salient Sentences

It is well established in the literature that not all potential scalar implicatures are actually attested. An illustrative example is (57), in which (a), but not (b) is an attested implicature:

(57) Bill was required to answer some of the questions
Scalar Implicatures:
a. He was not required to answer all of the questions
b. ~~He was not required to answer some but not all of the questions~~

(57) illustrates the symmetry problem for scalar implicatures (see Breheny et al., 2018; Chierchia et al., 2011; Fox & Katzir, 2011; Gotzner & Romoli, 2021; Katzir, 2014; Trinh & Haida, 2015; Trinh, 2019 etc.). An influential approach to deal with this problem is based on complexity. In particular Fox and Katzir (2011), Katzir (2014) propose that in general only material which is at most as complex as the focus element can substitute it in creating alternatives. This constraint is met when *some* is substituted by *all*, which are of the same complexity. The alternative is then negated by the covert *only*-like operator *exh* (see Chierchia et al., 2011 and much subsequent work). This leads to the implicature in (57a). In contrast, the constraint is not met with *some but not all,* which is more complex than *some,* so the implicature in (57b) is not attested.

However, as was also pointed out in this literature, the complexity-based constraint can be overridden when the more complex material is based on salient sentences, e.g., those which were previously uttered. This is illustrated by an example from Matsumoto (1995) in (58):

(58) It was warm yesterday, and it is a little bit more than warm today

Importantly, (58) can have the scalar implicature "It was a little bit more than warm yesterday". It is argued, then, that the salience of *a little bit more than warm* is what allows it to substitute *warm*, although it is clearly more complex than it.

Following such observations, then, Katzir (2014) formulates a complexity-based algorithm for formal alternatives, with a substitution source as in (1) above, repeated here as (59):

(59) X′ is at most complex as X if X′ can be derived from X by successive steps in which a sub-constituent *z* of X is replaced with an element of the substation source for s in C, SS(z,C), where () SS(z,C), is the union of
   a. The lexicon
   b. The sub-constituents of z
   c. **The set of salient constituents in C (that is, constituents of the structures of utterances made in recent discourse).** (My emphasis)

Indeed, as shown in Katzir (2014), this proposal correctly predicts that in cases *some but not all* is present in the salient sentence before the one with *some*, it can substitute *some* despite being more complex. That this prediction is borne out is seen in (60), where unlike what we saw in (57), both implicatures are attested:

(60) John was required to answer some but not all of the questions
   Bill was required to answer some of the questions
   Implicatures:
   a. He was not required to answer all of the questions
   b. He was not required to answer some but not all of the questions

7.7.2 Back to the Puzzling Data with Scalar Implicatures

Against this background, we now turn back to the puzzling cases pointed out in Sect. 7.2.2 above, and repeated here. Consider first (61):

(61) Some but not all of the kids arrived to class on time
   The teacher required that they answer some of the questions
   Implicatures:
   a. The teacher did not require them to answer all of the questions
   b. b. ~~The teacher did not require them to answer some but not all of the questions.~~

The puzzle is that unlike what we have just seen with (60), in this case only the implicature in (61a) arises. That is, the implicature in (61b) does not arise despite the fact that *some but all* is made salient in the first sentence.

One might attempt to attribute the difference between (60) and (61) to the fact that, unlike (60), where the nominal argument of *some* and *some but not all*, namely *questions*, is the same in both sentences, in (61) the nominal arguments of the quantifiers are different (*kids* vs. *questions*).

Crucially, however, we can also find such cases where the nominal arguments in the first and second sentences are the same, as in (62). Here the salience of *some but not all of the questions* cannot be used to substitute *some of the questions*, as can be seen from the fact that the implicature in (62b) is not attested:

(62) (Context: I spent 3 weeks at a math camp last year. We got 100 questions to solve.)
On the first day the instructors gave us some but not all of the questions. (The rest were given to us on the second day.)
The instructors required that we submit the answers to some of the questions already by the end of the first week
Implicatures:
a. They did not require that we submit the answers to all of the questions by the end of the first week

~~They did not require that we submit the answers to~~

~~some but not all of the questions by the end of the first~~

~~week.~~

This kind of data, then, poses a puzzle for current theories of scalar implicatures. We repeat the puzzle phrased in Sect. 7.2.2 here:

(63) **Why is it that scalar implicatures which are based on substitution of focused material with more complex material can arise in the presence of some salient sentences with this complex material, but not with all such salient sentences?**
What is the factor which teases these two types of salient sentences apart?

7.7.3 Alternatives with More Complex Material Are Allowable into the Set Only if the Salient Sentences Are Based on Obey the Answerability Constraint

In Sect. 7.6 above we proposed an answerability-based constraint on alternatives-introducing salient sentences, based on the (dis)appearance of evaluativity effects of *only* with some (but not all!) salient sentences.

If a constraint along these lines is operative with scalar implicatures as well, then in case *some but not all* is part of a salient sentence which does not answer the same question that the sentence with *some* answers, then this sentence will not be able to construct alternatives into C, crucially, despite being salient. In such a case no implicature along the lines of (b) above, where the alternative with *some but not all* is negated, will be attested.

We think that this is indeed what accounts for the data above. Consider first (60), where the (b) implicature is attested. In this case the salient sentence S_q and S_p can be taken to answer two sub-questions of the same super-question in the context, as seen in (64):

(64) How many questions were John and Bill required to answer?
Sub-questions:
How many questions was John required to answer?
How many questions was Bill required to answer?

The salient sentence, S_q, then, can be indeed taken in this case to answer the same question in the context that S_p is used to answer. Thus, the answerability-based constraint is met, and S_q can be used to introduce an alternative into C.

In contrast, consider (61). Here it is much harder to find a single super-questions with two sub-questions that each of two sentences (the salient S_q and the prejacent of *exh,* S_p) answer, namely *How many of the kids arrive on time?* And *How many of the questions did the teacher require us to answer?* Notice that a CT-FOCUS question does not seem to work here (*??How many kids arrived on time and questions were required by the teacher to answer*?), and broader questions (e.g., *What happened in class today?*) are problematic as well: Such a question would require much more narrowing down the stack to get to these sub-questions. For example, to get to the sub-question *How many of the kids arrive on time?* answered by S_q we will first need to ask 'higher' questions like *What happened with the kids today? What happened with the arrival of the kids today? What happened with the time of arrival of the kids today?* And only then *How many of the kids arrived on time?* Similarly, to get to the sub-question *How many of the questions did the teacher require us to answer?* we will first need to ask *What happened with the teacher today? What did the teacher require today? What did the teacher require today regarding the questions he gave us?* etc.). Thus, unlike what happens in (60), no reasonable single super-question in the context seems to have sub-questions that both S_q and S_p answer. A similar case can be made for (62).

We conclude, then, that while alternatives where an element is substituted by more complex material are indeed allowable into the set of alternatives if they are based on constituents made salient by previously uttered sentences, as proposed by Katzir, 2014 in the 'substitution source' in (59), this can only happen if the previously uttered sentences obey the answerability constraint developed in Sect. 7.6 above.

7.8 Conclusion

In this chapter we examined two types of novel data regarding salient (i.e., previously uttered) sentences, which on the surface do not seem to be very much related. The first is the effect of some, but crucially not all salient sentences on the disappearance of evaluativity ('smallness') effects of *only*, namely on the (in)felicity of *only* with 'large' focus associates. The second is the ability of some, but crucially not all salient sentences to lead to scalar implicatures with 'complex' substituting material, which are otherwise not attested.

We proposed that there is, in fact, an important similarity between the two types of data, namely that given current theories in both cases the salient sentences are supposed to be the only possible source of alternatives to p. In other words, in such cases alternatives to p cannot be based on the lexicon, due to clashes with some general—contextual or formal—constraints on forming actual alternatives.

Therefore, the novel observations we made indicate that, unlike what is predicted, only some, but crucially not all salient sentences can be used to construct alternatives into the set which are not allowable into it without them. We took this to indicate that in both kinds of phenomena, there are constraints on which salient sentences can vs. cannot be used to introduce alternatives into the set.

Importantly, we proposed that one and the same constraint, namely an answerability-based one, seems to be at work with both phenomena. In particular, in both cases salient sentences can only introduce alternatives into the set if they answer the same question in the context that the prejacent sentence answers, and more technically, only if there is a single super-question in the context, or one which is easy to accommodate, such that the salient sentence and the prejacent answer a sub-question of.

Integrating this proposal with the one made based on the mirror-imaged infelicity of *only* and *even* in Greenberg (2022), we conclude that alternatives based on salient sentences which obey the answerability-based constraint can and must be in C, crucially even if these alternatives (a) include material more complex than the original focused material (b) are not otherwise 'contextually plausible' and (c) lead to presupposition failure (e.g., to the failure of the 'superlative' scalar presuppositions of *only* and *even*).

The discussion above leaves several directions for future research. We would like to end this chapter by mentioning four such directions. First, as pointed out above, a more precise characterization of the answerability-based constraint still needs to be developed. Second, to the extent that the answerability-based constraint above is on the right track, we would expect to find its effects with additional alternative-sensitive phenomena. Is this indeed the case? Third, it will be interesting to examine whether the proposed constraint on alternative-introducing salient sentences has wider implication regarding the algorithm for constructing alternatives, and the division of labor between contextual and formal constraints on the set of alternatives. Fourth, an assumption which underlies our proposal is that when a salient sentence need not be the one which introduces alternatives to *p*, it is not subject to the answerability constraint. This can happen either because there is another possible source for the alternatives (e.g., the lexicon), or because no alternatives to p are required (e.g., because S_p does not involve any alternative-sensitive operator). In such cases, then, the prediction is that although S_p follows the salient sentence, the two sentences can be used to answer two unrelated questions, i.e., a 'question shift' can occur. To see whether such a prediction is borne out we need a precis way to identify and to model question shifts, and an understanding of the contextual constraints on this phenomenon (see Greenberg, 2022; Simons et al., 2010 for some discussions).

Acknowledgements For constructive comments regarding the observations and ideas in this paper and in previous versions of it, I would like to thank Sam Alxatib, Moshe Elyashiv Bar-Lev, Luka Crnič, Nicole Gotzner, Aynat Rubinstein, Benjamin Spector, Carla Umbach, Hedde Zeijlstra and Malte Zimmermann. Special thanks to Roni Katzir for discussions, suggestions and enjoyable brainstorming. Work on this paper was supported by ISF grant 682/22. All remaining errors are mine.

References

Alxatib, Sam. (2013). *'Only' and association with negative antonyms.* PhD thesis, MIT.

Alxatib, S. (2020). *Focus, evaluativity and antonymy.* Springer.

Beaver, D., & Brady, C. (2008). *Sense and sensitivity: How focus determines meaning.* (Explorations in Semantics). Blackwell.

Beltrama, A., & Emiliy, H. (2019). Marking imprecision, expressing surprise. *Like* between hedging and mirativity. *Journal of Linguistics. 55(1)*, 1–34

Breheny, R., Klinedinst, N., Romoli, J., & Sudo, Y. (2018). The symmetry problem: Current theories and prospects. *Natural Language Semantics, 26*, 85–110. https://doi.org/10.1007/s11050-017-9141-z

Büring, D. (2003). On D-trees, beans, and b-accents. *Linguistics and Philosophy, 26*, 511–545. https://doi.org/10.1023/A:1025887707652

Charnavel, I. (2017). How French sheds new light on scalar particles. In S. Perpiñán, D. Heap, I. Moreno-Villamar, & A. Soto-Corominas (Eds.),

Romance Languages and Linguistic Theory 11: Selected papers from the 44th Linguistic Symposium on Romance Languages (LSRL), London, Ontario (pp. 53–75). John Benjamins.

Chierchia, G., Fox, D., & Spector, B. (2011). The grammatical view of scalar implicatures and the relationship between semantics and pragmatics. In C. Maienborn, P. Portner, & K. von Heusinger (Eds.), *Handbook of semantics* (Vol. 3, pp. 2297–2331). Mouton de Gruyter.

Coppock, E., & Beaver, D. (2014). Principles of the exclusive muddle. *Journal of Semantics, 31*(3), 371–432. https://doi.org/10.1093/jos/fft007

Crnič, L. (2012). Focus particles and embedded exhaustification. *Journal of Semantics, 30*(4), 533–558. https://doi.org/10.1093/jos/ffs018

DeLancey, S. (1997). Mirativity: The grammatical marking of unexpected information. *Linguistic Typology, 1*, 33–52. https://doi.org/10.1515/lity.1997.1.1.33

Farkas, D. F., & Bruce, K. B. (2010). On reacting to assertions and polar questions. *Journal of semantics, 27*, 1–118.

Fox, D., & Katzir, R. (2011). On the characterization of alternatives. *Natural Language Semantics, 19*, 87–107. https://doi.org/10.1007/s11050-010-9065-3

Fraundorf, S. H., Benjamin, A. S., & Watson, D. G. (2013). What happened (and what didn't): Discourse constraints on encoding of plausible alternatives. *Journal of Memory and Language, 69*(3), 196–227. https://doi.org/10.1016/j.jml.2013.06.003

Gotzner, Nicole. (2015). What's included in the set of alternatives? Psycholinguistic evidence for a permissive view. In *Proceedings of Sinn und Bedeutung* 19, eds. Eva Csipak and Hedde Zeijlstra, 252–267.

Gotzner, N., Wartenburger, I., & Spalek, K. (2016). The impact of focus particles on the recognition and rejection of contrastive alternatives. *Language and Cognition, 8*(1), 59–95. https://doi.org/10.1017/langcog.2015.25

Gotzner, N., & Spalek, K. (2019). The life and times of focus alternatives: Tracing the activation of alternatives to a focused constituent in language comprehension. *Language and Linguistics Compass, 13*(2), e12310. https://doi.org/10.1111/lnc3.12310

Gotzner, N., & Romoli, J. (2021). Meaning and alternatives. *Annual Reviews in Linguistics, 8*, 213–234. https://doi.org/10.1146/annurev-linguistics-031220-012013

Greenberg, Y. (2015). *Even*, comparative likelihood and gradability. In T. Brochhagen, F. Roelofsen, & N. Theiler (Eds.), *Proceedings of the Amsterdam Colloquium 20* (pp. 147–156). UVA.

Greenberg, Y. (2016). A novel problem for the likelihood-based semantics of *even*. *Semantics and Pragmatics* 9, article 2: 1–28. https://doi.org/10.3765/sp.9.2

Greenberg, Y. (2018). A revised, gradability semantics for *even*. *Natural Language Semantics, 26*, 51–83. https://doi.org/10.1007/s11050-017-9140-0

Greenberg, Yael. (2019). *Even* and *only*: Arguing for parallels in scalarity and in constructing focus alternatives. In Maggie Baird & Jonathan Pesetsky (Eds.), *Proceedings of NELS 49*, (pp. 45–60). GSLA.

Greenberg, Y. (2022). On the scalar antonymy of *only* and *even*. *Nat Lang Semantics, 30*, 415–452. https://doi.org/10.1007/s11050-022-09200-x

Greenberg, Yael and Dina Orenstein. (2016). Typologies for *even*-like and *only*-like particles: Evidence from Modern Hebrew. Paper presented at ESSLLI 28, Bozen-Bolzano, Italy, August 15–26, 2016.

Guerzoni, Elena. (2003). *Why* even *ask? On the pragmatics of questions and the semantics of answers*. PhD thesis, MIT.

Homer, Vincent. (2019). That's *all*. *Proceedings of WCCFL* 36, eds. Richard Stockwell, Maura O'Leary, Zhongshi Xu, and Z.L. Zhou, 1–21. Somerville, MA: Cascadilla Proceedings Project.

Horn, L. (1969). A presuppositional analysis of only and even. In R. I. Binnick, A. Davison, G. M. Green, & J. L. Morgan (Eds.), *The 5th annual meeting of the Chicago Linguistic Society* (pp. 98–107). Chicago Linguistic Society.

Karttunen, L., & Peters, S. (1979). Conventional implicature. In D. A. Dinneen & C.-K. Oh (Eds.), *Syntax and semantics 11: Presupposition* (pp. 1–56). Academic Press.

Katzir, Roni. (2014). On the roles of markedness and contradiction in the use of alternative. In *Semantics, pragmatics, and the case of scalar implicatures*, ed. Salvatore Pistoia Reda, 40–71. London: Palgrave.

Kay, Paul. (1990). *Even*. *Linguistics and Philosophy* 13(1): 59–111. https://doi.org/10.1007/BF00630517

Kim, C. S., Gunlogson, C., Tanenhaus, M. K., & Runner, J. T. (2015). Context-driven expectations about focus alternatives. *Cognition, 139*, 28–49. https://doi.org/10.1016/j.cognition.2015.02.009

Klinedinst, N. (2004). Only scalar *only*. A paper presented at the Presupposition & Implicature Workshop, Paris, October 5, 2004.

Klinedinst, N. (2005). *Scales and* only. Master's thesis, UCLA.

Krifka, Manfred. (2000). Alternatives for aspectual particles: Semantics of *still* and *already*. In Lisa J. Conathan, Jeff Good, Darya Kavitskaya, Alyssa B. Wulf, and Alan C.L. Yu (Eds.), *Proceedings of the twenty-sixth annual meeting of the Berkeley Linguistics Society* (pp. 401–412). https://doi.org/10.3765/bls.v26i1.1125

Liu, M. (2017). Varieties of alternatives: Mandarin focus particles. *Linguistics and Philosophy, 40*, 61–95. https://doi.org/10.1007/s10988-016-9199-y

Magri, Giorgio. (2011). Another argument for embedded scalar implicatures based on oddness in downward entailing environments. *Semantics and Pragmatics* 4, article 6: 1–51. https://doi.org/10.3765/sp.4.6

Yo., & Matsumoto. (1995). The conversational condition on Horn Scales. *Linguistics and Philosophy, 18*, 21–60.

Orenstein, Dina. (2016). *The semantics, pragmatics and focus sensitivity of exclusive particles in Modern Hebrew.* PhD thesis, Bar Ilan University.

Orenstein, Dina and Yael Greenberg. (2013). A flexible exclusive particle: The case of the Hebrew 'be-sax ha-kol' (≈ 'all in all'). In *Proceedings of Sinn und Bedeutung* 17, eds. E. Chemla, V. Homer, and G. Winterstein, 381–397.

Rett, J. (2015). *The semantics of evaluativity*. Oxford University Press.

Roberts, Craige. (1996). Information structure in discourse: Towards an integrated formal theory of pragmatics. *Semantics and Pragmatics* 5, article 6: 1–69. https://doi.org/10.3765/sp.5.6

Roberts, Craige. (2011). *only*: A case study in projective meaning. *Baltic International Yearbook of Cognition, Logic and Communication* 6 (1), article 14. https://doi.org/10.4148/biyclc.v6i0.1581

Rooth, Mats. (1985). *Association with focus*. PhD dissertation, University of Massachusetts at Amherst.

Rooth, M. (1992). A theory of focus interpretation. *Natural Language Semantics, 1*, 75–116. https://doi.org/10.1007/BF02342617a

Rooth, Mats. (1996). Focus. In *The handbook of contemporary semantic theory*, ed. Shalom Lappin, 271–297. Hoboken, NJ: Blackwell Reference.

Simons, Mandy, Judith Tonhauser, David Beaver, and Craige Roberts. (2010). What projects and why. In *Proceedings of Semantics and Linguistic Theory (SALT)* 20, eds. Nan Li and David Lutz, 309–327.

Spector, Benjamin. (2007). Aspects of the pragmatics of plural morphology: On higher-order implicatures. In *Presupposition and implicature in compositional semantics*, eds. U. Sauerland and P. Stateva. (Palgrave Studies in Pragmatics, Language and Cognition.) London: Palgrave Macmillan. https://doi.org/10.1057/9780230210752_9

Trinh, T. (2019). Exhaustification and contextual restriction. *Frontiers in Communication, 4*, 47. https://doi.org/10.3389/fcomm.2019.00047

Trinh, T., & Haida, A. (2015). Constraining the derivation of alternatives. *Natural Language Semantics, 23*, 249–270. https://doi.org/10.1007/s11050-015-9115-y

Van Rooy, R. (2003). Questioning to resolve decision problems. *Linguistics and Philosophy, 26*, 727–763.

Xiang, Y. (2020). Function alternations of the Mandarin particle *dou*: Distributor, free choice licensor, and 'even.' *Journal of Semantics, 37*(2), 171–217. https://doi.org/10.1093/jos/ffz018

Zeevat, Henk. (2009). "Only" as a mirative particle. In *Proceedings of Focus at the Syntax–Semantics Interface,* eds. Arndt Riester and Edgar Onea, 121–141. Stuttgart: University of Stuttgart.

Zeevat, Henk. (2013). Expressing surprise by particles. In *Beyond expressives: Explorations in use-conditional meaning,* eds. Daniel Gutzmann and Hans-Martin Gärtner, 297–320. (Current Research in the Semantics/Pragmatics Interface, Vol. 28). Leiden: Brill. https://doi.org/10.1163/9789004183988_010

8

Any vs. *Or* and Indefinites vs. Modals

Sam Alxatib and Andreea Nicolae

8.1 Introduction

The question we ask in this paper is why *any* is licensed under possibility modals like *can* and *allowed*, but not licensed under indefinites like *some people* or adverbs of existential force like *sometimes*, as shown by the contrast below.

For discussion and feedback, we thank Anamaria Fălăuş, Takanobu Nakamura, Orin Percus, Yasutada Sudo, and audiences at the Nantes University SynSem seminar, and the 10th MACSIM in College Park, MD. A. Nicolae was supported by the DFG grant NI-1850/2-1.

S. Alxatib (✉)
CUNY Graduate Center, New York, NY, USA
e-mail: alxatib@alum.mit.edu

A. Nicolae
ZAS Berlin, Berlin, Germany
e-mail: nicolae@leibniz-zas.de

N. Gotzner et al. (eds.), *Alternatives in Grammar and Cognition*, Palgrave Studies in Pragmatics, Language and Cognition, https://doi.org/10.1007/978-3-031-76676-3_8

(1) a. Mary is allowed to bring any of her friends.
    b. Bill can take any of these subway lines to get to work.
    c. Our students can take any language class as elective.

(2) a. *Some people brought any of their friends.
    b. *Bill sometimes took any of these subway lines to work.
    c. *Some of our students take any language class as elective.

To our knowledge this question has not been discussed in the literature, and exhaustification-based accounts of *any* do not provide an answer to it. In this paper, we will propose an answer on which (a) exhaustification is dynamicized, so that an exhaustified sentence is dynamically conjoined with (the negations of) its formal alternatives, and (b) the formal alternatives to an indefinite/adverb must be anaphoric to the indefinite/adverb, while the formal alternatives to a modal may not be anaphoric to the modal.[1]

8.2 Background

The theoretical perspective we adopt is one where *any* denotes an existential quantifier that obligatorily projects subdomain alternatives, i.e., other existential quantifiers that have a subset of the original as their domain (Chierchia, 2013; Krifka, 1995, among many others). Under this view, the logical relation between *any* and its formal alternatives is therefore the same as the relation between a disjunction and its disjuncts. We will use this analogy throughout the paper to describe our basic theoretical assumptions and to explain our proposal.

8.2.1 Descriptive Background

Or is known to license free choice inferences (FC) under possibility modals, as shown in (3a–b). This is one of the contexts in which a disjunctive sentence intuitively implies its disjunct alternatives. The same inferential pattern is found in negated sentences, shown in (3c), as well as other DE-contexts like the *if*-clauses in (3d).

[1] This aspect of the proposal builds on the work of Sudo (2016, 2023).

(3) a. Mary is allowed to invite Susan or Louise.
$\rightsquigarrow$ Mary is allowed to invite Susan
$\rightsquigarrow$ Mary is allowed to invite Louise
b. Bill can take the B or the Q to get to work.
$\rightsquigarrow$ Bill can take the B to get to work
$\rightsquigarrow$ Bill can take the Q to get to work
c. Bill will not take the B or the Q to go to work.
$\rightsquigarrow$ Bill will not take the B to go to work
$\rightsquigarrow$ Bill will not take the Q to go to work
d. If Mary invites Susan or Louise, Bill will want to come.
$\rightsquigarrow$ If Mary invites Susan, Bill will want to come
$\rightsquigarrow$ If Mary invites Louise, Bill will want to come

Sentences where *any* appears in the same contexts—under possibility modals (4a–b) and under DE operators (4c–d)—are acceptable, and in parallel to the disjunctive sentences in (3), they imply their subdomain alternatives.

(4) a. Mary is allowed to invite any of her friends.
$\rightsquigarrow$ Mary is allowed to invite $friend_1$
$\rightsquigarrow$ Mary is allowed to invite $friend_2$, etc.
b. Bill can take any of these subway lines to go to work.
$\rightsquigarrow$ Bill can take $line_1$ to go to work
$\rightsquigarrow$ Bill can take $line_2$ to go to work, etc.
c. Bill will not take any of these subway lines to go to work.
$\rightsquigarrow$ Bill will not take $line_1$ to go to work
$\rightsquigarrow$ Bill will not take $line_2$ to go to work, etc.
d. If Mary invites any of her friends, Bill will want to come.
$\rightsquigarrow$ If Mary invites $friend_1$, Bill will want to come
$\rightsquigarrow$ If Mary invites $friend_2$, Bill will want to come, etc.

Of course, there are many sentence types that host *or* and that do not imply their disjunct alternatives. (5a), where *or* appears unembedded, is an example, as are (5b–c) where *or* appears in the scope of a universal quantifier and a necessity modal, respectively.

(5) a. Bill took the B or the Q today.
$\not\rightsquigarrow$ Bill took the B today
$\not\rightsquigarrow$ Bill took the Q today
b. Everyone took the B or the Q today.
$\not\rightsquigarrow$ Everyone took the B today
$\not\rightsquigarrow$ Everyone took the Q today
c. Mary needs to invite Susan or Louise.
$\not\rightsquigarrow$ Mary needs to invite Susan
$\not\rightsquigarrow$ Mary needs to invite Louise

Analogous sentences to these in which *any* replaces *or* are unacceptable.

(6) a. *Bill took any of these subway lines today.
b. *Everyone took any of these subway lines today.
c. *Mary needs to invite any of her friends.

From this, and building on Crnič (2019, 2022) (who in turn builds on Ladusaw [1979], Krifka [1999], Lahiri [1998], Chierchia [2013] among others), we write the following informal generalization. The generalization says that an *any* sentence is acceptable whenever the equivalent sentence where *any* is replaced with the equivalent disjunction implies its disjunct alternatives.

(7) **The *any-or* generalization**:
$[_S \ldots [any\ NP] \ldots]$ is acceptable whenever $[_S \ldots [P \text{ or } Q] \ldots]$ implies $[_S \ldots P \ldots]$ and implies $[_S \ldots Q \ldots]$.

(3) and (4) illustrate the positive side of (7): in (3) the disjunctive sentences imply their disjuncts, and in (4) *any* is licensed. (5) and (6) illustrate the negative side: the sentences in (5) do not imply their disjuncts, and in (6) *any* is not licensed.

Our concern is the set of examples in (8–9), which at first sight seem to run counter to the generalization in (7). Even though the *or*-sentences in (8) entail their disjunct alternatives, the *any*-analogs in (9) are not acceptable, contrary to what the generalization in (7) would have us expect.

(8) a. Some people brought their children or their pets (to the picnic).
$\rightsquigarrow$ Some people brought their children
$\rightsquigarrow$ Some people brought their pets
b. Bill sometimes took the B or the Q to work.
$\rightsquigarrow$ Bill sometimes took the B
$\rightsquigarrow$ Bill sometimes took the Q
c. Some of our students take French or German as elective.
$\rightsquigarrow$ Some of our students take French as elective
$\rightsquigarrow$ Some of our students take German as elective

(9) a. *Some people invited any of their friends. (repeated from (2))
b. *Bill sometimes took any of these subway lines to get to work.
c. *Some of our students take any language class as elective.

8.2.2 Theoretical Background

As we mentioned earlier, the generalization in (7) is based on Crnič's (2019) theory of *any*-licensing. The basics of the theory are as follows. *Any* denotes an existential quantifier over an implicitly provided domain *D* and has as formal alternatives existential quantifiers over subsets of *D*. *Any*, to its "subdomain" alternatives, is therefore like *or* is to its disjuncts. What is special about *any* is that it is acceptable only in constituents that are maximally informative among their subdomain alternatives, that is, constituents whose interpretation entails those of the alternatives (see 10). There is no such licensing condition on *or*, hence its unrestricted distribution compared to *any*.

(10) **The *Any* condition (Crnič 2019)**:
A DP headed by *any* is acceptable only if its domain is dominated by a constituent that is Strawson downward-entailing with respect to it, where ...

A constituent *S* is Strawson downward-entailing with respect to the domain *D* of an *any*-DP it dominates iff every D' such that $[\![D']\!] \subseteq [\![D]\!]$, $[\![S]\!] \models_s [\![S[D \rightarrow D']]\!]$ (where $S[D \rightarrow D']$ is identical to *S* except that every occurrence of *D* in *S* is replaced with an occurrence of D').

From the semantic/formal parallels between *any* and *or*, and given the additional constraint on the distribution of *any* in (10), we can make sense of most of the datapoints we saw earlier. A sentence in which *or* is negated, for example, entails (by the semantics of *or*) alternatives where the disjunction is replaced with either of its disjuncts. The same holds of sentences where *any* is negated and of the subdomain alternatives to these sentences. This is why *any* is licensed in (4c).

The cases that are not so straightforward are the ones where *or*/*any* appears under a possibility modal. While the noted free choice inferences are intuitively available in (3a) for the *or* examples, just as they are in (4a) for the *any* examples, it is not exactly clear what the source of the inference is. The inference does not follow from the boolean semantics of *or* or from what is typically assumed about the semantics of possibility modals; this is the famous problem of free choice disjunction.[2] Here we will adopt the view that FC can be generated as an entailment via the application of the exhaustification operator (Alonso-Ovalle, 2005;

[2] See Meyer (2020) for a comprehensive review.

Chierchia, 2013; Fox, 2007). It is from this perspective that the puzzle presented by (8–9) can best be discussed as we outline next.

In what follows we will review the most recent approach to exhaustification, namely Bar-Lev and Fox's (2020) characterization. We choose this particular proposal because it simplifies the task that we will take on later, namely recasting exhaustification in dynamic terms. In our review, we will also revisit Crnič's (2019) *any*-condition to remind our readers of the connection between the inference patterns of *or* and the licensing condition on *any*.

To Bar-Lev and Fox (B-L&F hereafter), exhaustification of a proposition p given a set of (alternative) propositions A conjoins p with its exclusions given A, and its inclusions given A. (Throughout this paper, we will follow Sauerland [2004] and assume that the set of relevant alternatives to a disjunction includes the individual disjuncts as well as the conjunctive alternative.)

(11) **Exhaustification**:
Given a proposition p and a set of propositions A,
$\text{Exh}(A)(p) = p \mathbin{\&} \textbf{\textit{exclusions}}(A)(p) \mathbin{\&} \textbf{\textit{inclusions}}(A)(p)$

The exclusions of p given A are the (joint) negations of the excludable alternatives of A (given p).

(12) **Exclusions**:
Given a proposition p and a set of propositions A,
$\textbf{\textit{exclusions}}(A)(p) = \bigcap\{\neg q : q \text{ is excludable given } A \text{ and } p\}$

The excludable elements of A are those whose negations are consistent with the negations of any other set of elements from A whose negations do not contradict p. The definition is in (13), and as the reader may verify, excludability here is none other than Fox's (2007) notion of innocent excludability:[3]

(13) **Excludability**:
Given a proposition p and a set of propositions A, q is excludable iff $q \in A$ and for all subsets B of A, if $p \mathbin{\&} \bigcap B^{\neg}$ is consistent, then $p \mathbin{\&} \neg q \mathbin{\&} \bigcap B^{\neg}$ is also consistent.

[3] $B^{\neg} = \{\neg q : q \in B\}$.

The inclusions of p given A is the conjunction of the includable alternatives of A (given p).

(14) **Inclusions**:
Given a proposition p and a set of propositions A,
inclusions$(A)(p) = \bigcap\{q : q \text{ is includable given } A \text{ and } p\}$

These are the element of A which are consistent with the conjunction of any other set of elements from A that do not contradict p and its exclusions:[4]

(15) **Includability**:
Given a proposition p and a set of propositions A, q is includable iff $q \in A$ and for all subsets B of A, if p & ***exclusions***$(A)(p)$ & $\bigcap B$ is consistent, then p & ***exclusions***$(A)(p)$ & q & $\bigcap B$ is also consistent.

In cases where the disjunction appears in a DE context, exhaustification is vacuous, since the disjunctive sentence is itself the strongest among its alternatives. In these cases the (exhaustified) disjunctive sentence entails its disjunct alternatives, as shown below.

(16) Given $A = \{\neg p, \neg q, \neg(p \wedge q)\}$,
$\text{Exh}(A)(\neg(p \vee q)) = \neg(p \vee q)$
$\vDash \neg p, \neg q$

Exhaustification of sentences of the form $\Diamond(p \vee q)$, like (17), is non-vacuous, and the resulting interpretation is one which entails the meaning of the disjunct alternatives.

(17) Bill can take the B or the Q to work (repeated from (8b))

Here the alternatives are $\Diamond p$, $\Diamond q$, and $\Diamond(p \wedge q)$. Of these, only the conjunctive alternative $\Diamond(p \wedge q)$ is excludable; the disjunct alternatives $\Diamond p$, $\Diamond q$ are includable.[5] By virtue of this inclusion, the entailment to the disjunct alternatives goes through trivially. The result is shown in (18):

(18) Given $A = \{\Diamond p, \Diamond q, \Diamond(p \wedge q)\}$,
$\text{Exh}(A)(\Diamond(p \vee q)) = \Diamond(p \vee q)\ \&\ \neg\Diamond(p \wedge q)\ \&\ \Diamond p\ \&\ \Diamond q$
$\vDash \Diamond p, \Diamond q$

[4] Includability is equivalent to Bar-Lev and Fox's (2020) "innocent includability".

[5] We leave it to readers to verify this.

Let's turn now to other environments where the disjunction may occur. In cases involving universal quantifiers and necessity modals as in (5b–5c), exhaustification generates the negations of the disjunct alternatives, as shown in (19a–19b). With unembedded disjunction as in (5a), exhaustification says nothing about the disjunct alternatives, as shown in (19c).[6] In other words, in these cases exhaustification does not entail the disjunct alternatives.

(19) a. Given $A=\{\forall xPx,\forall xQx,\forall x(Px\wedge Qx)\}$,
$\text{Exh}(A)(\forall x(Px\vee Qx)) = \forall x(Px\vee Qx)\ \&\ \neg\forall xPx\ \&\ \neg\forall xQx\ \&\ \neg\forall x(Px\wedge Qx)$
$\nvDash \forall xPx, \forall xQx$

b. Given $A=\{\Box p,\Box q,\Box(p\wedge q)\}$,
$\text{Exh}(A)(\Box(p\vee q)) = \Box(p\vee q)\ \&\ \neg\Box p\ \&\ \neg\Box q\ \&\ \neg\Box(p\wedge q)$
$\nvDash \Box p,\Box q$

c. Given $A=\{p,q,p\wedge q\}$,
$\text{Exh}(A)(p\vee q) = (p\vee q)\ \&\ \neg(p\wedge q)$
$\nvDash p,q$

Now, on the assumption that *any* is an existential quantifier over an implicitly provided domain *D*, and that its formal alternatives are existential quantifiers over subsets of *D*, exhaustification of an *any*-sentence is predicted to generate inferences that run parallel to those generated from disjunction. So the *any* condition so far leads to the (correct) prediction that the *any*-sentences in (4) are acceptable, while those in (6) are not. Let us see how this works in some detail. Consider a domain D that consists of four individuals, a, b, c, d, and assume that Mary's friends are a, b, c. Now consider (20), the exhaustification of (4a):

(20) Exh(Mary is allowed to invite any$_D$ of her friends) (=(Exh(4a)))

(20) itself has a number of subdomain alternatives. Some are equivalent to (20), e.g., where D is replaced with $D' = \{a, b, c\}$, and others, e.g.,

[6] Crnič et al. (2015) report experimental evidence that sentences of the form $\forall x(Px \vee Qx)$ license a weaker inference, namely $\exists x\,Px\ \&\ \exists x\,Qx$, and Ramotowska et al. (2022) report similar evidence for necessity modals. This does not affect the point that the disjunctive sentences $\forall x(Px \vee Qx)$ and $\Box(p \vee q)$ do not license their disjunct alternatives, namely $\forall x\,Px, \forall x\,Qx$ and $\Box p, \Box q$, respectively, so we will set these findings aside in our presentation.

where D is replaced with $D'' = \{a, b, d\}$, $D''' = \{a, c\}$, etc., are asymmetrically entailed by it, as we will discuss below. These alternatives to (20) are shown in (21):

(21) a. Exh(Mary is allowed to invite any$_{\{a,b,d\}}$ of her friends)
b. Exh(Mary is allowed to invite any$_{\{a,c\}}$ of her friends)
c. Exh(Mary is allowed to invite any$_{\{b,c\}}$ of her friends), etc.

On some additional assumptions that we will now make explicit, (20) entails each of its alternatives in (21); (20) is itself equivalent to exhaustifying a three-way disjunction $\Diamond(a \vee b \vee c)$, i.e., equivalent to the proposition $(\Diamond a \,\&\, \Diamond b \,\&\, \Diamond c) \,\&\, \neg\Diamond(a \wedge b) \,\&\, \neg\Diamond(b \wedge c) \,\&\, \neg\Diamond(a \wedge c)$. This follows provided that a disjunction is assumed to have the conjunction of any of its parts as alternatives, that is, that the alternatives to $(a \vee b \vee c)$ include the conjunctions $(a \wedge b \wedge c)$ as well as $(a \wedge b)$, $(a \wedge c)$, and $(b \wedge c)$. We assume this, and we extend it to *any*$_D$: the alternatives in that case are forms where D is replaced with its subsets, and where *any* is replaced with a universal quantifier.[7] With this assumption, the entailment from (20) to (21) should be clear: (21a), for instance, says that Mary is allowed to invite a and allowed to invite b, but not allowed to invite both; (21b) says the same thing about a and c, and (21c) about b and c. Each of these follows from (20), as do its other subdomain alternatives, so *any* is predicted to be licensed in (20), as desired. Notice, crucially, that the requisite entailment relation holds between (20) itself and its alternatives, not between the unexhaustified sentence (4a) and its alternatives.

By contrast, consider the case of necessity modals. Here the *any*-condition cannot be met, regardless of exhaustification. Look at (22), itself the exhaustification of (6c).

(22) Exh(Mary needs to invite any$_D$ of her friends) (=(Exh(6c)))

(22), in parallel to the disjunctive case in (19b), asserts its prejacent $\Box(a \vee b \vee c)$ and negates its excludable alternatives $\Box(a \vee b)$, $\Box(a \vee c)$,

[7] Chierchia (2013) divides these alternatives into domain (D) and scalar (σ) alternatives, respectively.

and $\Box(b \vee c)$. (22) thus entails the inferences $\neg\Box(a \vee b)$, $\neg\Box(a \vee c)$, and $\neg\Box(b \vee c)$. But these inferences contradict the subdomain alternatives of (22) seen in (23); (23a), for example, *asserts* the proposition $\Box(a \vee b)$, and (23b) asserts $\Box(a \vee c)$. We therefore predict *any* not to be licensed in (22), again as desired.[8]

(23) a. Exh(Mary needs to invite any$_{\{a,b,d\}}$ of her friends)
b. Exh(Mary needs to invite any$_{\{a,c\}}$ of her friends)
c. Exh(Mary needs to invite any$_{\{b,c\}}$ of her friends), etc.

8.2.3 Spelling Out the Problem

Let us now return to the sentences in (8), repeated in (24), where an indefinite/existential adverb embeds a disjunction:

(24) a. Some people brought their children or their pets (to the picnic). (=(8))
⇝ Some people brought their children
⇝ Some people brought their pets
b. Bill sometimes took the B or the Q to work.
⇝ Bill sometimes took the B
⇝ Bill sometimes took the Q
c. Some of our students take French or German as elective.
⇝ Some of our students take French as elective
⇝ Some of our students take German as elective

If these sentences, of the form $\exists x(Px \vee Qx)$, have as alternatives sentences where the disjuncts replace the disjunction, i.e., $\exists x Px$, $\exists x Qx$, then exhaustification is expected to produce the inferences noted under (24a, b, c) as inclusions, in parallel to the case of possibility modals. The result is shown in (25).

(25) Given $A = \{\exists x Px, \exists x Qx, \exists x(Px \wedge Qx)\}$,
$\text{Exh}(A)(\exists x(Px \vee Qx)) = \exists x(Px \vee Qx) \;\&\; \exists x Px \;\&\; \exists x Qx \;\&\; \neg\exists x(Px \wedge Qx)$
$\models \exists x Px, \exists x Qx$

[8] As we noted in Footnote 5, it is not a settled matter that, e.g., $\Box p$ and $\Box q$ are indeed excludable given $\Box(p \vee q)$. This does not affect our point however: any theory that derives the (attested) possibility inferences $\Diamond p, \Diamond q, \cdots$ from premises of the form $\Box(p \vee q \vee \cdots)$ must avoid the unattested inference to the disjuncts $\Box p, \Box q, \cdots$. By doing this, we derive the target failure of the *any* condition in examples like (22).

This is good. However, with this result, and given Crnič's condition on *any*, we also predict that the corresponding *any*-sentences in (26) should be acceptable, as the logic is identical to the case discussed above in (22).

(26) a. *Some people invited any of their friends. (=(9))
b. *Bill sometimes took any of these subway lines to get to work.
c. *Some of our students take any language class as elective.

This is bad. How can we avoid this prediction? Is there a difference that we have not yet noticed between the FC inference pattern we see with possibility modals and the one we see with quantifiers and adverbs? If there is, how does this difference interact with the *any*-condition?

Before we proceed, we want to introduce another related problem. While the mechanism of exhaustification appears to deliver a good result for sentences like the ones in (24) involving disjunctions in the scope of plural indefinite quantifiers, it makes the wrong prediction for sentences where a singular indefinite embeds a disjunction. The reader may verify that the disjunct alternatives to (27) are predicted to be includable by the same logic as in (24) and are thus predicted to fall out as inferences. Intuitively, however, these inferences do not seem to follow.[9]

(27) Someone took French or German as elective.
⇝ Someone took French as elective
⇝ Someone took German as elective

Interim summary. We have identified two problems: the problem of plural indefinites is that, *even though* they intuitively license FC-like inference with disjunctions, as they are predicted to, they do not license

[9] The problem of singular indefinites and disjunctions was noted and discussed in Fox (2007) (see Sect. 9). Fox speculates that the singular marking in a sentence like (27) implies non-multiplicity, that is, that only one person took French or German as elective. If true, this would stop the disjunct alternatives from being includable, because asserting them would entail that the relevant person took both courses, contradicting the predicted exclusive inference of the sentence (see Fox for details). We are not sure, however, that non-multiplicity is the crucial detail here; there are sentences which, unlike (27), do not have a non-multiplicity inference associated with them, and that still do not license FC. (1) is an example:

(1) At least one student took French or German as elective.
⇝̸ At least one student took French
⇝̸ At least one student took German
⇝̸ Exactly one student took French or German as elective

any; the problem of singular indefinites is that they are incorrectly predicted to license FC-like inferences when they embed disjunctions. Our proposed solution to the first problem will also provide a solution to the second, as we will explain soon.

The first hint we take as we develop our proposal comes from Klinedinst's (2007) theory of FC, modeled in fact on cases like (24). Klinedinst proposed that FC comes from an embedded distribution implicature: an existential quantifier/adverb introduces a plurality, and a distributive operator attributes the disjunctive VP to every part of that plurality. The predication is then enriched by local exhaustification in a similar way to universal quantification: every part of the relevant plurality must satisfy the disjunctive VP, but not every part must satisfy the first disjunct, and not every part must satisfy the second. Together, these inferences entail that some parts of the plurality satisfy one disjunct, and others satisfy the second, and so it follows that there exists a plurality of the first kind, and one of the second kind. This is the inference in (24).[10]

With Klinedinst's account, there are now two ways to derive FC, and in principle they are both applicable to the cases of existential quantifiers/adverbs ($\exists x(Px \vee Qx)$) and to modals ($\Diamond(p \vee q)$). While our account will eventually build on Klinedinst's insight, we want to briefly explain why this possibility of deriving FC as embedded distribution still does not correctly capture the unacceptability of *any* in (26).

Klinedinst's account requires LFs that look like (28), where Exh is embedded under the existential operator, and where it takes as its prejacent the proposition denoted by node $\boxed{\text{A}}$. Node $\boxed{\text{A}}$, in turn, must include what effectively amounts to a universal quantifier (the distributive operator) and a variable over pluralities.[11]

---

[10] We should note that Klinedinst proposed to explain all FC inferences in this way, that is, for both quantifiers and modals.

[11] The variable itself is not necessary if we allow a type-flexible definition of Exh. This would enrich the predicate denoted by [DIST [P or Q]] to the stronger predicate [[DIST [P or Q]] and not ...]. This aside, there is also a question of whether possibility modals can quantify over world pluralities—a necessary assumption if Klinedinst's view is to be applied to modals. For the sake of discussion we do not take a stance on this issue, though see Schmitt (2023).

(28)

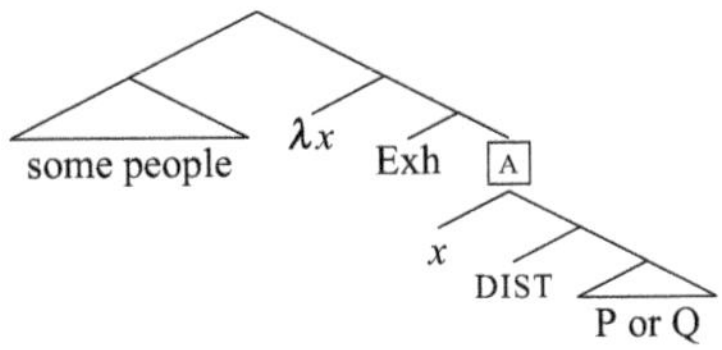

Exhaustifying the universal claim about the bound variable in (28) amounts to the claim that all of its parts satisfy the disjunction $P \vee Q$, but not all of them satisfy P, and not all of them satisfy Q. Putting these together yields the result that (28) entails its disjunct alternatives in (29a, b), which in effect amounts to the FC inference going through.

(29) a. Some people [λ*x* Exh [*x* DIST P]]
b. Some people [λ*x* Exh [*x* DIST Q]]

The result generalizes to larger disjunctions and (unfortunately) to *any*. Imagine an LF like (30) for (26c).[12]

(30)

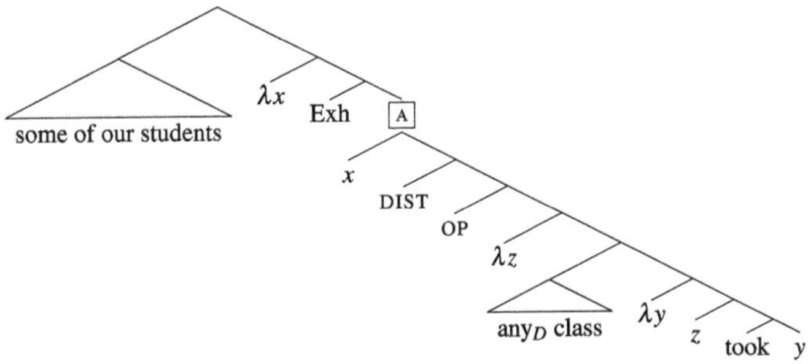

---

[12] (30) is slightly more complicated than (28). The *any*-phrase, by assumption, denotes a quantifier, and if we assume that quantifiers are not interpretable in object position (e.g., Heim & Kratzer, 1998), it is necessary for the *any*-phrase to adjoin to a propositional/truth-value-denoting constituent. At the same time, the reading that we are interested in requires that *any* takes scope below DIST operator. Notice that taking scope below DIST is something that we need to accommodate anyway, independently of *any*, as on, e.g., the following example:

(1) The students in my class presented at least one research paper.
(DIST>*at least one*)

We achieve this scopal configuration using the OP-abstraction. This complication is independent of our research question, as it arises whenever an object quantifier takes scope below a distributive operator. Here we make explicit one particular way of handling the issue, but we are open to others.

(30) denotes a similar proposition to (28). It says (i) that there exists a plurality of students x, (ii) that every part of x took some class in D, and (iii) that not every part of x took $class_1$, and not every part of x took $class_2$, and so on. And just as (28) entails its alternatives in (29), (30) entails its own subdomain alternatives, namely those sentences in which D is replaced with a subset of D. *Any* is therefore predicted to be acceptable under existential quantifiers, contrary to fact. The same point holds for adverbs like *sometimes*.

We have found, then, that on both paths to FC, whether by global exhaustification or by distribution (via exhaustification) under the existential quantifier, we make good predictions for disjunctions but bad predictions for *any*. This complicates our search for a solution. Imagine, however, that one could independently argue that the source of FC for modals is *always* global exhaustification, i.e., that the LF in (31a) is licit while (31b) is not.

(31) a. ✓[Exh [can/allowed/etc. ⋯ [⋯ {P or Q/*any*} ⋯]]]
b. *[can/allowed/etc. [λw ⋯ [Exh [w DIST ⋯ {P or Q/*any*} ⋯]]]]

Imagine also that one could independently argue the reverse for existential quantifiers and adverbs (32a vs. 32b), that is, that the FC-like inference in these cases is always due to embedded exhaustification along the lines of (28/30).

(32) a. *[Exh [some people ⋯ [DIST ⋯ {P or Q/*any*}] ⋯]]]
b. ✓[some people [λx ⋯ [Exh [x DIST ⋯ {P or Q/*any*} ⋯]]]]

Even if modals and quantifiers/adverbs differed along these lines, it would still not be clear why *any* should be licensed in LFs like (31a) but not in LFs like (32b). The mere fact that (28) is predicted to produce FC means that when analogous structures to it host *any* (as in, e.g., (30)), the subdomain alternatives to the structure will be entailed by it, and the structure will satisfy the *any* condition. There is a conceivable way of keeping (32b) from licensing *any*, but it requires complicating the *any* condition in a way that we do not think is desirable. We might say that the *any* condition is connected to the position at which exhaustification applies, so that in (31a) the *any*-condition must be satisfied at the topmost level of the structure, while in (32b) it needs to be satisfied at the level of the embedded constituent [x DIST $\cdots$ *any* $\cdots$]. Only then would the anti-licensing of *any* under existential quantifiers be explained; this is so due to the fact that exaustification immediately above the A node results in an interpretation whose entailments do contradict its subdomain alternatives, similarly to what we see in cases involving *any* embedded under a necessity modal. We think such an account is stipulative, however, and choose not to pursue it further here.

While we think that exhaustification does interact differently with modals than it does with existential quantifiers, we will talk about the difference in terms of binding between prejacent and alternatives, instead of syntactic location of Exh. We will say, specifically, that when Exh applies to a sentence that contains an indefinite (or an adverb of existential force), the participating formal alternatives behave as if they contained a bound pronoun—bound by the indefinite that is—instead of the indefinite itself. The same is not true of possibility modals. We state the details within dynamic semantics, in the next section.

8.3 Proposal

We begin with a brief informal overview of our proposal. By its semantics, a sentence S of the form [*some...* P'] says that P' holds of some entity x. If P' has a scalar alternative P', exhaustification does not add to S's literal meaning the implicature that [*some...* P'] is false. Instead it adds the implicature that x does not satisfy P'. This requires a mechanism by which the prejacent binds into its formal alternatives. As we will explain later, when the indefinite in S is singular and when P' is a disjunction, the prejacent will say that some non-plural entity x satisfies one of the disjuncts, and its implicature will say that x does not satisfy both of them. No further exclusions or inclusions are predicted, because adding the exclusions that x does not satisfy either disjunct will contradict the meaning of the prejacent, and adding the inclusions that x satisfies each disjunct will contradict the exclusive implicature. The mechanism thus evades the problem of singular indefinites noted above. When the indefinite in S is plural and when P' is a disjunction, the prejacent will say that some *plural* entity x consists of atoms that (each) satisfy one of P''s disjuncts, and its implicatures will say that the atoms of x do not each satisfy the first disjunct of P', and do not each satisfy its second disjunct, and so on. The result is a distribution inference: the relevant plurality must consist of atoms that all satisfy P, but that satisfy different disjuncts of P'. Crucially, the result of exhaustifying S in this case is predicted to not entail its disjunct alternatives (which are in fact negated), which means that *any* is predicted not to be licensed under plural indefinites. In the case of possibility modals we propose that the modal does not bind into its formal alternatives in the same way, a key detail that (unfortunately) we must leave as a stipulation for the time being.

8.3.1 Formal Details

We skip the details about sentence-internal semantic composition. We take sentences to be functions from information states to information states. Information states are sets of world-assignment pairs. Simple sentences that do not have any interesting anaphoric content map an input state C to a subset of C. A sentence is intuitively false in a state C whenever (the denotation of) S maps C to the empty set. A sentence S is informative given state C whenever it(s denotation) maps C to a (non-empty) proper subset of C. S is uninformative given C whenever S maps C to itself. For example, the sentence *it is warm* maps an input state C to the biggest subset of C in which the possible worlds are worlds where it is warm. Nothing changes in the assignment parts of the pairs that populate C. Below we follow common practice and write $C + p$ in place of $p(C)$, that is, the result of "updating" a state C with a proposition p. We will sometimes drop the semantic brackets $[\![\ ]\!]$ to ease readability.

We treat indefinites essentially as variables (following Heim, 1982). The semantics of an indefinite do not require either novelty or familiarity (see below for more on the novelty condition); a sentence containing an indefinite that carries index i may update states that have i in their domain, and may also update states that do not. (We say that i is in the domain of a state C whenever i is in the domain of every assignment that appears in the pairs in C.) When i is in the domain of C, a sentence containing an indefinite behaves as if it contained a pronoun in place of the indefinite. This is shown in the first line in (33). When i is not in the domain of C, the variable i undergoes random assignment, so that it is mapped by every assignment in the output to an individual that satisfies the restriction/scope of the indefinite. This is shown in the second line in (33).

(33) $C + [\![\textbf{someone}_i \ \textbf{XP}]\!] =$

$$\begin{cases} \{\langle w,g\rangle : \langle w,g\rangle \in C \ \& \ [\![\textbf{NP}]\!](w)(g(i)) = [\![\textbf{VP}]\!](w)(g(i)) = 1\} & \text{if } i \in Dom(C) \\ \{\langle w,g\rangle : \exists x([\![\textbf{NP}]\!](w)(x) = [\![\textbf{XP}]\!](w)(x) = 1 \ \& \\ \qquad \exists h(\langle w,h\rangle \in C \ \& \ h \sim_i g \ \& \ g(i) = x))\} & \text{if } i \notin Dom(C) \end{cases}$$

Although the definition in (33) leaves room for indefinites to play the role of pronouns, this (we propose) does not come up in linguistic *uses* of indefinites. Those uses are constrained by Heim's Novelty Condition, reformulated in (34). The pronoun-like character of indefinites is, for our purposes, relevant primarily in exhaustification, and in the notion of entailment used in our reformulation of Crnič's *any*-condition.

(34) **<u>The Novelty Condition:</u>**
An utterance of S is felicitous in a speech context c only if every indefinite in S is novel in c, where an indefinite XP_i is novel in a speech context c iff i is not in the domain of the information state in c.

We define exhaustification dynamically. In what follows, we will use the term "proposition" to mean a function from states to states, by assumption the denotation of a sentence. Given a set of propositions A and prejacent p, Exh updates a state C with three propositions; p, the exclusions of p given A, and the inclusions of p given A.

(35) **<u>Exhaustification (dynamic)</u>**:
Given a proposition p, set of propositions A, and state C,
$\text{Exh}(A)(p)(C) = C + p + \textbf{\textit{exclusions}}(A)(p) + \textbf{\textit{inclusions}}(A)(p)$, that is
$= \textbf{\textit{inclusions}}(A)(p)(\textbf{\textit{exclusions}}(A)(p)(p(C)))$

The proposition exclusions (A)(p) is the dynamic conjunction of the negations of the excludable elements of A, given p. To formulate the details of this in a way that parallels our earlier review (in Sect. 8.2.2), we will first provide dynamic(ized) definitions of consistency, negation, and grand conjunction.

We say that two propositions p, q are *consistent in sequence* (seq-consistent) iff there is a state C such that $C + p + q$ is non-empty:[13]

(36) **Seq-consistency**:
Two propositions p and q are seq-consistent iff $\exists C(C{+}p{+}q{\neq}\varnothing)$

Negation $\neg$ is defined as follows:

(37) **Negation (dynamic)**:
Given a proposition p and state C,
$[\neg p](C) = C - \{\langle w,g\rangle : \exists h(h{\geq}g \;\&\; \langle w,h\rangle \in p(C))\}$
where $h{\geq}g$ iff $\forall i(i{\in}Dom(g) \rightarrow i{\in}Dom(h) \;\&\; h(i){=}g(i))$

Note that (37) is stronger than standard definitions of negation in dynamic semantics.[14] On this definition, the negation of a sentence that contains a (novel) indefinite requires (correctly) that no entity in the domain satisfies the restriction and the scope of the indefinite.

Entailment is defined in terms of seq-consistency and negation: a proposition entails another iff the first is not seq-consistent with the negation of the second:

(38) **Entailment**:
A proposition p entails a proposition q iff p is not seq-consistent with $\neg q$, that is, iff for any state C, $C{+}p{+}\neg q{=}\varnothing$.

We also define $+$ as "grand dynamic conjunction". Given a set of propositions A, $+A$ is that proposition that maps a state C to the set of world-assignment pairs that appear in every individual update of C with an element of A:

(39) **Grand dynamic conjunction**:
$[+A](C) = \{\langle w,g\rangle : \forall q(q{\in}A \rightarrow \langle w,g\rangle{\in}q(C))\}$

We are now ready to redefine the propositions exclusions (A)(p) and inclusions (A)(p) in dynamic terms. The revisions are nearly identical to the static definitions provided in Sect. 8.2.2, the differences being that, here, $+$ replaces grand conjunction as grand set intersection, and

[13] Seq-consistency is not intended to be a dynamic surrogate of logical consistency. The notion, though perhaps limited in applicability, is sufficient for our goal of dynamicizing exhaustification.

[14] See Sudo (2023).

dynamic negation replaces static negation. The proposition exclusions (A)(p) is defined as follows,

(40) **Exclusions (dynamic)**:
Given a proposition p, set of propositions A, and state C,
$\textbf{\textit{exclusions}}(A)(p)(C) = \mathop{\Large +}\{\neg q : q \text{ is excludable given } A \text{ and } p\}$

... where ...

(41) **Excludability (dynamic)**:
Given a proposition p and a set of propositions A, a proposition q is excludable iff $q \in A$ and for all subsets R of A, if $p + \mathop{\Large +} R^{\neg}$ is seq-consistent, then $p + \mathop{\Large +} R^{\neg} + [\neg q]$ is also seq-consistent.

And inclusions (A)(p) is defined as follows:

(42) **Inclusions (dynamic)**:
Given a proposition p, set of propositions A, and state C,
$\textbf{\textit{inclusions}}(A)(p)(C) = \mathop{\Large +}\{q : q \text{ is includable given } A \text{ and } p\}$

... where...

(43) **Includability (dynamic)**:
A proposition q is includable given A and proposition p iff $q \in A$ and for all subsets R of A, if $p + \textbf{\textit{exclusions}}(A)(p) + \mathop{\Large +} R$ is seq-consistent, then $p + \textbf{\textit{exclusions}}(A)(p) + \mathop{\Large +} R + q$ is also seq-consistent.

We will now demonstrate the workings of dynamic exhaustification by applying it to three example types: first, a sentence like (44) where a singular indefinite accompanies a disjunction; second, a sentence like (45) where a plural indefinite accompanies a disjunction; and third, the negation of the first type sentence, e.g., (46). Notice that the VP in (45) includes a distributive operator, which we will hereafter represent as ∗.

(44) a. Prejacent: [someone$_i$ [A or B]]
b. Alternatives: [someone$_i$ A]
[someone$_i$ B]
[someone$_i$ [A and B]]

(45) a. Prejacent: [[some people]$_i$ ∗[A or B]]
b. Alternatives: [[some people]$_i$ ∗A]
[[some people]$_i$ ∗B]
[[some people]$_i$ ∗[A and B]]

(46) a. Prejacent: [not [someone$_i$ [A or B]]]
b. Alternatives: [not [someone$_i$ A]]
[not [someone$_i$ B]]
[not [someone$_i$ [A and B]]]

Here is a preview of the details that are about to come. First, in the case of (44a), exhaustification produces the inference that someone satisfies the disjunction [A or B], and that *that* person does not satisfy the conjunction—no unwanted FC-like inferences are predicted. Importantly, this means that neither (44a) nor its exhaustification is predicted to entail the disjunct alternatives in (44b), and given the parallel relation between disjunction and *any*, we predict (correctly) that singular indefinites do not license *any* in their scope. Second, in (45), exhaustification produces the inference that some plurality consists of people-atoms that (each) satisfy [A or B], but that the people-atoms of *that* plurality do not each satisfy A and do not each satisfy B. It follows that the atoms of the plurality are divided, some satisfying A and some satisfying B, and we generate the (attested) FC-like inference from the sentence that way—recall the examples in (8). The crucial point is that, despite this outcome, neither (45a) nor its exhaustification is predicted to entail the disjunct alternatives in (45b). The reason, speaking informally, is that it does not follow from (45a), or from its exhaustification, that the atoms of the plurality i satisfy A, or that they satisfy B. So even though plural indefinites are predicted to license an FC-like inference when they outscope disjunction, they are not predicted to license *any*.[15] Finally, in the case of (46), exhaustification is predicted to be vacuous, and as we will see, (46a) itself entails its alternatives in (46b), and is thus predicted to license *any*.

8.3.2 Application to Singular Indefinites

To begin, observe that, by the Novelty Condition, our sentences may not be uttered unless the variable i is novel in the input state. Such a state is shown in (47):

[15] Notice that, dynamics aside, the predicted inferential behavior of (44) and (45) largely matches that of Klinedinst's account. But here the predictions do not depend on application of Exh under the indefinite (recall discussion from Sect. 8.2.3).

(47)

	…	i	…
$\langle w_1, g_1 \rangle$	…		…
⋮			
$\langle w_1, g_n \rangle$	…		…
$\langle w_2, g_1 \rangle$	…		…
⋮			
$\langle w_2, g_n \rangle$	…		…
$\langle w_3, g_1 \rangle$	…		…
⋮			
$\langle w_3, g_n \rangle$	…		…

Call this state C_0, its elements being the pairs that appear in the left column. On the right, we gloss over the largely irrelevant details about what the given assignments map the different indices to. The only important detail is that the assignments do not have i in their domain.

Now imagine that there are three individuals that in w_1 are people that satisfy [A or B]. Call these individuals a, b, and c. Let's say that a satisfies A but not B; b satisfies B but not A; and c satisfies both. Imagine also that there are two individuals a', b' that, in w_2, are people that satisfy [A or B]: a' satisfies A but not B and b' satisfies B but not A. Finally, imagine that there are no individuals that are people that satisfy [A or B] in w_3.

When C_0 is updated with [someone$_i$ [A or B]], the output is a state in which the worlds are individually paired with assignments that map i to something that is an [A or B]-person in the given world. So w_1 will be paired with what we may call g_1^a—this is our shorthand for $g_1[i \rightarrow a]$, the assignment that is almost identical to g_1 in C_0 except in mapping i to *a*. The same possible world w_1 will also be paired with g_1^b, g_1^c, because these are also almost identical to g_1 and they also map i to something that is both a person and an "A or B" in w_1. The remaining details, as they appear in (48), should be clear. Importantly, w_3 will not paired with anything because there are no entities in it that are people that satisfy [A or B].

(48)

$$\begin{array}{l|ccc} & \cdots & i & \cdots \\ \hline \langle w_1, g_1 \rangle & \cdots & & \cdots \\ \vdots & & & \\ \langle w_1, g_n \rangle & \cdots & & \cdots \\ \langle w_2, g_1 \rangle & \cdots & & \cdots \\ \vdots & & & \\ \langle w_2, g_n \rangle & \cdots & & \cdots \\ \langle w_3, g_1 \rangle & \cdots & & \cdots \\ \vdots & & & \\ \langle w_3, g_n \rangle & \cdots & & \cdots \end{array} \quad + \quad [\text{someone}_i \text{ [A or B]]} \quad = \quad \begin{array}{l|ccc} & \cdots & i & \cdots \\ \hline \langle w_1, g_1^a \rangle & \cdots & a & \cdots \\ \langle w_1, g_1^b \rangle & \cdots & b & \cdots \\ \langle w_1, g_1^c \rangle & \cdots & c & \cdots \\ \vdots & & & \\ \langle w_1, g_n^a \rangle & \cdots & a & \cdots \\ \langle w_1, g_n^b \rangle & \cdots & b & \cdots \\ \langle w_1, g_n^c \rangle & \cdots & c & \cdots \\ \langle w_2, g_1^{a'} \rangle & \cdots & a' & \cdots \\ \langle w_2, g_1^{b'} \rangle & \cdots & b' & \cdots \\ \vdots & & & \\ \langle w_2, g_n^{a'} \rangle & \cdots & a' & \cdots \\ \langle w_2, g_n^{b'} \rangle & \cdots & b' & \cdots \end{array}$$

Call the output state in (48) C_1. What happens if C_1 is updated with the alternative [someone$_i$ A]? By our assumption that the Novelty Condition does not apply internally to exhaustification, and by our pronoun-like semantics of indefinites in cases where the index is old, the update preserves from C_1 those pairs in which i is mapped to an entity that satisfies A in the relevant world. We therefore get:

(49)

$$\begin{array}{l|ccc} & \cdots & i & \cdots \\ \hline \langle w_1, g_1^a \rangle & \cdots & a & \cdots \\ \langle w_1, g_1^b \rangle & \cdots & b & \cdots \\ \langle w_1, g_1^c \rangle & \cdots & c & \cdots \\ \vdots & & & \\ \langle w_1, g_n^a \rangle & \cdots & a & \cdots \\ \langle w_1, g_n^b \rangle & \cdots & b & \cdots \\ \langle w_1, g_n^c \rangle & \cdots & c & \cdots \\ \langle w_2, g_1^{a'} \rangle & \cdots & a' & \cdots \\ \langle w_2, g_1^{b'} \rangle & \cdots & b' & \cdots \\ \vdots & & & \\ \langle w_2, g_n^{a'} \rangle & \cdots & a' & \cdots \\ \langle w_2, g_n^{b'} \rangle & \cdots & b' & \cdots \end{array} \quad + \quad [\text{someone}_i \text{ A}] \quad = \quad \begin{array}{l|ccc} & \cdots & i & \cdots \\ \hline \langle w_1, g_1^a \rangle & \cdots & a & \cdots \\ \langle w_1, g_1^c \rangle & \cdots & c & \cdots \\ \vdots & & & \\ \langle w_1, g_n^a \rangle & \cdots & a & \cdots \\ \langle w_1, g_n^c \rangle & \cdots & c & \cdots \\ \langle w_2, g_1^{a'} \rangle & \cdots & a' & \cdots \\ \vdots & & & \\ \langle w_2, g_n^{a'} \rangle & \cdots & a' & \cdots \end{array}$$

Given this, what is the predicted result of updating C_1, i.e., the output state in (48), with the negation of [someone$_i$ A]? We must remove from C_1 every pair whose assignment element is extended in the output in (49). In this case, the domains of the assignments are not meaningfully extended, so the effect is simply subtraction: Updating C_1 with the negation of [someone$_i$ A] is the result of subtracting the output of (49) from C_1:

(50)

$$\begin{array}{c|ccc} & \cdots & i & \cdots \\ \hline \langle w_1, g_1^a\rangle & \cdots & a & \cdots \\ \langle w_1, g_1^b\rangle & \cdots & b & \cdots \\ \langle w_1, g_1^c\rangle & \cdots & c & \cdots \\ \vdots & & & \\ \langle w_1, g_n^a\rangle & \cdots & a & \cdots \\ \langle w_1, g_n^b\rangle & \cdots & b & \cdots \\ \langle w_1, g_n^c\rangle & \cdots & c & \cdots \\ \langle w_2, g_1^{a'}\rangle & \cdots & a' & \cdots \\ \langle w_2, g_1^{b'}\rangle & \cdots & b' & \cdots \\ \vdots & & & \\ \langle w_2, g_n^{a'}\rangle & \cdots & a' & \cdots \\ \langle w_2, g_n^{b'}\rangle & \cdots & b' & \cdots \end{array} + [\neg[\text{someone}_i\ \text{A}]] = \begin{array}{c|ccc} & \cdots & i & \cdots \\ \hline \langle w_1, g_1^b\rangle & \cdots & b & \cdots \\ \vdots & & & \\ \langle w_1, g_n^b\rangle & \cdots & b & \cdots \\ \langle w_2, g_1^{b'}\rangle & \cdots & b' & \cdots \\ \vdots & & & \\ \langle w_2, g_n^{b'}\rangle & \cdots & b' & \cdots \end{array}$$

By similar steps we derive the following results:

(51)

$$\begin{array}{c|ccc} & \cdots & i & \cdots \\ \hline \langle w_1, g_1^a\rangle & \cdots & a & \cdots \\ \langle w_1, g_1^b\rangle & \cdots & b & \cdots \\ \langle w_1, g_1^c\rangle & \cdots & c & \cdots \\ \vdots & & & \\ \langle w_1, g_n^a\rangle & \cdots & a & \cdots \\ \langle w_1, g_n^b\rangle & \cdots & b & \cdots \\ \langle w_1, g_n^c\rangle & \cdots & c & \cdots \\ \langle w_2, g_1^{a'}\rangle & \cdots & a' & \cdots \\ \langle w_2, g_1^{b'}\rangle & \cdots & b' & \cdots \\ \vdots & & & \\ \langle w_2, g_n^{a'}\rangle & \cdots & a' & \cdots \\ \langle w_2, g_n^{b'}\rangle & \cdots & b' & \cdots \end{array} + [\neg[\text{someone}_i\ \text{B}]] = \begin{array}{c|ccc} & \cdots & i & \cdots \\ \hline \langle w_1, g_1^a\rangle & \cdots & a & \cdots \\ \vdots & & & \\ \langle w_1, g_n^a\rangle & \cdots & a & \cdots \\ \langle w_2, g_1^{a'}\rangle & \cdots & a' & \cdots \\ \vdots & & & \\ \langle w_2, g_n^{a'}\rangle & \cdots & a' & \cdots \end{array}$$

(52)

$$\begin{array}{c|ccc} & \cdots & i & \cdots \\ \hline \langle w_1, g_1^a\rangle & \cdots & a & \cdots \\ \langle w_1, g_1^b\rangle & \cdots & b & \cdots \\ \langle w_1, g_1^c\rangle & \cdots & c & \cdots \\ \vdots & & & \\ \langle w_1, g_n^a\rangle & \cdots & a & \cdots \\ \langle w_1, g_n^b\rangle & \cdots & b & \cdots \\ \langle w_1, g_n^c\rangle & \cdots & c & \cdots \\ \langle w_2, g_1^{a'}\rangle & \cdots & a' & \cdots \\ \langle w_2, g_1^{b'}\rangle & \cdots & b' & \cdots \\ \vdots & & & \\ \langle w_2, g_n^{a'}\rangle & \cdots & a' & \cdots \\ \langle w_2, g_n^{b'}\rangle & \cdots & b' & \cdots \end{array} + [\neg[\text{someone}_i\ [\text{A and B}]]] = \begin{array}{c|ccc} & \cdots & i & \cdots \\ \hline \langle w_1, g_1^a\rangle & \cdots & a & \cdots \\ \langle w_1, g_1^b\rangle & \cdots & b & \cdots \\ \vdots & & & \\ \langle w_1, g_n^a\rangle & \cdots & a & \cdots \\ \langle w_1, g_n^b\rangle & \cdots & b & \cdots \\ \langle w_2, g_1^{a'}\rangle & \cdots & a' & \cdots \\ \langle w_2, g_1^{b'}\rangle & \cdots & b' & \cdots \\ \vdots & & & \\ \langle w_2, g_n^{a'}\rangle & \cdots & a' & \cdots \\ \langle w_2, g_n^{b'}\rangle & \cdots & b' & \cdots \end{array}$$

Now we can determine which alternatives to the prejacent [someone$_i$ [A or B]] are predicted to be (dynamically) excludable. (50) shows us that the prejacent can be seq-consistently updated with [¬[someone$_i$ A]], but updating the outcome with [¬[someone$_i$ B]] produces the empty state (notice that the outputs in (50) and (51) are disjoint). Therefore [someone$_i$ B] is not excludable. Similar reasoning with (51) shows us that [someone$_i$ A] is not excludable either. By contrast, the negation of the alternative [someone$_i$ [A and B]] is consistent with the output in (50) and with the output in (51), and is therefore excludable. This gives us the following result:

$$
(53)\quad C_0 \;+\; \text{[someone}_i\text{ [A or B]]} \;+\; \textbf{\textit{exclusions}}(A)(\cdots) \;=\;
\begin{array}{l|ccc}
 & \cdots & i & \cdots \\
\hline
\langle w_1, g_1^a\rangle & \cdots & a & \cdots \\
\langle w_1, g_1^b\rangle & \cdots & b & \cdots \\
\vdots & & & \\
\langle w_1, g_n^a\rangle & \cdots & a & \cdots \\
\langle w_1, g_n^b\rangle & \cdots & b & \cdots \\
\langle w_2, g_1^{a'}\rangle & \cdots & a' & \cdots \\
\langle w_2, g_1^{b'}\rangle & \cdots & b' & \cdots \\
\vdots & & & \\
\langle w_2, g_n^{a'}\rangle & \cdots & a' & \cdots \\
\langle w_2, g_n^{b'}\rangle & \cdots & b' & \cdots
\end{array}
$$

The output state in (53), then, is the result of updating C_0 with our disjunctive prejacent and with its exclusions. It is also the state that we must consider when determining which formal alternatives are includable. In this example it turns out that none of them are. Why? Observe first that the result of updating (53) with [someone$_i$ A] preserves those pairs in which i is mapped to something that satisfies A in the world element. Observe second that a subsequent update with [someone$_i$ B] is empty, since the previous update keeps only those pairs in which i is mapped to something that satisfies A, and none of those individuals satisfy B. This makes [someone$_i$ B] not includable. The same consideration (in reverse order) shows that [someone$_i$ A] is also not includable. Finally, updating (53) with the conjunctive alternative will lead directly to an empty state, because none of the entities under i above satisfy both A and B. It follows that the conjunctive alternative is not includable either, and that what we see in (53) is in fact the result of updating C_0 with the full exhaustification of the sentence [someone$_i$ [A or B]]:

$$(54)\quad C_0 \;+\; [\text{Exh}\,[\text{someone}_i\,[\text{A or B}]]] \;=\; \begin{array}{l|ccc} & \cdots & i & \cdots \\ \hline \langle w_1, g_1^{a}\rangle & \cdots & a & \cdots \\ \langle w_1, g_1^{b}\rangle & \cdots & b & \cdots \\ \vdots & & & \\ \langle w_1, g_n^{a}\rangle & \cdots & a & \cdots \\ \langle w_1, g_n^{b}\rangle & \cdots & b & \cdots \\ \langle w_2, g_1^{a'}\rangle & \cdots & a' & \cdots \\ \langle w_2, g_1^{b'}\rangle & \cdots & b' & \cdots \\ \vdots & & & \\ \langle w_2, g_n^{a'}\rangle & \cdots & a' & \cdots \\ \langle w_2, g_n^{b'}\rangle & \cdots & b' & \cdots \end{array}$$

So, for this example, exhaustification produces nothing more than an exclusive inference: a sentence of the form [someone [A or B]] is predicted to say (by its literal semantics) that there is an individual that satisfies A or B, and (by its implicature) that *that* individual does not satisfy both A and B. This matches intuition as far as we can see.[16]

Connection to the *any*-condition. This result, and the ones we will see below, makes correct predictions about the licensing of *any*. The key detail is that, in this example, neither of the alternatives [someone$_i$ A] and [someone$_i$ B] is entailed by the exhaustification of the disjunctive sentence [someone$_i$ [A or B]]. That is, speaking in the terms used in our definition of entailment, there are states that can be updated with [Exh [someone$_i$ [A or B]]] and subsequently with [¬[someone$_i$ A]] without producing an empty result. A brief look at the output in (53) should make this clear: updating that output with [¬[someone$_i$ A]] would not remove the pairs in which i is mapped to b and b', and updating it with [¬[someone$_i$ B]] would likewise not remove the pairs in which i is mapped to a, a'. It follows from this, *a fortiori*, that [Exh [someone$_i$ [A or B]]] does not entail [Exh [someone$_i$ [A]]] or [Exh [someone$_i$ [B]]], and by extension, that given a domain of quantification D, [Exh [someone$_i$ [... *any* $_D$ ...]]] does not entail [Exh [someone$_i$ [... *any* $_{D'}$ ...]]] for any D' that is a proper subset of D. Assuming Crnič's *any*-condition, then, we also predict correctly that *any* should not be licensed under (unnegated) singular indefinites.

16 We think that the case of singular indefinites tells us that such views of exhaustification are necessary, because capturing the intuitive inferences without appealing to this sort of binding requires one of two moves: either we stipulate that exhaustification cannot apply above indefinites (building on Klinedinst), or we attribute to singular indefinites an overly strong inference (like Fox proposes, see Footnote 8 above).

8.3.3 Application to Plural Indefinites

Now we turn to the case of disjunctions and *any* embedded under plural indefinite quantifiers. To keep things simple, we take the multiplicity of plural marking for granted.[17] Assuming that multiplicity is encoded in the semantics of plural marking, we have something like the following: remember that each of a, b, c satisfies the disjunction [A or B] in w_1, as do a', b' in w_2, so (by assumption) their sums will consist of atoms that (each) satisfy the disjunction. When a sum consists of atoms that individually satisfy a predicate, we will say that the sum "$*$-satisfies" that predicate.

(55)

$$
\begin{array}{l|ccc}
 & \cdots & i & \cdots \\
\hline
\langle w_1, g_1 \rangle & \cdots & & \cdots \\
\vdots & & & \\
\langle w_1, g_n \rangle & \cdots & & \cdots \\
\langle w_2, g_1 \rangle & \cdots & & \cdots \\
\vdots & & & \\
\langle w_2, g_n \rangle & \cdots & & \cdots \\
\langle w_3, g_1 \rangle & \cdots & & \cdots \\
\vdots & & & \\
\langle w_3, g_n \rangle & \cdots & & \cdots
\end{array}
\quad + \quad [[\text{some people}]_i \ *[\text{A or B}]] \quad = \quad
\begin{array}{l|ccc}
 & \cdots & i & \cdots \\
\hline
\langle w_1, g_1^{ab} \rangle & \cdots & ab & \cdots \\
\langle w_1, g_1^{bc} \rangle & \cdots & bc & \cdots \\
\langle w_1, g_1^{ac} \rangle & \cdots & ac & \cdots \\
\langle w_1, g_1^{abc} \rangle & \cdots & abc & \cdots \\
\vdots & & & \\
\langle w_1, g_n^{ab} \rangle & \cdots & ab & \cdots \\
\langle w_1, g_n^{bc} \rangle & \cdots & bc & \cdots \\
\langle w_1, g_n^{ac} \rangle & \cdots & ac & \cdots \\
\langle w_2, g_1^{a'b'} \rangle & \cdots & a'b' & \cdots \\
\vdots & & & \\
\langle w_2, g_n^{a'b'} \rangle & \cdots & a'b' & \cdots
\end{array}
$$

Let's now update this outcome with [[some people]$_i$ $*$A], so we can later check whether the alternative can be excluded. The update with [[some people]$_i$ $*$A] preserves those pairs in which i is mapped to a plurality that $*$-satisfies A in the relevant world. This is shown in (56):

(56)

$$
\begin{array}{l|ccc}
 & \cdots & i & \cdots \\
\hline
\langle w_1, g_1^{ab} \rangle & \cdots & ab & \cdots \\
\langle w_1, g_1^{bc} \rangle & \cdots & bc & \cdots \\
\langle w_1, g_1^{ac} \rangle & \cdots & ac & \cdots \\
\langle w_1, g_1^{abc} \rangle & \cdots & abc & \cdots \\
\vdots & & & \\
\langle w_1, g_n^{ab} \rangle & \cdots & ab & \cdots \\
\langle w_1, g_n^{bc} \rangle & \cdots & bc & \cdots \\
\langle w_1, g_n^{ac} \rangle & \cdots & ac & \cdots \\
\langle w_2, g_1^{a'b'} \rangle & \cdots & a'b' & \cdots \\
\vdots & & & \\
\langle w_2, g_n^{a'b'} \rangle & \cdots & a'b' & \cdots
\end{array}
\quad + \quad [[\text{some people}]_i \ *\text{A}] \quad = \quad
\begin{array}{l|ccc}
 & \cdots & i & \cdots \\
\hline
\langle w_1, g_1^{ac} \rangle & \cdots & ac & \cdots \\
\vdots & & & \\
\langle w_1, g_n^{ac} \rangle & \cdots & ac & \cdots
\end{array}
$$

[17] There are important accounts in the literature on plurals that derive multiplicity as an implicature, but to keep the complications to a minimum, we will have to look at these on another occasion.

And so the negation of [[some people]$_i$ $*$A] subtracts the result in (56) from (55):

(57)
$$\begin{array}{cccc} & \cdots & i & \cdots \\ \hline \langle w_1,g_1^{ab}\rangle & \cdots & ab & \cdots \\ \langle w_1,g_1^{bc}\rangle & \cdots & bc & \cdots \\ \langle w_1,g_1^{ac}\rangle & \cdots & ac & \cdots \\ \langle w_1,g_1^{abc}\rangle & \cdots & abc & \cdots \\ \vdots & & & \\ \langle w_1,g_n^{ab}\rangle & \cdots & ab & \cdots \\ \langle w_1,g_n^{bc}\rangle & \cdots & bc & \cdots \\ \langle w_1,g_n^{ac}\rangle & \cdots & ac & \cdots \\ \langle w_2,g_1^{a'b'}\rangle & \cdots & a'b' & \cdots \\ \vdots & & & \\ \langle w_2,g_n^{a'b'}\rangle & \cdots & a'b' & \cdots \end{array} + [\neg[[\text{some people}]_i *\text{A}]] = \begin{array}{cccc} & \cdots & i & \cdots \\ \hline \langle w_1,g_1^{ab}\rangle & \cdots & ab & \cdots \\ \langle w_1,g_1^{bc}\rangle & \cdots & bc & \cdots \\ \langle w_1,g_1^{abc}\rangle & \cdots & abc & \cdots \\ \vdots & & & \\ \langle w_1,g_n^{ab}\rangle & \cdots & ab & \cdots \\ \langle w_1,g_n^{bc}\rangle & \cdots & bc & \cdots \\ \langle w_2,g_1^{a'b'}\rangle & \cdots & a'b' & \cdots \\ \vdots & & & \\ \langle w_2,g_n^{a'b'}\rangle & \cdots & a'b' & \cdots \end{array}$$

By the same process we get the result in (58): updating (55) with the negation of [[some people]$_i$ $*$B] removes those pairs in which i is mapped to an all-B plurality (i.e., bc):

(58)
$$\begin{array}{cccc} & \cdots & i & \cdots \\ \hline \langle w_1,g_1^{ab}\rangle & \cdots & ab & \cdots \\ \langle w_1,g_1^{bc}\rangle & \cdots & bc & \cdots \\ \langle w_1,g_1^{ac}\rangle & \cdots & ac & \cdots \\ \langle w_1,g_1^{abc}\rangle & \cdots & abc & \cdots \\ \vdots & & & \\ \langle w_1,g_n^{ab}\rangle & \cdots & ab & \cdots \\ \langle w_1,g_n^{bc}\rangle & \cdots & bc & \cdots \\ \langle w_1,g_n^{ac}\rangle & \cdots & ac & \cdots \\ \langle w_2,g_1^{a'b'}\rangle & \cdots & a'b' & \cdots \\ \vdots & & & \\ \langle w_2,g_n^{a'b'}\rangle & \cdots & a'b' & \cdots \end{array} + [\neg[[\text{some people}]_i *\text{B}]] = \begin{array}{cccc} & \cdots & i & \cdots \\ \hline \langle w_1,g_1^{ab}\rangle & \cdots & ab & \cdots \\ \langle w_1,g_1^{ac}\rangle & \cdots & ac & \cdots \\ \langle w_1,g_1^{abc}\rangle & \cdots & abc & \cdots \\ \vdots & & & \\ \langle w_1,g_n^{ab}\rangle & \cdots & ab & \cdots \\ \langle w_1,g_n^{ac}\rangle & \cdots & ac & \cdots \\ \langle w_2,g_1^{a'b'}\rangle & \cdots & a'b' & \cdots \\ \vdots & & & \\ \langle w_2,g_n^{a'b'}\rangle & \cdots & a'b' & \cdots \end{array}$$

Finally, updating (55) with the negation of the conjunctive sentence [[some people]$_i$ $*$[A and B]] does not do anything, because by assumption there are no (non-atomic) pluralities that $*$-satisfy both A and B:

(59)
$$\begin{array}{cccc} & \cdots & i & \cdots \\ \hline \langle w_1,g_1^{ab}\rangle & \cdots & ab & \cdots \\ \langle w_1,g_1^{bc}\rangle & \cdots & bc & \cdots \\ \langle w_1,g_1^{ac}\rangle & \cdots & ac & \cdots \\ \langle w_1,g_1^{abc}\rangle & \cdots & abc & \cdots \\ \vdots & & & \\ \langle w_1,g_n^{ab}\rangle & \cdots & ab & \cdots \\ \langle w_1,g_n^{bc}\rangle & \cdots & bc & \cdots \\ \langle w_1,g_n^{ac}\rangle & \cdots & ac & \cdots \\ \langle w_2,g_1^{a'b'}\rangle & \cdots & a'b' & \cdots \\ \vdots & & & \\ \langle w_2,g_n^{a'b'}\rangle & \cdots & a'b' & \cdots \end{array} + \begin{array}{l}[\neg[[\text{some people}]_i \\ \quad *[\text{A and B}]]]\end{array} = \begin{array}{cccc} & \cdots & i & \cdots \\ \hline \langle w_1,g_1^{ab}\rangle & \cdots & ab & \cdots \\ \langle w_1,g_1^{bc}\rangle & \cdots & bc & \cdots \\ \langle w_1,g_1^{ac}\rangle & \cdots & ac & \cdots \\ \langle w_1,g_1^{abc}\rangle & \cdots & abc & \cdots \\ \vdots & & & \\ \langle w_1,g_n^{ab}\rangle & \cdots & ab & \cdots \\ \langle w_1,g_n^{bc}\rangle & \cdots & bc & \cdots \\ \langle w_1,g_n^{ac}\rangle & \cdots & ac & \cdots \\ \langle w_2,g_1^{a'b'}\rangle & \cdots & a'b' & \cdots \\ \vdots & & & \\ \langle w_2,g_n^{a'b'}\rangle & \cdots & a'b' & \cdots \end{array}$$

Now notice that, in this example, all of the alternatives are excludable; updating our initial state with the prejacent and with the negations of its alternatives does not lead to an empty state: the output consists of pairs whose assignments map i to a plurality that neither $*$-satisfies A nor $*$-satisfies B. This is simply the intersection of the outputs in (57–59):

(60)
$$
\begin{array}{l|ccc}
 & \cdots & i & \cdots \\
\hline
\langle w_1, g_1^{ab}\rangle & \cdots & ab & \cdots \\
\langle w_1, g_1^{bc}\rangle & \cdots & bc & \cdots \\
\langle w_1, g_1^{ac}\rangle & \cdots & ac & \cdots \\
\langle w_1, g_1^{abc}\rangle & \cdots & abc & \cdots \\
\vdots & & & \\
\langle w_1, g_n^{ab}\rangle & \cdots & ab & \cdots \\
\langle w_1, g_n^{bc}\rangle & \cdots & bc & \cdots \\
\langle w_1, g_n^{ac}\rangle & \cdots & ac & \cdots \\
\langle w_2, g_1^{a'b'}\rangle & \cdots & a'b' & \cdots \\
\vdots & & & \\
\langle w_2, g_n^{a'b'}\rangle & \cdots & a'b' & \cdots
\end{array}
\quad + \ \boldsymbol{exclusions}(A)(p) \quad = \quad
\begin{array}{l|ccc}
 & \cdots & i & \cdots \\
\hline
\langle w_1, g_1^{ab}\rangle & \cdots & ab & \cdots \\
\langle w_1, g_1^{abc}\rangle & \cdots & abc & \cdots \\
\vdots & & & \\
\langle w_1, g_n^{ab}\rangle & \cdots & ab & \cdots \\
\langle w_2, g_1^{a'b'}\rangle & \cdots & a'b' & \cdots \\
\vdots & & & \\
\langle w_2, g_n^{a'b'}\rangle & \cdots & a'b' & \cdots
\end{array}
$$

Given this output, we are left with no alternatives that can be included; the alternatives [[some people]$_i$ $*$A], [[some people]$_i$ $*$B], and [[some people]$_i$ $*$[A and B]] are each inconsistent with the result in (60), in which i is mapped only to pluralities that have a mix of A-atoms and B-atoms. It follows that the output in (60) is the result of updating C_0 with the exhaustification of the sentence [[some people]$_i$ [A or B]]:

(61)
$$
C_0 \ + \ [\text{Exh [[some people]}_i \ *\text{[A or B]]]} \quad = \quad
\begin{array}{l|ccc}
 & \cdots & i & \cdots \\
\hline
\langle w_1, g_1^{ab}\rangle & \cdots & ab & \cdots \\
\langle w_1, g_1^{abc}\rangle & \cdots & abc & \cdots \\
\vdots & & & \\
\langle w_1, g_n^{ab}\rangle & \cdots & ab & \cdots \\
\langle w_2, g_1^{a'b'}\rangle & \cdots & a'b' & \cdots \\
\vdots & & & \\
\langle w_2, g_n^{a'b'}\rangle & \cdots & a'b' & \cdots
\end{array}
$$

So, unlike the case of singular indefinites, exhaustifying sentences of the form [some people [A or B]] is predicted to produce more than an exclusive inference: the result says (by the literal semantics of the sentence) that there is a plurality that satisfies A or B, and (by the implicatures) that the atoms of *that* plurality do not all satisfy A and do not all satisfy B. This entails that there is at least one individual that satisfies A and at least one that satisfies B, as intuitions indicate. However, neither the sentence [[some people]$_i$ [A or B]] nor its exhaustification entails the alternatives [[some people]$_i$ A] and [[some people]$_i$ B], because as we saw above it is possible to update a non-empty state with [[some people]$_i$ [A or B]], and with the negation of [[some people]$_i$ A], without producing an empty result. It follows that [Exh [[some people]$_i$ [A or B]]] does not entail [Exh [[some people]$_i$ [A]]] or [Exh [someone$_i$ [B]]], and by extension, that given a domain of quantification D, [Exh [[some people]$_i$ [... *any* $_D$ ...]]] does not entail [Exh [[some people]$_i$ [... *any* $_{D'}$ ...]]] for any subdomain D' of D. Like in the case of singular indefinites, then, we predict correctly that *any* is not licensed under (unnegated) plural indefinites.

8.3.4 Application to Negated Indefinites

We turn finally to negated indefinites. These are predicted to license *any*, as desired, because a sentence of the form (62) entails its disjunct alternatives. We will show this with a singular indefinite, so as to avoid the (otherwise orthogonal) issue of how plural marking interacts with negation.

(62) a. Prejacent: [not [someone$_i$ [A or B]]]
b. Alternatives: [not [someone$_i$ A]]
[not [someone$_i$ B]]
[not [someone$_i$ [A and B]]]

Consider first the result of updating our state C_0 with [not [someone$_i$ [A or B]]]. The update subtracts from C_0, shown on the left below, every pair whose assignment is extended in C_1, C_1 being the result of updating C_0 with the unnegated [someone$_i$ [A or B]]:

(63)
$$\begin{array}{l|ccc} & \cdots & i & \cdots \\ \hline \langle w_1, g_1\rangle & \cdots & & \cdots \\ \vdots & & & \\ \langle w_1, g_n\rangle & \cdots & & \cdots \\ \langle w_2, g_1\rangle & \cdots & & \cdots \\ \vdots & & & \\ \langle w_2, g_n\rangle & \cdots & & \cdots \\ \langle w_3, g_1\rangle & \cdots & & \cdots \\ \vdots & & & \\ \langle w_3, g_n\rangle & \cdots & & \cdots \end{array} \quad + \quad [\text{someone}_i\ [\text{A or B}]] \quad = \quad \begin{array}{l|ccc} & \cdots & i & \cdots \\ \hline \langle w_1, g_1^a\rangle & \cdots & a & \cdots \\ \langle w_1, g_1^b\rangle & \cdots & b & \cdots \\ \langle w_1, g_1^c\rangle & \cdots & c & \cdots \\ \vdots & & & \\ \langle w_1, g_n^a\rangle & \cdots & a & \cdots \\ \langle w_1, g_n^b\rangle & \cdots & b & \cdots \\ \langle w_1, g_n^c\rangle & \cdots & c & \cdots \\ \langle w_2, g_1^{a'}\rangle & \cdots & a' & \cdots \\ \langle w_2, g_1^{b'}\rangle & \cdots & b' & \cdots \\ \vdots & & & \\ \langle w_2, g_n^{a'}\rangle & \cdots & a' & \cdots \\ \langle w_2, g_n^{b'}\rangle & \cdots & b' & \cdots \end{array}$$

Therefore C_0 + [not [someone$_i$ [A or B]]] will not contain any pairs that have w_1 or w_2 as their world element, since these are the pairs that have extended assignments in C_1.

(64)
$$\begin{array}{l|ccc} & \cdots & i & \cdots \\ \hline \langle w_1, g_1\rangle & \cdots & & \cdots \\ \vdots & & & \\ \langle w_1, g_n\rangle & \cdots & & \cdots \\ \langle w_2, g_1\rangle & \cdots & & \cdots \\ \vdots & & & \\ \langle w_2, g_n\rangle & \cdots & & \cdots \\ \langle w_3, g_1\rangle & \cdots & & \cdots \\ \vdots & & & \\ \langle w_3, g_n\rangle & \cdots & & \cdots \end{array} \quad + \quad [\text{not [someone}_i \text{ [A or B]]]} \quad = \quad \begin{array}{l|ccc} & \cdots & i & \cdots \\ \hline \langle w_3, g_1\rangle & \cdots & & \cdots \\ \vdots & & & \\ \langle w_3, g_n\rangle & \cdots & & \cdots \end{array}$$

Call the output state in (64) C_2. What happens if we update C_2 with the negation of [not [someone$_i$ A]]? As before, we first have to check what happens when we update it with [not [someone$_i$ A]]. But [not [someone$_i$ A]] is itself the negation of another sentence, so we must first check the result of updating C_2 with the negatum [someone$_i$ A]. Since i is new in the state, [someone$_i$ A] triggers random assignment: we put in the output state pairs where the assignment maps i to something that is an A-person in w_3. There are no such individuals as it happens, so there are no such assignments, and no such pairs. So the result of updating C_2 with [someone$_i$ A] is the empty set:

(65) $C_2 + [\text{someone}_i \text{ A}] = \varnothing$

Given (65) we can now determine the result of updating C_2 with [not [someone$_i$ A]]: we must remove from the state those pairs that contain an assignment that is extended in (65). Since no assignment is extended in the empty set, we remove nothing. Therefore updating C_2 with [not [someone$_i$ A]] returns C_2 itself:

(66) $C_2 + [\text{not [someone}_i \text{ A]]} = C_2$

From (66) it is clear that updating C_2 with the *negation* of [not [someone$_i$ A]] produces the empty set; the update removes from C_2 those pairs that contain an assignment that is extended in the output in (66), i.e., in C_2. These are the elements of C_2 themselves:

(67) $C_2 + [\neg[\text{not [someone}_i \text{ A]]}] = C_2 - C_2 = \varnothing$

The result, then, is that [not [someone$_i$ [A or B]]] is predicted to be inconsistent with the negation of its alternative [not [someone$_i$ A]], that is, that [not [someone$_i$ [A or B]]] entails [not [someone$_i$ A]], and by the same reasoning, [not [someone$_i$ B]] and [not [someone$_i$ [A and B]]]. *Any* is therefore predicted to be licensed under negated indefinites, as desired.

Taking Stock. The previous three subsections showed the formal details of how (a) dynamicizing the operation of exhaustification, coupled with (b) a view of indefinites wherein their formal alternatives are interpreted as bound pronouns, allows us to correctly derive facts regarding the licensing of *any*. Specifically, we showed why the *any* condition is only satisfied in the case of negated indefinites, but not unnegated ones: in the former case the subdomain alternatives are entailed by the (exhaustified) sentence; in the latter they are not.

We next turn to the case of modals which, unlike indefinite quantifiers/adverbs, license *any* in their scope. In the following subsection we will offer a suggestion as to how modals can be made to fit within this view of dynamic exhaustification.

8.3.5 Modals

With possibility modals we propose a semantics that is partly similar to the semantics of indefinites, and partly different. The similarity is that the update depends on whether or not the index (on the modal in this case) is in the domain of the input state. The difference is that the output state, when the index is not novel, is determined on a purely quantificational basis; recall that with indefinites the semantics for "old" indices was effectively pronominal. The entry is shown in (68).[18]

[18] Although we do not focus on necessity modals here, we can provide a semantics that parallels (68) for completeness:

(1) $C + [\![\textbf{necessary/required S}]\!] = \{\langle w, g\rangle : \langle w, g\rangle \in C \ \&\ \mathrm{Acc}(w, g) + [\neg[\![\mathbf{S}]\!]] = \varnothing\}$.

(68) $C + [\![\textbf{possible}_i\ \textbf{S}]\!] =$

$$\begin{cases} \{\langle w,g\rangle : \langle w,g\rangle \in C \ \&\ \mathrm{Acc}(w,g) + [\![\mathbf{S}]\!] \neq \varnothing\} & \text{if } i \in Dom(C) \\ \{\langle w,g\rangle : \exists h(h \sim_i g \ \&\ \langle w,h\rangle \in C \ \&\ \\ \qquad \exists u(\langle u,h\rangle \in \mathrm{Acc}(w,h) + [\![\mathbf{S}]\!] \ \&\ g(i) = \langle u,h\rangle))\} & \text{if } i \notin Dom(C) \end{cases}$$

We assume that Acc(w, g) is a state; a set of world-assignment pairs that are related in some way to (the occupants of) the input pair $\langle w, g\rangle$. We set aside the details of how Acc itself is defined (how it draws on conversational background and ordering source(s), etc.). The first line of (68) says that updating a context C with a possibility statement [possible/allowed$_i$ S] preserves from C those pairs whose accessible states are not neutralized upon update with S. In other words, $\langle w, g\rangle$ survives the update iff S is not impossible given what is accessible from $\langle w, g\rangle$. The line has no dynamic consequences. The second line says nearly the same thing, except that it also stores the possibilities that instantiate the modal's prejacent in the i slot in the output state. We do not discuss the details of this, since our goal is not to present this particular semantics as an account of modal subordination. The goal is to propose a semantics that can, at least in principle, capture modal subordination phenomena by making it possible for modals to introduce their own discourse referents. To keep things simple, we assume that Novelty applies to modals the same way it applies to indefinites, namely along the lines in (34) which constrains the application of novelty to utterances.

Turning back to our immediate interests, we will now show that FC results from applying Exh to something like (69a), given the alternatives in (69b). This means that *any* is predicted to be licensed under possibility modals, as desired.

(69) a. [possible$_i$/allowed$_i$ [A or B]]
b. [possible$_i$/allowed$_i$ A]
[possible$_i$/allowed$_i$ B]
[possible$_i$/allowed$_i$ [A and B]]

Before we work through the details we want to make a few things clear. First, we will assume that the disjunctive prejacent in our example, [A or B], is index-free. We assume this to keep the presentation simple—the reader may verify afterwards that having indices in [A or B] does not affect the important predictions. Second, we assume that for any given world w and any two assignments g, h, the worlds that appear in Acc(w, g), that is, the worlds that appear in the pairs that populate Acc(w, g), are the same as the worlds that appear in Acc(w, h). The intuition here is that accessibility between one world and another world is independent of assignments; what is possible given a set of laws, goals, etc., is not affected by the anaphoric details of the context of speech (e.g., which index is in the domain of the given state, and which indices are mapped to which entities in the domain, etc.). Third, we assume that these anaphoric details persist through accessibility: for any assignment g and world w, the pairs that populate Acc(w, g) all have g as their second element. This means that the anaphoric information encoded in a pair $\langle w, g\rangle$ does not change in the pairs that are accessible from $\langle w, g\rangle$. Finally, we will use the same visuals that we used in our earlier discussion of indefinites, but as the reader will notice, some (irrelevant) technical detail will be omitted. Recall that we used the letters *a*, *b*, *c*, etc., to designate our "discourse referents" in the case of indefinites. Here, going by the semantics in (68), the discourse referents are world-assignment pairs, not individuals. So, when a state is updated with a possibility statement, the index in the output state should be mapped by the various assignment functions to (possibly) various world-assignment pairs. However, instead of spelling out the contents of these pairs in our tables, we will use the letters *a*, *b*, *c* like we did in the indefinite example.

Now consider the following set-up. Let C_0 contain the world-assignment pairs below:

(70)

	…	i	…
$\langle w_1, g_1\rangle$	…		…
⋮			
$\langle w_1, g_n\rangle$	…		…
$\langle w_2, g_1\rangle$	…		…
⋮			
$\langle w_2, g_n\rangle$	…		…
$\langle w_3, g_1\rangle$	…		…
⋮			
$\langle w_3, g_n\rangle$	…		…
$\langle w_4, g_1\rangle$	…		…
⋮			
$\langle w_4, g_n\rangle$	…		…
$\langle w_5, g_1\rangle$	…		…
⋮			
$\langle w_5, g_n\rangle$	…		…

Let the elements of C_0 each be in the domain of an accessibility relation Acc. Let $\mathrm{Acc}(w_1, g_1)$ contain *a*, *b*, and *c*; $\mathrm{Acc}(w_2, g_1)$ contain a' and b'; $\mathrm{Acc}(w_3, g_1)$ contain d, e; $\mathrm{Acc}(w_4, g_1)$ contain a''; $\mathrm{Acc}(w_5, g_1)$ contain b''. The letters a, b, c are short for the pairs $\langle v_1, g_1\rangle$, $\langle u_1, g_1\rangle$, $\langle z_1, g_1\rangle$, a', b' are short for $\langle v_2, g_1\rangle$, $\langle u_2, g_1\rangle$, a'', b'' are short for $\langle v_4, g_1\rangle$, $\langle u_5, g_1\rangle$, and d, e are not important as will soon be clear:

(71) a. $\mathrm{Acc}(w_1,g_1) = \{a,b,c\} = \{\langle v_1,g_1\rangle, \langle u_1,g_1\rangle, \langle z_1,g_1\rangle\}$
b. $\mathrm{Acc}(w_2,g_1) = \{a',b'\} = \{\langle v_2,g_1\rangle, \langle u_2,g_1\rangle\}$
c. $\mathrm{Acc}(w_3,g_1) = \{d,e\}$
d. $\mathrm{Acc}(w_4,g_1) = \{a''\} = \{\langle v_4,g_1\rangle\}$
e. $\mathrm{Acc}(w_5,g_1) = \{b''\} = \{\langle u_5,g_1\rangle\}$

Our two assumptions about accessibility above guarantee two things: first, that only g_1 will appear in the pairs in $\mathrm{Acc}(w_1, g_1)$, and likewise for $\mathrm{Acc}(w_2, g_1)$, as shown in (71a,b) respectively; second, that the same worlds from $\mathrm{Acc}(w_1, g_1)$ appear in $\mathrm{Acc}(w_1, g_n)$, and the same worlds from $\mathrm{Acc}(w_2, g_1)$ appear in $\mathrm{Acc}(w_2, g_n)$. This is not to say that the two sets of *pairs* are identical; although the worlds in $\mathrm{Acc}(w_1, g_1)$ and $\mathrm{Acc}(w_1, g_n)$ are the same, in $\mathrm{Acc}(w_1, g_1)$ they are paired with g_1, while in $\mathrm{Acc}(w_1, g_n)$ they are paired with g_n. This is not a trivial difference by any means: g_1 and g_n may map the same index, say *k*, to two different individuals, and as a result it may turn out that the pair $\langle u, g_1\rangle$—for some world *u*—survives update with a sentence S, while the pair $\langle u, g_n\rangle$ does not. But in our example the prejacent [A or B] is by assumption index-free, so for our purposes $\mathrm{Acc}(w_1, g_1)$ and $\mathrm{Acc}(w_1, g_n)$ are identical; the worlds that appear in the two sets are the same, and the semantic content of [A or B], our prejacent, depends only on the world elements of the two sets.

Now let us say more about the accessible pairs in (71). Assume that $\langle v_1, g_1\rangle$, aka a, is an element of $\mathrm{Acc}(w_1, g_1) + [A]$ but not of $\mathrm{Acc}(w_1, g_1) + [B]$. This is what makes a the "A" possibility that is accessible from $\langle w_1, g_1\rangle$. Assume also that b is an element of $\mathrm{Acc}(w_1, g_1) + [B]$ but not of $\mathrm{Acc}(w_1, g_1) + [A]$, and that c is an element of $\mathrm{Acc}(w_1, g_1) + [A]$ and $\mathrm{Acc}(w_1, g_1) + [B]$: b is the w_1-accessible "B" possibility and c is the "A and B" possibility. The pairs that are accessible from w_2 are like a and b: $\langle v_2, g_1\rangle$, aka a', is an element of

$\text{Acc}(w_2, g_1) + [\text{A}]$ but not $\text{Acc}(w_2, g_1) + [\text{B}]$, and b' is an element of $\text{Acc}(w_2, g_1) + [\text{B}]$ but not $\text{Acc}(w_2, g_1) + [\text{A}]$. Furthermore, assume that $\text{Acc}(w_3, g_1) + [\text{A}]$ and $\text{Acc}(w_3, g_1) + [\text{B}]$ are empty (this is why d and e in (71c) were not worth spelling out). Finally, assume that the only pairs accessible from w_4 are like a, aka a'', and the only pairs accessible from w_5 are like b, aka b''. These details are spelled out below:

(72) $a \in \text{Acc}(w_1,g_1)+[\text{A}]$ $a \notin \text{Acc}(w_1,g_1)+[\text{B}]$	(73) $a' \in \text{Acc}(w_2,g_1)+[\text{A}]$ $a' \notin \text{Acc}(w_2,g_1)+[\text{B}]$	(74) $a'' \in \text{Acc}(w_4,g_1)+[\text{A}]$ $a'' \notin \text{Acc}(w_4,g_1)+[\text{B}]$
$b \notin \text{Acc}(w_1,g_1)+[\text{A}]$ $b \in \text{Acc}(w_1,g_1)+[\text{B}]$	$b' \notin \text{Acc}(w_2,g_1)+[\text{A}]$ $b' \in \text{Acc}(w_2,g_1)+[\text{B}]$	(75) $b'' \notin \text{Acc}(w_5,g_1)+[\text{A}]$ $b'' \in \text{Acc}(w_5,g_1)+[\text{B}]$
$c \in \text{Acc}(w_1,g_1)+[\text{A}]$ $c \in \text{Acc}(w_1,g_1)+[\text{B}]$		

Given all of this, what is the result of updating C_0 with a sentence of the form in (69a), i.e., $[\Diamond_i\ [\text{A or B}]]$? The definition in (68) says that, in the assignments in the output state, the index i must be mapped to a pair that appears in $\text{Acc}(w, g) + [\text{A or B}]$, where $\langle w, g \rangle$ appears in C_0, and where the assignments in the output must differ from g at most with respect to i. For example, the pair $\langle w_1, g_1[i \rightarrow a] \rangle$, hereafter $\langle w_1, g_1^a \rangle$, will appear in the output state, because its assignment element is identical to g_1, except that it maps i to a, i.e., the "A" pair $\langle v_1, g_1 \rangle$, which is an element of $\text{Acc}(w_1, g_1)$. The pair $\langle w_1, g_1^b \rangle$ will also appear in the result of the update, for similar reasons, and so on. The result of the update is therefore a state where i is mapped to accessible pairs that have the indicated property (a being the "A" pair, b being the "B" pair, etc., as described above). Now we will see that, like in the static case, the conjunctive alternative $[\Diamond_i\ [\text{A and B}]]$ is predicted to be excludable, and the disjunct alternatives $[\Diamond_i\ \text{A}]$, $[\Diamond_i\ \text{B}]$ are predicted to be includable.

(76)

	…	i	…
$\langle w_1, g_1\rangle$	…		…
⋮			
$\langle w_1, g_n\rangle$	…		…
$\langle w_2, g_1\rangle$	…		…
⋮			
$\langle w_2, g_n\rangle$	…		…
$\langle w_3, g_1\rangle$	…		…
⋮			
$\langle w_3, g_n\rangle$	…		…
$\langle w_4, g_1\rangle$	…		…
⋮			
$\langle w_4, g_n\rangle$	…		…
$\langle w_5, g_1\rangle$	…		…
⋮			
$\langle w_5, g_n\rangle$	…		…

$+ \ [\Diamond_i \text{ [A or B]]} \ =$

	…	i	…
$\langle w_1, g_1^a\rangle$	…	a	…
$\langle w_1, g_1^b\rangle$	…	b	…
$\langle w_1, g_1^c\rangle$	…	c	…
⋮			
$\langle w_1, g_n^a\rangle$	…	a	…
$\langle w_1, g_n^b\rangle$	…	b	…
$\langle w_1, g_n^c\rangle$	…	c	…
$\langle w_2, g_1^{a'}\rangle$	…	a'	…
$\langle w_2, g_1^{b'}\rangle$	…	b'	…
⋮			
$\langle w_2, g_n^{a'}\rangle$	…	a'	…
$\langle w_2, g_n^{b'}\rangle$	…	b'	…
$\langle w_4, g_1^{a''}\rangle$	…	a''	…
⋮			
$\langle w_4, g_n^{a''}\rangle$	…	a''	…
$\langle w_5, g_1^{b''}\rangle$	…	b''	…
⋮			
$\langle w_5, g_n^{b''}\rangle$	…	b''	…

Let us work through the first prediction first. Call the output state in (76) C_1. What is the result of updating C_1 with the negation of [$\Diamond_i$ [A and B]]? To find out, we must first consider the update with the unnegated sentence [$\Diamond_i$ [A and B]]. Notice that, because the index i is in the domain of C_1, the update (as formulated in the definition in (68)) will make requirements that depend only on the world element of the pairs in C_1, not the assignment element. For instance, the condition on keeping the pair $\langle w_1, g_1^a\rangle$ is that Acc(w_1, g_1^a) permit [A and B], that is, that Acc(w_1, g_1^a) + [A and B] is non-empty. By assumption we know that this is indeed the case, because the possibilities that are accessible from $\langle w_1, g_1^a\rangle$ have the same worlds as the ones that are accessible from $\langle w_1, g_1\rangle$. And because by assumption Acc(w_1, g_1) + [A and B] is non-empty—it contains the pair we designate as c—it follows that Acc(w_1, g_1^a) + [A and B] is also non-empty.[19] Therefore $\langle w_1, g_1^a\rangle$, and by the same reasoning $\langle w_1, g_1^b\rangle$ and $\langle w_1, g_1^c\rangle$ are predicted to survive updating C_1 with [$\Diamond_i$ [A and B]]. By contrast, the pairs containing w_2

[19] Is it possible for Acc(w_1, g_1) + [A and B] to be non-empty but for Acc(w_1, g_1^a) + [A and B] to be empty because g_1 maps i to a? The only way for this difference between g_1 and g_1^a to matter is if part of the conjunction [A and B] has an expression that carries index i. Suppose that this is the case. Then our sentence would have to be of the form [$\Diamond_i$ [A and [B … X$_i$ …]]].

do not survive the update, because the accessible possibilities from them do not permit [A and B], nor do the pairs containing w_4 or w_5.

From this it follows that (76) can be updated with [¬ [$\Diamond_i$ [A and B]]], with the following result:

(77)

$$
\begin{array}{llll}
 & \cdots & i & \cdots \\
\hline
\langle w_1, g_1^a \rangle & \cdots & a & \cdots \\
\langle w_1, g_1^b \rangle & \cdots & b & \cdots \\
\langle w_1, g_1^c \rangle & \cdots & c & \cdots \\
\vdots & & & \\
\langle w_1, g_n^a \rangle & \cdots & a & \cdots \\
\langle w_1, g_n^b \rangle & \cdots & b & \cdots \\
\langle w_1, g_n^c \rangle & \cdots & c & \cdots \\
\langle w_2, g_1^{a'} \rangle & \cdots & a' & \cdots \\
\langle w_2, g_1^{b'} \rangle & \cdots & b' & \cdots \\
\vdots & & & \\
\langle w_2, g_n^{a'} \rangle & \cdots & a' & \cdots \\
\langle w_2, g_n^{b'} \rangle & \cdots & b' & \cdots \\
\langle w_4, g_1^{a''} \rangle & \cdots & a'' & \cdots \\
\vdots & & & \\
\langle w_4, g_n^{a''} \rangle & \cdots & a'' & \cdots \\
\langle w_5, g_1^{b''} \rangle & \cdots & b'' & \cdots \\
\vdots & & & \\
\langle w_5, g_n^{b''} \rangle & \cdots & b'' & \cdots
\end{array}
\quad + \quad [\neg[\Diamond_i \text{ [A and B]]]} \quad = \quad
\begin{array}{llll}
 & \cdots & i & \cdots \\
\hline
\langle w_2, g_1^{a'} \rangle & \cdots & a' & \cdots \\
\langle w_2, g_1^{b'} \rangle & \cdots & b' & \cdots \\
\vdots & & & \\
\langle w_2, g_n^{a'} \rangle & \cdots & a' & \cdots \\
\langle w_2, g_n^{b'} \rangle & \cdots & b' & \cdots \\
\langle w_4, g_1^{a''} \rangle & \cdots & a'' & \cdots \\
\vdots & & & \\
\langle w_4, g_n^{a''} \rangle & \cdots & a'' & \cdots \\
\langle w_5, g_1^{b''} \rangle & \cdots & b'' & \cdots \\
\vdots & & & \\
\langle w_5, g_n^{b''} \rangle & \cdots & b'' & \cdots
\end{array}
$$

It should now be clear that updating this outcome with [¬[$\Diamond_i$ [A]]] produces a state where i is mapped to pairs involving w_5 and nothing else. A subsequent update with [¬[$\Diamond_i$ [B]]] will produce an empty result. The second prediction, that the disjunct alternatives are includable, should be easy to see. If the state is updated with [$\Diamond$ [A]], all but the pairs involving w_5 will be preserved, and a subsequent update with [$\Diamond$ [B]] will further eliminate any pairs involving w_4, leaving us with pairs involving w_2.

What we have shown here is how this semantics for modals, integrated within a dynamicized version of exhaustification, correctly predicts that *any* should be licensed given that the formal alternatives are shown to be includable, and thus, entailed.

8.4 A (Potential) Problem for Future Work

The main point of interest in this paper has been the contrast between existential quantifiers and possibility modals in terms of their ability to license *any* in their scope; we repeat this contrast below:

(78) a. Mary is allowed bring any friends to the party.
b. *Some people brought any friends to the party.

In the previous section we argued for an analysis wherein indefinites bind into their formal alternatives while modals do not, and we formulated the details in terms of dynamic exhaustification. The resulting pronoun-like behavior of (the alternatives to) indefinites limited their potential of licensing FC, and in consequence stopped them from licensing *any*. Modals, by contrast, do not behave like pronouns in the context of exhaustification, so their FC licensing potential, and therefore their ability to license *any*, is not affected by the dynamic switch.

A question that arises at this point is the following: do we expect existential quantifiers to disrupt the licensing of FC *any* when *any* occurs in the scope of the possibility modal licensor? We predict that sentences following the schemata in (79) where the disjunction is replaced by *any* should indeed be unacceptable if what is at stake is whether or not the alternatives to the prejacent of the exhaustivity operator are includable.

(79) a. Prejacent: [allowed$_j$ [[some people]$_i$ [A or B]]]
b. Alternatives: [allowed$_j$ [[some people]$_i$ A]]
[allowed$_j$ [[some people]$_i$ B]]
[allowed$_j$ [[some people]$_i$ [A and B]]]

The presence of an existential quantifier in the scope of the exhaustification operator, regardless of whether there is a possibility modal intervening, means that the indefinite in (79) will bind into the alternatives in (79b). Intuitively, a sentence following the structure in (79) will have as strengthened meaning the result in (80), which amounts to a distributive reading such that of the group of people who did A or B, only some did A and only some did B.

(80) *it's possible that some people did A or B* and
it's not possible that these people did both and
it's not possible that these people all did A and
it's not possible that these people all did B.

The example in (81) illustrates the same point. The relevant subdomain alternatives in (81a–81b) are excludable, meaning that (81) entails that grandpa is not allowed to send all those toys to Mary and he's not allowed to send all those toys to Sue. A sentence such as (81) can be uttered truthfully in a scenario in which grandpa is allowed to send a toy train and a toy car to Mary and a doll and a puzzle to Sue.

(81) Grandpa is allowed to send some toys to Mary or Sue.
a. Grandpa is allowed to send those toys to Mary.
b. Grandpa is allowed to send those toys to Sue.
c. Grandpa is allowed to send those toys to Mary and Sue.

What these examples show is that the subdomain alternatives are not entailed, a fact which, following Crnič's *Any* generalization, should mean that *any* is not acceptable in such configurations. And yet examples like the following appear to be acceptable.

(82) a. Bill is allowed to introduce some students to any faculty members.
b. Marta is allowed to buy some gifts for any of her cousins.
c. Paula is allowed to give some sweets to any kids.
d. Kai is allowed to send some threatening emails to any of his enemies.

We claim that the acceptability of these sentences is due to the fact that the underlying representation does not respect the c-commanding relations in (79), either because the indefinite outscopes the modal, receiving a specific indefinite interpretation, or because it scopes below *any*. If either of these conditions holds, then for purposes of exhaustification the alternatives will become includable and thus entailed, thereby satisfying Crnič's condition. Below we consider each possibility in turn.

The first case involving a specific indefinite interpretation is straightforward. For a sentence such as (82b), the paraphrase we are after is the following: There is a specific set of gifts such that Marta is allowed to buy them for any of her cousins. The subdomain alternatives, which are of the form *Marta is allowed to buy them for cousin A, Marta is allowed to buy them for cousin B, ...,* cannot be excluded without giving rise to a contradiction; they can, however, be included, thus giving rise to the expected FC inferences characteristic of configurations involving *any* in the scope of a possibility modal.

The second case involves a low indefinite, namely a configuration where the FCI *any* scope above the indefinite. Let's consider (82c) in a context with two relevant kids: Mary and Sue. The interpretation we are after is one where the scope relations respect the surface structure of the double object construction variant of (82c), namely (83). We will see that while the conjunctive alternative is excludable, the disjunctive ones are not and in fact can be included, therefore satisfying Crnič's generalization and thus helping us understand why *any* can appear in such sentences.

(83) Paula is allowed to give any kids some sweets.
  a. Paula is allowed to give Mary some sweets.
  b. Paula is allowed to give Sue some sweets.
  c. Paula is allowed to give Mary and Sue some sweets.

Negating the conjunctive alternative amounts to saying that while Paula is allowed to give Mary or Sue some sweets, she's not allowed to give them both those sweets. This is of course consistent. Notice, however, that if we try to exclude the subdomain alternatives, we run into a contradiction, since *she's not allowed to give Mary those sweets* and *she's not allowed to give Sue those sweets* is not consistent with the assertion in (83). Their inclusion, however, is consistent, and it leads to the expected FC inference that *Paula is allowed to give Sue some sweets* and *Paula allowed to give Mary some sweets*.

What we showed above is that the problem introduced by intervening indefinites is only a problem on a non-specific reading of the indefinite where it outscopes the FCI; the moment the indefinite is allowed to escape the scope of the modal, or scope below the FCI, there no longer is an issue of intervening discourse referents. The question then is the following: Can we create a context that forces the indefinite to be interpreted in the scope of the modal while at the same time outscoping the FCI?

In order to exclude a non-specific interpretation, we can appeal to verbs of creation which would force the indefinite to be interpreted in the scope of the modal. In order to guarantee that the FCI does not outscope the indefinite we can introduce a bound pronoun in the argument headed by *any*. Some such attempts are shown below in (84).

(84) a. Bill is allowed to write [some letters]$_i$ to anyone who wants them$_i$.
b. Noa is allowed to bake [some muffins]$_i$ for anyone who orders them$_i$.

Possibly not surprisingly, the examples above appear to be acceptable, despite the fact that they involve a FCI in a scope position where it should not be acceptable according to Crnič's generalization. Notice, however, that in our attempt to trap the scope of the FCI we had to overload it, leading to a possible subtrigging configuration. Subtrigging is a well-known problem faced by theories of FCIs as it involves FCIs occurring in configurations where they would otherwise be ruled out, e.g., the contrast in (85a) vs (85b) (cf. Crnič, 2019; Dayal, 2013).

(85) a. *Bill talked to any student.
b. Bill talked to any student who came to his office hours.

We have to leave a more detailed discussion of this potential issue for another occasion.

8.5 Conclusion

We began this paper by identifying a previously undiscussed contrast between indefinite quantifiers and modals in terms of their varying ability to license FC *any*, despite seemingly parallel licensing of FC inferences. We argued that current exhaustification-based accounts of *any* cannot provide a solution to this problem without stipulating unjustified conditions on the licensing conditions for *any*. We proposed, instead, to dynamicize exhaustification and, building on Sudo (2016, 2023), to argue that the formal alternatives to an indefinite must be anaphoric to it, a condition that need not apply to modals. In doing so, we were also able to provide a solution to a different but related problem concerning disjunctions embedded under singular indefinites.

Before we conclude, we would like to point that the contrast discussed in this paper between indefinite quantifiers and modals is not restricted to the issue of FC *any* covered in this paper. In fact, a split along the same lines has been previously identified in the following domains:

Intervention:	universal quantifiers but not universal modals intervene in NPI licensing (Chierchia, 2004; Linebarger, 1987).
Comparatives:	according to the Heim-Kennedy generalization (Kennedy, 1997; Heim, 2000), degree operators cannot bind into the scope of quantifiers, but can into the scope of modals.
Distributivity:	the strength of distributive inferences of disjunctions embedded under universal quantifiers on the one hand and universal modals on the other varies greatly (Crnič et al., 2015; Ramotowska et al., 2022).
Local implicatures:	existential quantifiers, but not existential modals, give rise to embedded/local implicatures (Sudo, 2016).

For the observation that quantifiers and modals behave differently with respect to their ability to give rise to local implicatures Sudo (2016) offers an account couched within dynamic semantics, not dissimilar to what we presented in this paper. Future work should try to investigate how this system can be extended to account for some of the other contrasts mentioned above.

References

Alonso-Ovalle, L. (2005). Distributing the disjuncts over the modal space. In L. Bateman & C. Ussery (Eds.), *Proceedings of the 35th meeting of the North East Linguistic Society* (pp. 75–86). GLSA Publications.

Bar-Lev, M. E., & Fox, D. (2020). Free choice, simplification, and Innocent Inclusion. *Natural Language Semantics, 28*, 175–223.

Chierchia, G. (2004). Scalar implicatures, polarity phenomena, and the syntax/pragmatics interface. In A. Belletti (Ed.), *Structure and beyond: The cartography of syntactic structures* (pp. 39–103). Oxford University Press.
Chierchia, G. (2013). *Logic in grammar: Polarity, free choice, and intervention.* Oxford University Press.
Crnič, L. 2019. *Any*: Logic, likelihood, and context (pt. 1). *Language and Linguistics Compass* 13, e12354.
Crnič, L. (2022). Number in NPI licensing. *Natural Language Semantics, 30,* 1–46.
Crnič, L., Chemla, E., & Fox, D. (2015). Scalar implicatures of embedded disjunction. *Natural Language Semantics, 23,* 271–305.
Dayal, V. (2013). A viability constraint on alternatives for free choice. In A. Fălău (Ed.), *Alternatives in semantics* (pp. 88–122). Palgrave Studies in Pragmatics: Language and Cognition.
Fox, D. (2007). Free choice and the theory of scalar implicatures. In U. Sauerland & P. Stateva (Eds.), *Presupposition and implicature in compositional semantics* (pp. 71–120). Palgrave Macmillan.
Heim, I. (1982). *The semantics of definite and indefinite noun phrases.* Doctoral Dissertation, UMass, Amherst.
Heim, I. (2000). Degree operators and scope. In B. Jackson & T. Matthews (Eds.), *SALT X.* . CLC Publications.
Heim, I., & Kratzer, A. (1998). *Semantics in generative grammar*. Blackwell.
Kennedy, C. (1997). *Projecting the adjective*. Doctoral Dissertation, UC Santa Cruz. Published as Kennedy (1999).
Klinedinst, N. (2007). *Plurality and possibility*. Doctoral Dissertation, UCLA.
Krifka, M. (1995). The semantics and pragmatics of polarity items. *Linguistic Analysis, 25,* 209–257.
Krifka, M. (1999). At least some determiners aren't determiners. In K. Turner (Ed.), *The semantics/pragmatics interface from different points of view, Volume 1: Current research in the semantics/pragmatics interface.* Elsevier Science Ltd.
Ladusaw, W. (1979). *Polarity sensitivity as inherent scope relations.* Doctoral Dissertation, University of Texas at Austin.
Lahiri, U. (1998). Focus and negative polarity in Hindi. *Natural Language Semantics, 6,* 57–125.
Linebarger, M. (1987). Negative polarity and grammatical representation. *Linguistics and Philosophy, 10,* 325–387.

Meyer, M-C. (2020). Free choice disjunction. In D. Gutzmann, L. Matthewson, C. Meier, H. Rullmann, & T. Ede Zimmermann (Eds.), *The Wiley Blackwell companion to semantics*. Wiley-Blackwell.

Ramotowska, S., Marty, P., Romoli, J., Sudo, Y., & Breheny, R. (2022). Diversity with universality. In M. Degano, T. Roberts, G. Sbardolini, & M. Schouwstra (Eds.), *Proceedings of the 23rd Amsterdam Colloquium*. ILLC.

Sauerland, U. (2004). Scalar implicatures in complex sentences. *Linguistics and Philosophy, 27*, 367–391.

Schmitt, V. (2023). Are there pluralities of worlds? *Journal of Semantics, 40*, 153–178.

Sudo, Y. 2016. The existential problem of scalar implicatures and anaphora across alternatives. In C. Piñón (Ed.), *Empirical issues in syntax and semantics* (Vol. 11; pp. 225–244). CSSP.

Sudo, Y. (2023). Scalar implicatures with discourse referents: A case study on plurality inferences. *Linguistics and Philosophy, 46*, 1161–1217.

Part IV

Commentary

9

Monotonicity, Substitution Sources, and the Robustness of Disjunct Alternatives

Raj Singh

9.1 Introduction

In my commentary, I will aim to synthesize and sharpen various claims in the literature that have been made about the interaction between grammar (formal alternatives, exhaustification) and context (relevance considerations and quantity reasoning that is free of syntactic stipulations). I will in particular focus on questions of optionality: What, if any, are the options when considering which formal or relevant alternatives ought to enter into grammatical exhaustification or pragmatic quantity reasoning? Which consequences of alternative-sensitive reasoning must remain, and which may be cancelled? Is exhaustification required? What, if anything, do processing and acquisition data have to say about these questions?

R. Singh (✉)
Department of Cognitive Science, Carleton University, 1125 Colonel By Drive, K1S 5B6, Ottawa, ON, Canada
e-mail: raj.singh@carleton.ca

N. Gotzner et al. (eds.), *Alternatives in Grammar and Cognition*, Palgrave Studies in Pragmatics, Language and Cognition, https://doi.org/10.1007/978-3-031-76676-3_9

I will use disjunctive sentences and their disjunct alternatives as a place from which to address these questions. Along the way, I will tie together some observations that have previously been treated separately and I will generalize the characterization of oddness in Magri (2009) to extend to pragmatically generated ignorance inferences (and will hint at possible extensions to Condition B effects). Very roughly, I will conclude (i) that alternatives from different substitution sources have variable robustness in terms of their resistance to pruning (constituents are most robust, salient discourse constituents least, and lexical replacements are in-between), and (ii) pragmatically computed ignorance inferences, like grammatically computed exhaustification inferences, are monotonic (cannot be cancelled). For those who want to skip ahead to the fuller punchline, you can see my summary in (22) in Sect. 9.5.

The papers in this volume are concerned with alternatives, mechanisms that reason with alternatives, intonational cues speakers give to hearers to help them figure out which inferences ought to be drawn about which alternatives, the psycholinguistic mechanisms that perform operations specified by the competence systems of grammar and pragmatics, and the vexing matter of the interaction between salience and relevance. I hope that my discussion will provide a useful perspective from which to consider these matters, and I will allude to connections to papers in this volume in relevant places (mostly in scattered footnotes; much of this paper had been written when I saw the other papers in this volume).

I end the paper with some questions raised by numerals for theories of alternatives and exhaustification. Specifically, numerals suggest that alternatives can have more structure to them than the utterance itself, hence suggesting that there ought to be a limited role for structure building operations in the generation of alternatives. In processing and acquisition data, numerals seem to pattern more like free-choice implicatures than like scalar implicatures (cf. Sauerland et al., 2017). Neither source of alternative (subconstituent versus lexical substitution, cf. Bar-Lev, 2018; Bar-Lev & Fox, 2020; Chemla, 2009a; Chemla & Bott, 2014) nor manner of inference (like inclusion versus exclusion; cf. Bar-Lev, 2018; Bar-Lev & Fox, 2017) leads to placing numerals and free-choice on the one side and scalar implicatures on the other, but a general pressure relating parsing preferences to answers to questions does (Singh, 2019; Singh et al., 2016).

9.2 Reasoning with Alternatives

9.2.1 Disjuncts are Robust Alternatives

I begin by connecting three observations about the interpretation of disjunctive sentences and lead to some preliminary conclusions about their alternatives and the way they are reasoned with in conversation. First, it has been noted that disjunctive sentences $p \vee q$ do not license the scalar implicature (SI) that just one of the disjuncts is false. For example, Fox and Katzir (2011) note that (1) does not license the SI that yesterday John didn't talk to Mary.

(1) Yesterday John talked to Mary or Sue, and today he talked to Mary.

Note that even an overt *only* can't target just one of the disjuncts, even if it is made salient:[1]

(2) A: Did John talk to Mary?
No! He only talked to Mary or Sue!

This observation is relevant to the question of which alternatives may be pruned. Assume (following Fox, 2007; Sauerland, 2004; Katzir, 2007) that $p \vee q$ has the following formal alternatives: $F = \{p, q, p \wedge q\}$. We know $p \wedge q$ can be pruned from the set, given that $p \vee q$ doesn't always imply $\neg(p \wedge q)$. But which other subsets of F are possible as actual alternatives to $p \vee q$? The observations above suggest that $F' = \{p\}$ is not a possible set of alternatives.

Second, the ignorance inferences associated with disjunctive sentences appear to be extremely robust, to the point that they appear to be mandatory. For example, consider the following contrast from Singh (2008b):

[1] I assume (following Singh, 2008a) that in response to utterance s, the response *No!* r is felicitous only if r contradicts s.

(3) a. #I have three or more daughters.
b. I have more than two daughters.

The content of each sentence in (3) is the same: each sentence tells you that the speaker has at least three daughters. But the disjunctive way of expressing this is extremely odd, presumably because it suggests that the speaker is ignorant about whether they have exactly three daughters or more than three daughters. Note that there is nothing strange about the content of the disjunction itself; changing the subject to a third person eliminates the oddness, presumably because there is nothing odd about being ignorant about how many daughters someone else has.[2]

(4) a. Sandy has three or more daughters.
b. Sandy has more than two daughters.

The only way out of oddness in (3-a) seems to be to give up the usual assumption that any given person will know how many daughters they have. For example, we might learn that they have a problem with their memory or worse because they actually haven't kept track. Without this exceptional information, we stick to our default common knowledge assumption that someone knows the number and gender distribution of their children. As we will see in more detail below, under the architecture in Fox (2007) the contrast in (3) would suggest that each disjunct must be relevant and furthermore that the ignorance implicatures computed by the Maxim of Quantity cannot be cancelled.

Third, when we embed the odd disjunction in (3) under a universal operator the oddness disappears:

(5) (In order to make my parents happy) it is required that I have three or more daughters.

---

[2] In particular, (3-a) is likely not a Hurford Disjunction (Hurford, 1974). A Hurford Disjunction is one in which one of the disjuncts entails the other, and such disjuncts are known to be odd (e.g., # *John was born in Paris or France*). The oddness can be obviated if one of the disjuncts implicates that the other is false (e.g., Gazdar, 1979), such as *Sandy ate some or all of the cookies* or *the first two students passed or all of them did*. Such cases have been used to argue for local implicatures (e.g., Chierchia et al., 2012 and much other work; see also Chemla et al., 2016 for processing evidence). We assume that numerals have a basic 'at least meaning' that can be strengthened to an 'exactly' meaning (see, e.g., Spector, 2013 for discussion). Thus, disjuncts like *three or more* will be understood as 'exactly' three or more than three.

Note that in (5) we have replaced ignorance inferences with SIs. Specifically, (5) implies that the speaker is not required to have exactly three daughters and is not required to have more than three daughters. So long as they reach at least three, all will be well with their parents. There are two observations I'd like to highlight here. First, the existence of these SIs suggests that each of *it is required that I have three daughters* and *it is required that I have more than three daughters* is an alternative. Crucially, it is not possible to have just one of these as an SI. For example, (5) cannot convey that the speaker is not required to have exactly three daughters but leave open whether they are required to have more than three. Note for example that it would be odd for the hearer to respond like in (6); their response suggests that there is something they didn't quite grasp about the speaker's intention.

(6) S: (In order to make my parents happy) it is required that I have three or more daughters.
H:# Okay, so you're allowed to have more than three daughters. But are you required to?

Second, it appears that each of these SIs is mandatorily generated. For example, the speaker cannot in the same breath utter (5) and then try to cancel the SI:

(7) H: How many daughters are you required to have (in order to make your parents happy)?
S: It is required that I have three or more daughters. # In fact, it is required that I have at least four daughters.

I take the above as evidence that disjuncts are 'robust' alternatives insofar as it appears very hard to ignore them during conversational reasoning. It is commonly assumed that *some* alternatives to a sentence may be pruned in some contexts in which they are not relevant, and hence may not turn into SIs or ignorance inferences. But if the above is right, disjunct alternatives are much harder to ignore in this way. Claims to this effect have been made in the prior literature, such as that the reasoning associated with disjunct alternatives is somehow special (e.g., Bar-Lev, 2018; Bar-Lev & Fox, 2017; Chemla, 2009a) or that disjunct alternatives are as a default included in conversational reasoning (e.g., Bar-Lev, 2018; Bar-Lev & Fox, 2020; Chemla & Bott, 2014). I will return to the connection between alternatives and reasoning shortly. For now, let me write down a version of the claim about the robustness of alternatives here; I will later generalize this to a claim about the robustness of alternatives from the various substitution sources proposed in Fox and Katzir (2011).

(8) Disjuncts are robust alternatives (revised in (15) below): When a sentence S is used in context c, assume (with Fox and Katzir, 2011) that S has a set of formal alternatives, F, and that there is a set of contextually relevant alternatives, C, and that the input to exhaustification is $A = C \cap F$ and that the Maxim of Quantity operates over C. Then:

a. When a sentence ϕ that contains a disjunction, $A \vee B$, call it $\phi(A \vee B)$, is used in context c, the alternatives $\phi(A)$ and $\phi(B)$ are *robust*.

b. Robust alternatives: An alternative T to S is *robust* if T must be in F and must be in C.

9.2.2 Reasoning and (Non-)Monotonicity

What (8) means, in effect, is that it is a safe bet that disjunct alternatives will enter into exhaustification computations in the grammar as well as into pragmatic reasoning. Versions of the claim in (8) are also often coupled with specific stipulations about reasoning with alternatives. These stipulations have proven useful in making sense of the relative robustness of free-choice inferences compared with 'some but not all' type scalar implicatures in adult processing and child acquisition.[3] A free-choice inference takes a sentence like *you're allowed to eat cake or ice-cream* and concludes that you're allowed to eat cake and you're allowed to eat ice-cream; it takes disjunct alternatives and concludes that each is true. A scalar implicature takes a sentence like *Sandy ate some of the cookies* and concludes that it is false that Sandy ate all of the cookies. In comparing free-choice inferences with scalar implicatures, free-choice inferences have been found to be faster to process, easier to embed, and earlier to develop in children (see references in Footnote 3).

One obvious difference between these inferences is that free-choice is derived using subconstituents as alternatives while scalar implicatures are derived using alternatives generated by lexical substitutions (*some* is replaced with the lexical item *all*). There are also claims that systems

[3] There is interesting and relevant typological data (e.g., Bowler, 2014; Davidson, 2013) and experimental data (e.g., Chemla, 2009b; Singh et al., 2016; Tieu et al., 2016, 2017; Zhou et al., 2013) that I will not get into here. For discussion, see, e.g., Chemla and Singh (2014a, 2014b), Meyer (2016), Singh et al. (2016), Sauerland et al. (2017), Bar-Lev (2018), Singh (2019) and Aloni (2022).

that reason with alternatives operate differently with these alternatives. For example, Bar-Lev and Fox (2017) propose that innocent inclusion—the output of their strengthening of Fox's (2007) exhaustive operator and responsible for computing free-choice—is mandatory while innocent exclusion (capturing various other SIs) is optional.[4] Elsewhere there are arguments that exclusion by parsing with *Exh* is mandatory (e.g., Magri, 2009). As we discuss in more detail in later sections, these apparently conflicting views on exclusion can be reconciled by assuming that sentences are always parsed with *Exh* and that constraints on pruning of alternatives capture when exclusion is or is not mandatory (see Bar-Lev & Fox, 2017; Magri, 2009). There is also a common assumption that the output of pragmatic reasoning is cancellable.

I will propose something different. Specifically, I will propose:

(9) Claim about reasoning (updated in (22)):
  a. The consequences of the Maxim of Quantity are not cancellable.
  b. An independent pressure to parse with Exh may not be required (building on ideas found in Singh et al., 2016; Singh, 2019).

In what follows, to fix ideas I will situate the discussion above within a specific approach to the division of labor between grammar and pragmatics. We will try to make some conceptual sense of (8) and (9), generalize (8) to a statement about the relative robustness of alternative types, and more importantly we will see that the approach has some additional welcome predictions, such as accounting for other cases of oddness that don't quite follow from principles that have been articulated elsewhere (e.g., Magri, 2009).

[4] The system in Chemla (2009a) reasons with disjunct alternatives separately from those derived by lexical substitutions. There is an epistemic 'similarity' principle under which the speaker is assumed to have the same epistemic status with respect to similar alternatives. It follows that disjunct alternatives—which are similar alternatives because they are derived by a 'connective split'—give rise to ignorance inferences in matrix disjunctions but a conjunctive free-choice inference. There are two levels of similarity here: disjuncts are syntactically similar and have similar pragmatic consequences. These similarities are stipulated primitives in Chemla (2009a) and are accidental in the framework we are assuming (see [10]). A principled account of this observation would seem to be called for in any event.

9.3 Assumed Background

I will assume without comment an approach to implicature computation that involves the following assumptions:[5,6]

(10) When sentence S is uttered in context c:

a. The scalar implicatures of S are computed by parsing the sentence as $Exh(A)(S)$, where Exh is the exhaustive operator defined in Fox (2007).[5]

b. The set of alternatives, A, is derived by a contextual restriction of S's formal alternatives F (Fox and Katzir, 2011). That is, where F is the set of S's formal alternatives (computed following Fox and Katzir, 2011), and C is the set of contextually relevant alternatives, $A = F \cap C$.[6]

c. The maxim of quantity that governs pragmatics is the 'pure' version (free of any syntactic stipulations), called the 'Basic Maxim of Quantity' in Fox (2007). Under the Basic Maxim of Quantity (hf. 'B-MQ'), the speaker is required to assert the strongest relevant alternative that they believe to be true (without concern for form, and in particular without access to the Horn scales stipulated in Horn, 1972). It follows from B-MQ that any alternative in C whose truth-value is not decided by the meaning of the sentence will receive an ignorance inference (see Fox, 2007).

Consider how (10) might apply to a disjunctive sentence like *Sam ate cake or ice-cream*. The sentence has two salient inferences: (i) the SI that Sam didn't eat both cake and ice-cream, and (ii) the ignorance inferences that the speaker does not know whether Sam ate cake and does not know whether Sam ate ice-cream. Schematically, suppose that a disjunctive sentence $p \vee q$ has formal alternatives $F = \{p, q, p \wedge q\}$ (Fox, 2007; Fox & Katzir, 2011; Katzir, 2007; Sauerland, 2004). The SI in (i) is derivable if $p \wedge q$ is also *relevant*, and hence a member of C. Under this assumption, $p \wedge q$ will belong to $A = F \cap C$. Consider the parse $Exh(A)(p \vee q)$. The exhaustive operator in Fox (2007) aims to deny as many members of A as it can while maintaining consistency with the prejacent, in this case with $p \vee q$. If in this context $A = F$, that is, C does

---

[5] For what I have to say here, it will not matter whether we assume this operator or its strengthened version that computes both exclusion and inclusion (Bar-Lev, 2018; Bar-Lev & Fox 2017, 2020).

[6] This formulation suggests that F and C are generated independent of one another, but see Fox and Katzir (2011) for evidence that this independence assumption might need to be revisited. Note also that this formulation doesn't imply any ordering of operations during processing, nor does it spell out all the factors that enter into determining C. What is needed is a set of auxiliary assumptions about how performance systems realize this computation. See Footnote 14.

not end up restricting F in any way, then *Exh* finds two maximal exclusions: one is the set $\{p, p \wedge q\}$ and the other is the set $\{q, p \wedge q\}$ (denying a set involves denying each element of the set). Excluding $\{p, q, p \wedge q\}$ would end up contradicting the prejacent $p \vee q$. It would be arbitrary to pick one of the two maximal exclusions over the other, and a core principle in Fox 's (2007) approach is that exclusions must be non-arbitrary. The only non-arbitrary exclusion would be $p \wedge q$, given that this is the only alternative that shows up in each of the maximal exclusions. It is therefore 'innocently excludable', and the SIs of a sentence in a given context are all the innocently excludable elements of A in that context.[7]

Consider now the ignorance inferences about each disjunct. We saw above that neither p nor q is innocently excludable when both belong to A. We will return shortly to the possibility of excluding one or the other or both from A, but for now what is important is that under the assumed architecture in (10) the ignorance inferences can only arise by pragmatic reasoning under the Basic Maxim of Quantity (though cf. Meyer, 2013). Under that version of the maxim, a speaker is expected to provide all the information that is relevant and that they believe to be true (you must speak the truth, the whole truth, and nothing but; note that there is no mention of alternatives or syntactic complexity in this classical formulation). In particular, if r and s are both relevant, the speaker believes each to be true, and r is more informative than s, the speaker is required to assert r. Each disjunct is stronger than the disjunction in which it participates. Thus, if p and q are both relevant, a speaker can convey that they don't believe p and don't believe q simply by uttering $p \vee q$ (given *B-MQ*). We can furthermore conclude that the speaker also doesn't believe that p is false, for if they did we would conclude (given that they believe $p \vee q$) that they believe q, which would contradict our earlier conclusion that the speaker doesn't believe q. Hence, we can only conclude that the speaker is ignorant about the truth-value of p. A similar reasoning leads to the conclusion that the speaker is ignorant about the truth-value of q.

[7] It is an easy exercise to show that any restriction A of F that contains $p \wedge q$ will have $\neg(p \wedge q)$ as an SI.

The fact that these predicted ignorance inferences are attested is evidence that p and q are in C, the set of relevant sentences.[8]

What we have seen so far, then, is that when $p \vee q$ is uttered each member of $F(p \vee q)$ needs to also be in C for the attested SI and attested ignorance inferences to arise.[9] It is commonly assumed, however, that SIs are optional, that alternatives can sometimes be ignored or pruned from conversational reasoning, and that pragmatic reasoning is non-monotonic and not as strict as the semantic entailments that follow from the output of grammar itself. At the same time, we saw evidence in Sect. 9.2 that there are limits to this optionality. Specifically, we learned that alternatives sometimes *must* enter into conversational reasoning and that the reasoning—once executed—cannot be cancelled. In the next section, we will examine these choices in more detail. We identify choice points in the architecture in (10) that might naturally allow for optionality in the inferences that it generates, and we will identify empirically how these choices are actually set.

9.4 Optionality and Rigidity

9.4.1 Alternatives

The architecture in (10) makes various choice points available concerning the way in which sentences will be interpreted in context. One is the decision to add *Exh* to the parse. Either you parse the sentence as S, or you parse it as $Exh(A)(S)$. I will return to this matter shortly, but for now note that when the sentence is parsed with *Exh* there needs to be a decision about the makeup of A. We take Fox and Katzir (2011) as our starting point. According to their proposal, the set A is the intersection of two sets: the set of formal alternatives to the sentence and the

[8] I put aside here whether these are sets of sentences or propositions or LFs or concepts. So far as I can tell nothing I have to say hinges on this distinction.

[9] I put aside for now the possibility of parsing the sentence as $Exh(A)(p) \vee Exh(A)(q)$, with $A = \{p, q\}$. The availability of this parse is not relevant to anything I say here, other than that its availability is consistent with my main claims.

set of contextually relevant alternatives (often identified with the question under discussion; cf. Groenendijk & Stokhof, 1984; Lewis, 1988; Roberts, 1996). The formal alternatives $F(S)$ of a sentence S are generated by substituting focused constituents in S with elements from various substitution sources:

(11) Substitution sources:
  a. The Lexicon
  b. Subconstituents
  c. Salient material in the surrounding context

We saw evidence of the lexicon and subconstituents acting as substitution sources with our discussion of disjunction earlier. We get the conjunctive alternative $p \wedge q$ by substituting *and*—retrieved from the lexicon—in place of *or*. And we get each disjunct as an alternative by substituting it for the matrix. Thus, we get $F(p \vee q) = \{p, q, p \wedge q\}$.

Fox and Katzir (2011) present evidence that salient constituents in the surrounding context can also become alternatives. They present as an example the following from Matsumoto (1995):

(12) It was warm yesterday, and it is a little bit more than warm today.

(12) has an SI that it was not a little bit more than warm yesterday. This, in turn, is possible only if *it was a little bit more than warm yesterday and it is a little bit more than warm today* can be an alternative to (12). This teaches us that the constituent *a little bit more than warm* in the second conjunct of (12) can replace *warm* in the first conjunct of (12) even though it isn't a subconstituent of it.

The system thus presents three substitution sources, and the union of all of the sentences generated by editing the sentence S by making substitutions from these sources is the set $F(S)$ of formal alternatives to S. This set F gives an upper bound to the sentences that *Exh* may search for innocent exclusion. It is an upper bound because context also makes a set of alternatives available, those sentences C that are *relevant* in context, and the intersection of F and C yields the set $A \subseteq F$ that is input to *Exh* (together with S).

Although the alternatives in A are derived by substituting elements in A from multiple substitution sources, members of A are not labeled with the substitution source that was used in generating them. Nevertheless, Fox and Katzir (2011) note some generalizations that pertain to the substitution sources. First, they note that alternatives derived by lexical substitution and by salient constituents in the context are not robust. That is, it is not very difficult to prune them from F and hence to not have them become SIs. For example, *Sandy ate some of the cookies* only sometimes implies that Sandy didn't eat all of the cookies or that Sandy didn't eat many of the cookies. These SIs are generated from alternatives derived by lexical substitution (*some* is replaced by *all* or by *many*).

A similar optionality appears with SIs generated from alternatives that are derived from salient constituents, but there are also interesting differences between alternatives derived by lexical substitution and those derived by substitution from salient constituents. Fox and Katzir (2011) raise the following as a case in point:

(13) John did some of the homework yesterday, and he did just some of the homework today.

The sentence in (13) does not have the SI that John did not do just some of the homework yesterday, that is, it does not have the strengthened meaning that he did all of the homework yesterday. This is because the salient *John did just some of the homework yesterday* is not the only alternative available (Katzir, 2007).

(14) Alternatives to (13):
  a. John did all of the homework yesterday... (lexical substitution)
  b. John did just some of the homework yesterday... (substitution from salient constituents)

Under the definition of symmetry proposed by Fox and Katzir (2011), these are 'symmetric alternatives' to S: their disjunction is equivalent to S and their conjunction is contradictory. Thus, neither alternative in (14) is innocently excludable, so $Exh(A)(S)$ will be equivalent to S when $S = (13)$ and $A = \{(14 - a), (14 - b)\}$. Fox and Katzir (2011) present this (and other examples) as evidence that context is unable to break symmetry in F. (14-a) enters F via (11-a) and (14-b) enters F via (11-c), and once symmetry is present in F context cannot eliminate it by pruning one or the other symmetric alternative. In particular, note that the salience and relevance of (14-b) somehow can't dislodge (14-a) from being an alternative. In some contexts *all* might be pruned from the alternatives to *some*, but if there is a symmetric alternative *some but not all* in F the pruning option is no longer available as evidenced by the fact that (13) cannot be used to convey that John did all of the homework yesterday.

However, as Fox and Katzir (2011) note, there is an important distinction between the alternatives in (14). Specifically, *all* is always in $F(some)$, but only in some contexts—such as the one in (13)—is *just some* in $F(some)$. And this distinction appears to have important consequences. For example, they note that it is possible to read (13) as implying that John did not do all of the homework yesterday.[10] This, in turn, suggests that it is possible—despite its contextual salience—for (14-b) to be absent from F, and hence from A (even if (though?) it is in C). They suggest a way to accommodate this optionality by allowing a single sentence to have sets of salient constituents available for substitution, among which some particular set is chosen in the generation of F (see their Footnotes 16 and 23).[11]

I will not have much to say about this other than to note that this direction acknowledges a certain ordering of robustness of substitution sources. In particular, the above discussion teaches us that the lexicon is a more robust substitution source than salience. Lexical substitutions are always in F and may or may not be pruned by context (subject to the requirement that context cannot break symmetry), but salient constituents may or may not even enter F in the first place.

I will propose that this ordering of robustness of substitution sources extends to subconstituents. Specifically, subconstituents are maximally robust (cf. Chemla & Bott, 2014; Bar-Lev, 2018; Bar-Lev & Fox, 2020): they are always in F and appear extremely hard for context to prune.[12]

---

[10] They attribute this observation to a personal communication from Micha Breakstone.

[11] Greenberg (2024) notes that not all salient constituents are candidates for entering F, and suggests that a salient constituent may enter F only if it answers the same question under discussion as the utterance (or prejacent of a focus-sensitive operator like *only* or *even*).

[12] So far as I can tell, something like this assumption would also be needed in Alxatib and Nicolae 's proposal for solving various puzzles pertaining to disjunctions and free-choice *any* under various existential embeddings. They employ a mechanism for binding into alternatives to prevent a sentence like 'some student read *Syntactic Structures* or *Aspects*' from generating a conjunctive inference that some student read *Syntactic Structures* and some student read *Aspects* (see also Fox, 2007) for disjunctions under singular indefinites). If it were possible to have just

This is so even though the disjuncts to a disjunction are not symmetric (because in the general case the disjuncts in a disjunction do not contradict each other).[13] Hence there is a total order of substitution sources (ordered by robustness).

(15) Robustness of alternatives:

a. Those derived from sub-constituents are always in F and are always in C.
b. Those derived from the lexicon are always in F and may or may not be be in C.
c. Salient constituents in the surrounding discourse may or may not be in F.

It is worth reflecting somewhat on the claim that subconstituents, and disjuncts in particular, are always in C. This is a very strong claim. It may need to be weakened, say to being 'nearly always in C', or to have 'cost' functions for edit operations with low costs for subconstituent substitutions. But for now the assumption stated in (15) gives us what we need to make sense of the data in Sect. 9.2.[14] Note, for example, that even attempts to somehow make the question under discussion explicitly about the disjunction alone—and not about the disjuncts—aren't enough to remove the associated inferences about the disjuncts:

(16) A: Everyone with at least three daughters is invited to fill out this survey. Who here has at least three daughters?

a. B: Sandy has three or more daughters.
b. B': # I have three or more daughters.

---

one disjunct as an alternative, it should be possible to understand this sentence to be saying that there is a student who read *Syntactic Structures* and not *Aspects* (it should be possible to strengthen $\exists x(P(x) \vee Q(x))$ to $\exists x((P(x) \vee Q(x) \wedge \neg P(x))$ if one could have just one disjunct as an alternative). This is not a possible reading of the sentence, so if Alxatib and Nicolae (2024) are right about binding into alternatives this is additional evidence that it is not possible to prune one of the disjuncts.

[13] If Singh (2008a) is right about the statement of Hurford's Constraint (that it demands mutual inconsistency, and not merely non-entailment—see Footnote 2), then disjuncts in general will be symmetric alternatives. Under weaker definitions of symmetry, such as in Bar-Lev and Fox (2020), both $\{p, q\}$ and $\{p, q, p \wedge q\}$ contain symmetry with respect to $p \vee q$.

[14] See Husband and Patson (2024) for evidence that lexical replacements are processed differently than salient constituents, giving additional support for the idea that alternatives from different substitution sources have different cognitive status. They suggest that lexical alternatives are accessed using activation and selection mechanisms (cf. Gotzner & Lacina, 2024) while salient alternatives are accessed using retrieval mechanisms from discourse memory. These mechanisms appear to be triggered very early in processing. See Muxica and Harris (2024) for additional evidence for the early availability of mentioned focus alternatives, along with evidence that mentioning alternatives in prior context supports probe word recognition even when the mentioned alternative is semantically distant from the probe. So far I know, performance mechanisms pertaining to subconstituent alternatives have not been studied.

In (16), the question has no concern with whether the speaker has exactly three daughters or more than three. The only concern is with the content of the disjunction itself: does the person in question have at least three? The contrast in (16) suggests that there is nothing particularly odd about a disjunctive answer itself; it is only if the subject is first-person that the oddness arises. The oddness here, again, is plausibly attributable to the oddness of the ignorance inferences the sentence generates. We normally expect someone to know how many daughters they have (if any), and oddness is expected if the sentence necessarily implies that the speaker is ignorant about how many daughters they have and is puzzling otherwise.

There *is* a way in which one can express a disjunctive answer to a disjunctive question without implying ignorance, namely, by giving a positive 'yes' answer without spelling out the disjunction. But as soon as you actually represent the disjunction overtly, the oddness reappears (or at best you are being 'funny').

(17) A: Do you have three or more daughters?

a. B: Yes.

b. B': # Yes. I have three or more daughters.

This suggests that despite our explicit attempt to make the QUD only care about the truth of the disjunction, there is still a pressure to understand an overt expression $p \vee q$ as being uttered in a context in which p and q are both relevant. It appears that, against all sense, there is a pressure to compute the associated ignorance implicatures. This in turn means that each disjunct must be in C. The disjuncts are already in F, and hence they must be in A. This tells us why in (1) you cannot get $\neg p$ (say) as an SI of $p \vee q$: each of p and q is in A, and negation of one entails the truth of the other (given the disjunction $p \vee q$). Hence, neither disjunct is innocently excludable, so there is no SI for either disjunct. But since each disjunct is in C, the Basic Maxim of Quantity will apply and will imply that the speaker is ignorant about the truth-value of each disjunct.[15] Embedding of the disjunction under a universal

[15] It is an easy exercise to show that this is so whether or not the disjunctive utterance is strengthened by negating the conjunctive alternative.

operator, such as under *require* in (5), will then trigger the implicatures that the speaker is not required to have exactly three daughters and is not required to have more than three. Because *it is required that I have three daughters* and *it is required that I have more than three daughters* will both be in F and C (cf. [15]), and each is innocently excludable, the mandatory SIs follow as does the pattern in (5)–(7) discussed in Sect. 9.2.

Why should constituent alternatives be so robust? It clearly somehow matters that the speaker has chosen to represent their intended content with these constituents. They have set a certain complexity level in the context by using this form and have highlighted certain sentences/propositions in the creation of the disjunctive thought. Various rules of inference will be sensitive to the form of the sentence independent of its content. For example, without knowing the content of p and q, you can conclude that q is true if you learn that $p \vee q$ is true and learn that $\neg p$ is true. Thus, the disjunctive form itself is relevant to how the listener can reason with what was said: it matters that p was used, that q was used, and that they were connected with a disjunction. Furthermore, with disjunct subconstituents all the information needed for substitutions in the generation of alternatives is contained within the sentence. With the other substitution sources, like the lexicon and other surrounding salience material, you need to go outside of the sentence itself to find the right substitutions (see Chemla & Bott, 2014). And it might make sense for lexical substitutions to be more robust than salient ones given that lexical substitutions (and subconstituent ones) stay within the workspace of the language faculty (the current structure and the lexicon). Katzir (2007) notes that these are sources that need to be accessed for further linguistic operations in any event.

Thus, there are various reasons to think it might be natural for disjuncts to be highly accessible and important to systems that reason with what was said. Nevertheless, there is still a question that I think hasn't yet received a satisfactory answer: just because a constituent alternative is highly accessible and can enter into various rules of inference, why should that make it necessarily relevant in context and hence input to exhaustification and to *B-MQ*? You will recall from (16) that we encountered difficulty when we tried to force the question under discussion to concern itself only with whether the disjunction was true and to not be concerned about the truth of the disjuncts. Why should the salience, accessibility, and importance of disjuncts make them necessarily relevant in context?

We can make partial progress by thinking through the notion of relevance. Suppose that "*p* or *q*" is relevant (speaker and hearer want to jointly settle whether the disjunction is true). If the truth-values of *p* and *q* were already known, then the disjunction's truth-value could be computed and it wouldn't be relevant. Thus, if is relevant, then at least one of the disjuncts must be too (say, *p*). Thus, speaker and hearer want to jointly settle whether the disjunction "*p* or *q*" is true and whether "*p*" is true (the truth-value of *p* isn't settled in the common ground). Unfortunately, this doesn't on its own demand that the truth-value of *q* also be unsettled. For example, you can know that *q* is false while still being uncertain whether *p* is true and whether the disjunction is true (this does not hold when *q* is known to be true). However, although there isn't a logical requirement that *q* also be relevant, it is (for whatever reason) pragmatically strange to be in a situation in which *q* is known to be false while raising the question whether "*p* or *q*" is true. For example, it is odd to say "Mary wasn't at the party, but was at least one of John or Mary at the party?" Whatever is behind this oddness may then rule out a scenario in which the disjunction is relevant and only one of its disjuncts is. Futhermore, it is commonly assumed that relevance is closed under negation and conjunction (Chierchia et al., 2012; Fox, 2007; Groenendijk & Stokhof, 1984; Katzir, 2007; Lewis, 1988; von Fintel & Heim, 1999). [16]

[16] These closure conditions on relevance might help make sense of experimental findings in Marty et al. (2024). The authors find that *salience* of an alternative supports its eventual SI only insofar as the salience suggests *relevance* of the alternative. For example, in response to a sentence like *some of the students passed the exam*, three different probes showed similar rates of SI responses. Specifically, the following three paraphrases had the same rate of SI responses: *Would you conclude from this that, according to George*: (i) Not all of the students passed the exam? (ii) Some of the students failed the exam? (iii) There were students who failed the exam? Note that the probes all make the proposition $\neg\forall$ relevant, and by closure under negation $\forall$ is relevant also. Only in (i), however, is *all of the students passed the exam* a salient *sentence*, given that it is part of the probe (presumably, if X is salient, and Y is a part of X, then Y is also salient). Thus, in all three conditions, (a) *all of the students passed the exam* is in F (lexical replacement of *some* by *all*), (b) $\forall$ is relevant (the probe makes $\neg\forall$ relevant and relevance is closed under negation). Thus, each condition gives you the ingredients necessary to compute the SI. The salience of the probes raises questions about what enters F. Specifically, their introduction into F has the potential to introduce symmetry into F. Recall from (15)

However, closure under conjunction also leads to a problem in our setup. Specifically, once $p \vee q$, p, and q are relevant, so too is $p \wedge q$ (Bar-Lev, 2018). We clearly want to allow $p \wedge q$ to be pruned, given that it doesn't robustly show up as an SI. What we don't have yet is a non-stipulative statement that allows $p \wedge q$ to be pruned while preventing p and q from being pruned.[17] Continuing our line of reasoning from above, we want to examine whether it is logically or pragmatically reasonable to have settled on the truth-value of the conjunction while remaining ignorant of the truth-value of the disjunction and of each constituent. Of course if the conjunction is true the disjunction and each constituent is also. If the conjunction is known to be false, this doesn't impose any truth-value on the disjunction and it doesn't impose any truth-value on any constituent. There is also nothing pragmatically strange about knowing that the conjunction is false and wondering about whether the disjunction is true: "John and Mary didn't both show up to the party, but did at least one of them show up?" Logical considerations alone don't demand that each disjunct be relevant when the disjunction is. Our discussion here makes appeal to pragmatic judgments about what is sensible to raise as a question under different knowledge states. These considerations suggest that when logic alone doesn't demand the relevance of a formal alternative, pragmatics can rule out pruning of a disjunct but not pruning of the conjunction. Why should this be? I will have to leave the matter unanswered here and move on to questions about reasoning with alternatives.

that listeners have a choice point in whether a salient constituent is selected for F; perhaps this choice was relevant to which participants computed the SI (those that excluded them from F) and those that didn't (those that selected them for F and hence were faced with symmetry). Following Greenberg (2024), this might have to do with whether the listener perceives the alternative as answering the same question as the assertion. See our discussion in Sect. 9.5.

[17] Bar-Lev (2018) follows Katzir (2013) in assuming that pruning is a matter of deciding which of the innocently excludable propositions (operating over the entire set of formal alternatives) to delete because the corresponding alternative is irrelevant. This would capture the relevant distinction while also capturing why the irrelevance of $p \wedge q$ doesn't lead to free-choice inferences in the adult (given that closure under conjunction of formal alternatives is what prevents conjunctive scalar implicatures for disjunction; Bar-Lev, 2018; Bar-Lev & Fox, 2017, 2020; Bowler 2014; Chemla, 2009a; Franke, 2011; Fox, 2007; Meyer, 2016; Singh et al., 2016).

9.4.2 Reasoning with Alternatives and Monotonicity

Given a set of alternatives in our hand, there is still the question of how reasoning mechanisms use them. There are two that we are considering. One is the exhaustive operator in the grammar. The other is the Maxim of Quantity, *B-MQ*, in the pragmatics. We have seen evidence throughout this paper of apparently mandatory SIs and ignorance inferences. The SIs only appear if the sentence is parsed with *Exh*. So why not simply leave *Exh* off the parse? And ignorance implicatures are computed by *B-MQ*. But so what? Aren't pragmatic inferences cancellable (cf. Hom, 1972)? In the face of a strange ignorance inference, as with a strange sentence like *#I have three or more daughters*, why not simply cancel the ignorance inference so that the sentence ends up sounding more like the still not perfect but much better *I have more than two daughters*?

I will argue here that there is actually no rationale for pragmatic quantity inferences to be cancellable. I believe it is a mistake to think about the maxims as being flimsy enough to permit cancellation. Conceptually, note that *B-MQ* is a *requirement* on good speech. It is your duty as a cooperative speaker to obey it. And note the conditional formulation: if r and s are both relevant in context (a matter of common knowledge), and r entails s (also a matter of common knowledge), then if the speaker believes both are true the speaker must utter r. There is no room for cancellation here. Following Magri (2009), it is plausible that classic arguments for cancellation have really taught us more about relevance and pruning than about the nonmonotonicity of the reasoning. For example, if we fix the relevance of *all*, it is no longer possible to get away with uttering *some* and then (in the same breath) asserting *all*:

(18) A: How many of the cookies did Sam eat?
B: Sam ate some of them. # In fact, Sam ate all of them.

The only way *B* might get away with this is if they display that they are correcting themselves, say by inserting a *sorry* between the two sentences. Otherwise, it is just an odd way to answer the question if you know (and remembered the whole time) that Sam ate all of the cookies.

Zeroing in on relevance, then, Magri (2009) finds that in contexts in which *some* and *all* are contextually equivalent—and hence if one is relevant both are—*some* is odd.

(19) Prof. Smith gave the same grade to all of her students.
a. #She gave some of them an A.
b. She gave all of them an A.

Magri (2009) takes the above contrast to be teaching us that *Exh* must be present in the parse of (19-a). Furthermore, no pruning of alternatives is possible here. The prejacent is relevant (by assumption) and is equivalent in context to the alternative *all*. Hence *all* can't be pruned. The oddness is therefore explained if there's an *Exh* in the parse. With this assumption, the sentence means 'some but not all', and this contradicts the context-specific common knowledge in (19) that 'some if and only if all'. Without the assumption of an obligatory *Exh*, the oddness of the sentence is puzzling (given the assumption that the output of grammar is monotonic and the output of pragmatics is non-monotonic).

Unless, of course, we are right that the output of *B-MQ* is also monotonic. If you leave *Exh* off the parse, then you are left with a relevant alternative—*Prof. Smith gave all of them an A*—whose truth-value is left unaddressed by the content of the utterance. This then receives an ignorance inference under the architecture in (10), and this inference contradicts common knowledge. Note, for example, that the following are odd even though they do not have a 'some but not all' implicature (Katzir & Singh, 2014):

(20) Prof. Smith gave the same grade to all of her students.
a. #She gave some or all of them an A.
b. #She gave at least some of them an A.

What the sentences in (20) do have are ignorance implicatures that speaker doesn't know whether Prof. Smith gave all of her students an A. Again, together with the quality-based inference that the speaker knows the content of her utterance, $K_S\exists$, and the contextual assumption that $K_S\exists \iff K_S\forall$, we derive a contradiction between the ignorance inferences triggered by (20) and the information in the context.

For this to work as outlined above, pragmatic ignorance inferences would have to be computed *blind* to common knowledge. This would make them somewhat similar to exhaustivity inferences insofar as both are encapsulated from common knowledge. Exhaustivity inferences belong to the grammatical system, and ignorance inferences to the pragmatic system. It would appear, then, that there is a 'pragmatics module' that interfaces with grammar (receives the form and content of the utterance as an input) as well as with context (to determine what is salient and relevant to determine the makeup of *C*) but then computes its inferences in a way that is otherwise informationally encapsulated from common knowledge. This might seem unnatural in light of common assumptions about the place of pragmatics in the organization of the mind, but given the robustness of the inferences and oddness judgments we have seen, and our conceptual reassessment that maxims like *B-MQ* are rightly thought to be stricter than commonly conceived, it might make sense to think of the pragmatics module as a natural place within which various conversational inferences are drawn and whose consequences are then monotonically added to the context.[18]

It is not just these highly conventionalized implicatures that display this kind of robustness. Consider, for example, Grice's (1967) petrol example:

(21) Context: A is standing by an obviously immobilized car and is approached by B; the following exchange takes place:
A: I am out of petrol.
B: There is a garage around the corner.

There are various implicatures attached to *B*'s utterance, such as that the garage is open and has petrol to sell. What is noteworthy in the context of our discussion is how strong this implicature is. Consider how justifiably irate *A* would be if they were to learn that the garage is closed or has no petrol to sell and that *B* actually knew this at the time of *B*'s

[18] See Meyer (2013) for arguments that considerations like this lead instead naturally to the conclusion that there is a covert *K* operator in the grammar and that ignorance implicatures are computed with the interaction of *Exh* and *K*. Under this view, the monotonicity of ignorance inferences would follow from the monotonicity of grammar. I will try to paint an alternative picture here under which pragmatic inferences ought also to be conceptualized as monotonic and in which *B-MQ* is responsible for ignorance. I hope to return to a comparison of approaches in future work.

utterance. Furthermore, suppose that B in fact knows that the garage is open and has petrol to sell when A makes their utterance. It seems to me that B is *required* to share that there is a garage around the corner. It would not do to simply express a sympathetic 'Oh, I'm sorry, well good luck' and move on. It would be extremely uncooperative of B to not share the relevant information about the garage, and (again) A would be justifiably irate if they were to learn later that B had this information and failed to share it. Under *B-MQ*, the speaker is required to share all the information that is relevant, and this appears to be a very strict requirement that in turn has strict consequences. Monotonicity is expected in semantics and in pragmatics; whatever nonmonotonicity there appears to be will have to do with uncertainty (a failure to coordinate) about what is relevant in context, and not with the strength of the inference itself.

9.5 Summary and Further Remarks

What we have, then, is evidence for the following statements about optionality and obligatoriness in the framework of (10):

(22) When sentence S is uttered in context c:

a. The sentence may either be parsed as S or as $Exh(A)(S)$.
b. Whatever the LF associated with S, called it $\lambda(S)$, any relevant alternative in C whose truth-value is not settled by $[[\lambda(S)]]$ will receive a mandatory ignorance inference.
c. $[[\lambda(S)]]$ and its associated pragmatic ignorance inferences are computed blind to common knowledge.
d. Neither $[[\lambda(S)]]$ nor its associated pragmatic ignorance inferences are cancellable.
e. Among substitution sources, subconstituents are the most robust (always in F and C), salient non-subconstituents are the least robust (may but need not be in F), and lexical substitutions are in between (always in F and may be pruned from C so long as there is no symmetric alternative in F).

We are still left with a stipulation about *why* subconstituents must be in C. A slightly different way to formulate this question might provide a useful reframing of the question. Subconstituents are also salient, and hence it might be that there are just two categories of substitution sources: the lexicon and salience. Assuming this, why—among salient constituents—do subconstituents play a privileged role? Greenberg 's (2024) proposal might be relevant (cf. Footnote 11). Specifically, suppose (reformulating Greenberg, 2024) that salient constituents must be in F

if they answer the same question as the assertion. Since they answer the same question, these constituents would also be in C (they are relevant). The question, of course, is whether disjuncts as a rule answer the same question as the assertion, and more generally whether alternatives derived by deletion as a rule answer the same question as the assertion. To answer this, we would need to fix a suitable notion of what counts as answering the same question. In any event, the fact that these constituents are parts of the uttered sentence seems central to their privileged status.[19] I hope future work will make analytical sense of this observation.

We are also left for now with the question of how to make sense of the robustness of free-choice inferences. As we noted earlier, there is significant evidence that free-choice inferences are extremely robust. A sentence like *you're allowed to eat cake or ice-cream* is very naturally understood as implying that you have free-choice: you're allowed to eat cake and you're allowed to eat ice-cream. Compared to SI's of the 'some but not all' variety, this SI is fast, is easy to embed, and arises earlier in acquisition (cf. Footnote 3). More generally, disjunctive sentences $\phi(A \vee B)$ can receive conjunctive SIs $\phi(A) \wedge \phi(B)$ whenever their alternatives are not closed under conjunction (see references in Footnote 17), and for some reason this kind of inference is extremely preferred and fast to compute. But if *Exh* is responsible for this inference, and it is optional, what is responsible for the conjunctive SI? Merely being pressured to consider $\phi(A)$ and $\phi(B)$ isn't enough to conclude that they are true. For that you need *Exh* (within our assumed framework).

Here we follow Singh et al. (2016) and Singh (2019) in assuming that such parsing decisions are governed by preferences relating to questions under discussion (QUD). In short, if there is a parse of the sentence that provides a complete answer to the QUD, that parse will (*ceteris paribus*) be preferred.[20] For disjunctive sentences $\phi(p \vee q)$, a conjunctive

19 The current sentence seems relevant to other context-sensitive operations, such as setting 'lifespans' for discourse referents (e.g., Heim, 1982) or windows within which disambiguation decisions are to be made (e.g., Fodor et al., 1974).

20 It is plausible that different parses with different levels of commitment to speaker certainty/answer completeness come with detectable intonational differences. For example, $L + H^*$ may signal certainty/completeness and $L^* + H$ (and Rise-Fall-Rise more generally in which it is a part) may signal some level of speaker uncertainty/answer incompleteness. See Göbel (2024) for discussion and for unnoticed interpretations of $L^* + H$ and their connection to 'at least'.

SI $\phi(p)\wedge\phi(q)$ would completely answer the question whether $\phi(p)$ and whether $\phi(q)$, but something like an exclusive disjunction SI $\neg\phi(p\wedge q)$ would not.

There are proposals that would take a different stance. For example, Bar-Lev and Fox (2017) propose that innocent inclusion (responsible for free-choice) is mandatory while innocent exclusion (responsible for 'some but not all' type SIs) is not. And Chemla (2009a) would treat disjunct alternatives separately, with similarity principles applying to them separately from lexical substitutions, making room for differences for inferences of this kind. A general preference for complete answers strikes me as more natural than stipulations that tie preferences to certain kinds of inference mechanism, but more importantly SIs involving numerals pattern like free-choice. They are also fast in processing, easy to embed, and early to develop in children (for discussion see Aloni, 2022; Chemla & Singh, 2014a, 2014b; Sauerland et al., 2017; Singh, 2019; Singh et al., 2016). A preference for complete answers captures this parallel. The assumption that innocent inclusion is faster than innocent exclusion doesn't (the SIs of numerals are derived by denying alternatives) nor does the assumption that the manner in which alternatives are derived is an indicator of the processing pattern. For note that the alternatives to numerals aren't derived as constituents. For example, suppose that *Sandy has four daughters* is an alternative to *Sandy has three daughters.* There is no reason to think the former is a subconstituent of the latter. Furthermore, it is unlikely to be derived by lexical substitution either. There is an infinite set of natural numbers, and hence they cannot be stored in the lexicon. They must be derived.[21]

[21] These considerations also call into question Sauerland et al.'s (2017) argument against Sudo's (2014) analysis of conjunctive readings of the Japanese disjunctive coordinator *ya*. Sauerland et al. (2017) find that the conjunctive reading of *ya* has a similar mouse-tracking profile as the *exactly* reading of numerals (as expected based on other findings in the literature). Sudo (2014) proposes an analysis under which the conjunctive SI is derived using lexical substitutions, and Sauerland et al. (2017) argue that the processing profile is evidence that only subconstituents are used as alternatives to *ya*. But if we are right, it is only the quality of the answer that is relevant, not the manner in which it is derived. See also Footnote 24.

More plausible, then, is that—if *four* is an alternative to *three*—it is derived using the successor function on *three*.[22] As Chomsky points out (e.g., Chomsky, 2005), the successor function can be defined in terms of Merge. Hence, structure building operations can also be used to derive alternatives. This does raise interesting questions about complexity and alternatives. Specifically, there is a very real sense in which any number $n + 1$ is structurally more complex than its predecessor n.[23] This might seem to go against the spirit of Katzir's (2007) proposal, but I think the predicament we find ourselves in is not as severe as it might appear. Specifically, so long as we restrict ourselves to Internal Merge in the generation of alternatives—reusing elements in the structure itself to extend it rather than merging objects that sit outside the structure to extend it—that may well keep to the conceptual idea that the form of the sentence imposes a very serious constraint on what else you may consider when reasoning about why the speaker decided to use this structure with this meaning in this context.[24]

The possible use of Internal Merge like operations raises new empirical questions. For example, consider an operation like Quantifier Raising (Heim & Kratzer, 1998) in relation to a sentence like (23):

[22] It does not matter that there might be a smallish set of numbers that are stored as primitive and available for substitution. At some point that possibility will have to end to accommodate the entire infinite set of natural numbers (see, e.g., Piantadosi et al., 2012, 2016; Riley et al., 2023) on the interaction between primitives and Bayesian learning of number systems; as in all number systems (see Footnote 23), here too a small set of primitives gives way eventually to operations that derive numbers, with larger numbers requiring more complex derivations). And large numbers—which are unlikely to be stored as primitive—appear to follow the same implicatures as smaller ones. *Sandy has two-thousand daughters* still implicates that Sandy has no more than two-thousand, and the same will be true for any number *n*. Of course this sentence is implausible but that is irrelevant (one could find contexts in which it might become plausible). For interesting data pertaining to oddness and its contextual obviation involving prejacents to *only* that contain large numbers, see Greenberg (2024).

[23] Under one common set-theoretic characterization of numbers (see, e.g., Halmos, 1960 for a textbook treatment), 0 is identified as the empty set and the successor of any given number n, $s(n)$, is the union of n and the set containing $n : s(n) = n \cup \{n\}$. Thus, a number n is both an element of and a subset of its successor. For example, under this definition $2 = \{0, 1\}$ and $3 = 2 \cup \{2\} = \{0, 1, 2\}$.

[24] This might make sense of the assumption in Sauerland et al. (2017) that subconstituent alternatives and the alternatives to numerals ought to cluster together as what they call 'explicit alternatives' or ones with 'inherent scales'. They didn't spell out a characterization that ties them together, but mere reuse of existing material in the structure could be relevant (see Footnote 21).

(23) Every faculty member met some prospective student.

The inverse scope reading in which *some* outscopes *every* identifies some particular prospective student that met with each faculty member. When we teach intro semantics and want the students to zero in on the narrow scope reading under which every faculty member met some prospective student or other, the way we often paraphrase that reading is by denying the inverse scope reading. If that is not merely a pedagogical technique and indicates an actual reading of the sentence, it might be evidence that a QR operation is available to generate alternatives.

If this is indicative, it might be useful to look elsewhere for QR'd alternatives. Consider binding principles from syntax like Condition B, which rule out sentences like (24) with *him* understood as John, say by use of a contextual assignment function that assigns to 1 the individual John (see, e.g., Heim & Kratzer, 1998).

(24) #John sam him_1

Reinhart (1983) initiated various attempts to derive Condition B effects from a comparison of a sentence and its alternatives instead of through stipulations about syntactic principles. In a case like (24), her proposal would require that if there is an alternative available to express (24) with a *bound* variable instead, that would be preferred. In this light, consider (25):

(25) John 1 t_1 saw himself_1

(25) can be derived from (24) with two edits: (i) replace *him* with *himself* (lexical substitution and keep the index the same) and (ii) QR the subject *John*. This yields the LF in (25) (following the implementation of QR in (Heim & Kratzer, 1998). What is relevant for us, then, is that if QR is a legitimate way to generate an alternative, then (25) would be an alternative to (24). It is natural to think of the LF in (25) as non-weaker

than (24).[25] In the given context, though, the two are equivalent if we assume (e.g., Heim, 1983) that contexts are world-assignment pairs and that in the given context all assignments map 1 to John in (24). Hence, following Magri (2009), (25) cannot be pruned. If (24) is parsed with *Exh*, then it would entail that (25) is false, which would contradict the contextual equivalence of (24) and (25). Without *Exh* on (24), *B-MQ* would lead to the conclusion that the speaker is ignorant about whether (25) is true. Again, this would contradict the contextual information that the speaker in fact knows its truth-value (given that it is equivalent in context to [24] and the quality-based conclusion that speaker knows that [24] is true).[26] These contradictions arise—and the oddness of (24) is therefore explained—if QR is a mechanism for generating alternatives and if (22-c) is true.

I cannot do more with these initial observations than merely raise them as speculations about the possible role of an additional route to alternatives that adds structure through movement.

References

Aloni, M. (2022, June). Logic and conversation: The case of free choice. *Semantics and Pragmatics, 15*(5), 1–60. https://doi.org/10.3765/sp.15.5

Alxatib, S., & Nicolae, A. (2024). *Any* vs. *or* and indefinites vs. modals. This volume.

Bar-Lev, M. (2018). *Free-choice, homogeneity, and innocent inclusion* (Doctoral Dissertation), The Hebrew University of Jerusalem.

Bar-Lev, M., & Fox, D. (2017). Universal free choice and innocent inclusion. In *Proceedings of SALT 27*.

Bar-Lev, M., & Fox, D. (2020). Free choice, simplification, and innocent inclusion. *Natural Language Semantics, 28*, 175–223.

25 For example, a natural definition of semantic entailment that makes room for assignment functions would be that A entails B iff for all world-assignment pairs $< g, w >$, $[[A]]^{g,w} = 1 \rightarrow [[B]]^{g,w} = 1$.

26 See Katzir and Singh (2011) for a proposal connecting these observations to a maxim calling on speakers to avoid ambiguity.

Bowler, M. (2014). Conjunction and disjunction in a language without 'and'. *Proceedings of SALT, 24*, 137–155.

Chemla, E. (2009a). *Similarity: Towards a unified account of scalar implicatures, free choice permission, and presupposition projection*. Manuscript, ENS.

Chemla, E. (2009b). Universal implicatures and free choice effects: Experimental data. *Semantics and Pragmatics, 2*, 1–33.

Chemla, E., & Bott, L. (2014). Processing inferences at the semantics/pragmatics frontier: Disjunctions and free choice. *Cognition, 130*, 380–396.

Chemla, E., & Singh, R. (2014a). Remarks on the experimental turn in the study of scalar implicature. *Part I. Language and Linguistics Compass, 8*(9), 373–386.

Chemla, E., & Singh, R. (2014b). Remarks on the experimental turn in the study of scalar implicature. *Part II. Language and Linguistics Compass, 8*(9), 387–399.

Chemla, E., Cummins, C., & Singh, R. (2016). Training and timing local scalar enrichments under global pragmatic pressures. *Journal of Semantics, 34*(1), 107–126.

Chierchia, G., Fox, D., & Spector, B. (2012). Scalar implicature as a grammatical phenomenon. In P. Portner, C. Maienborn, & K. von Heusinger (Eds.), *Handbook of semantics* (Vol. 3, pp. 2297–2331). Mouton de Gruyter.

Chomsky, N. (2005). Three factors in language design. *Linguistic Inquiry, 36*(1), 1–22.

Davidson, K. (2013). 'And' and 'or': General use coordination in ASL. *Semantics and Pragmatics, 6*, 1–44.

Fodor, J. A., Bever, T. G., & Garrett, M. F. (1974). *The psychology of language*. MgGraw-Hill.

Fox, D. (2007). Free choice disjunction and the theory of scalar implicature. In U. Sauerland & P. Stateva (Eds.), *Presupposition and implicature in compositional semantics* (pp. 71–120). Palgrave Macmillan.

Fox, D., & Katzir, R. (2011). On the characterization of alternatives. *Natural Language Semantics, 19*, 87–107.

Franke, M. (2011). Quantity implicatures, exhaustive interpretation, and rational conversation. *Semantics and Pragmatics, 4*(1), 1–82. https://doi.org/10.3765/sp.4.1

Gazdar, G. (1979). *Pragmatics*. Academic Press.

Göbel, A. (2024). How to operate over alternatives: The place of the L*+H pitch accent among possible focus meanings. This volume.

Gotzner, N., & Lacina, R. (2024). Generating and selecting alternatives for scalar implicature computation: The alternative activation account and other theories. This volume.

Greenberg, Y. (2024). Answerability constraints on alternative-introducing salient sentences: Support from the evaluativity effects of only and from scalar implicatures. This volume.

Grice, H. P. (1967). *Logic and conversation.* William James Lectures, Harvard University.

Groenendijk, J., & Stokhof, M. (1984). *Studies on the semantics of questions and the pragmatics of answers* (Doctoral Dissertation), University of Amsterdam.

Halmos, P. R. (1960). *Naive set theory*. Van Nostrand.

Heim, I. (1982). *On the semantics of definite and indefinite noun phrases* (Doctoral Dissertation), University of Massachusetts at Amherst.

Heim, I. (1983). On the projection problem for presuppositions. *WCCFL, 2*, 114–125.

Heim, I., & Kratzer, A. (1998). *Semantics in generative grammar*. Blackwell.

Horn, L. R. (1972). *On the semantic properties of logical operators in English* (Doctoral Dissertation), UCLA.

Hurford, J. (1974). Exclusive or inclusive disjunction. *Foundations of Language, 11*, 409–411.

Husband, E. M., & Patson, N. D. (2024). Informational sources and discourse in the generation and maintenance of alternatives. This volume.

Katzir, R. (2007). Structurally defined alternatives. *Linguistics and Philosophy, 30*, 669–690.

Katzir, R. (2013). On the role of markedness and contradiction in the use of alternatives. In S. P. Reda (Ed.), *Semantics, pragmatics, and the case of scalar implicatures*. Palgrave, Basingstoke.

Katzir, R., & Singh, R. (2011). *Avoid ambiguity!* Talk presented to the Dept. of Psychology at Stanford University.

Katzir, R., & Singh, R. (2014). Hurford disjunctions: Embedded exhaustification and structural economy. In U. Etxeberria, A. Falaus, A. Irurtzun, & B. Leferman (Eds.), *Proceedings of Sinn und Bedeutung* (Vol. 18, pp. 201–216).

Lewis, D. (1988). Relevant implication. *Theoria, 54*, 161–174.

Magri, G. (2009). A theory of individual level predicates based on blind mandatory scalar implicatures. *Natural Language Semantics, 17*, 245–297.

Marty, P., Romoli, J., & Sudo, Y., & Breheny, R. (2024). Probing the probe: Why inference tasks may inflate response rates for Scalar Implicature. This volume.

Matsumoto, Y. (1995). The conversational condition on Horn scales. *Linguistics and Philosophy, 18*, 21–60.

Meyer, M.-C. (2013). *Ignorance and grammar* (Doctoral Dissertation), MIT, Cambridge, MA.

Meyer, M.-C. (2016). Generalized free choice and missing alternatives. *Journal of Semantics, 33*(4), 703–754.

Muxica, C. J., & Harris, J. A.. (2024). Constructing alternatives: Evidence for the early availability of contextually relevant focus alternatives. This volume.

Piantadosi, S. T., Tenenbaum, J. B., & Goodman, N. D. (2012). Bootstrapping in a language of thought: A formal model of numerical concept learning. *Cognition, 123*, 199–217.

Piantadosi, S. T., Tenenbaum, J. B., & Goodman, N. D. (2016). The logical primitives of thought: Empirical foundations for compositional cognitive models. *Psychological Review, 123*(4), 392–424.

Reinhart, T. (1983). *Anaphora and semantic interpretation.* Croon Helm.

Riley, S. N., Savelson, Z., & Singh, R. (2023). Cognitive primitives and Bayesian number word learning. In M. Goldwater, F. K. Anggoro, B. K. Hayes, & D. C. Ong (Eds.), *Proceedings of the 45th Annual Conference of the Cognitive Science Society* (pp. 2924–2930).

Roberts, C. (1996). Information structure and discourse: Towards an integrated formal theory of pragmatics. In J. H. Yoon & A. Kathol (Eds.), *OSU working papers in linguistics* (pp. 91–136). The Ohio State University.

Sauerland, U. (2004). Scalar implicatures in complex sentences. *Linguistics and Philosophy, 27*, 367–391.

Sauerland, U., Tamura, A., Koizumi, M., & Tomlinson, J. M. (2017). Tracking down disjunction. In *New Frontiers in Artificial Intelligence: JSAI International Symposium on Artificial Intelligence* (pp. 109–121). Springer.

Singh, R. (2008a). On the interpretation of disjunction: Asymmetric, incremental, and eager for inconsistency. *Linguistics and Philosophy, 31*, 245–260.

Singh, R. (2008b). *Modularity and locality in interpretation* (Doctoral Dissertation), MIT.

Singh, R. (2019). Context, content, and the occasional costs of implicature computation. *Frontiers in Psychology*. https://doi.org/10.3389/fpsyg.2019.02214

Singh, R., Wexler, K., Astle-Rahim, A., Kamawar, D., & Fox, D. (2016). Children interpret disjunction as conjunction: Consequences for theories of implicature and child development. *Natural Language Semantics, 24*(4), 305–352.

Spector, B. (2013). Bare numerals and scalar implicatures. *Language and Linguistics Compass, 7*(5), 273–294.

Sudo, Y. (2014). Higher-order scalar implicatures of 'ya' in japanese. Handout, TEAL 9, University of Nantes.

Tieu, L., Romoli, J., Zhou, P., & Crain, S. (2016). Children's knowledge of free choice inferences and scalar implicatures. *Journal of Semantics, 33*(2), 269–298.

Tieu, L., Yatsuhiro, K., Cremers, A., Romoli, J., Sauerland, U., & Chemla, E. (2017). On the role of alternatives in the acquisition of simple and complex disjunctions in French and Japanese. *Journal of Semantics, 34*(1), 127–152.

von Fintel, K., & Heim, I. (1999). *Notes on implicature. Lecture Notes, 24.954: Pragmatics in linguistic theory*. MIT.

Zhou, P., Romoli, J., & Crain, S. (2013). Children's knowledge of free choice inferences. *Proceedings of SALT, 23*, 1–15.

Index

N. Gotzner et al. (eds.), *Alternatives in Grammar and Cognition*, Palgrave Studies in Pragmatics, Language and Cognition, https://doi.org/10.1007/978-3-031-76676-3

www.ingramcontent.com/pod-product-compliance
Lightning Source LLC
Chambersburg PA
CBHW072312040325
22980CB00004B/46
9783031766756